STUDIES IN SOCIAL HISTORY

issued by the

INTERNATIONAL INSTITUTE OF SOCIAL HISTORY
AMSTERDAM

1. W. H. ROOBOL. *Tsereteli – A Democrat in the Russian Revolution. A Political Biography.*
2. ZVI ROSEN. *Bruno Bauer and Karl Marx. The Influence of Bruno Bauer on Marx's Thought.*

BRUNO BAUER AND KARL MARX

THE INFLUENCE OF BRUNO BAUER ON MARX'S THOUGHT

by

ZVI ROSEN

MARTINUS NIJHOFF / THE HAGUE / 1977

To my mother

© *1977 by Martinus Nijhoff, The Hague, Netherlands*

ISBN 90 247 1948 8

PRINTED IN THE NETHERLANDS

CONTENTS

Foreword   VII

Abbreviations   IX

PART ONE

BRUNO BAUER AS A YOUNG HEGELIAN   I

    I. The problem   3
   II. Literature on Bruno Bauer   7
  III. Bauer's life until the publication of Strauss' *Leben Jesu*   17
  IV. The split in the Hegelian school – emergence of the Young
       Hegelians   21
    V. Bruno Bauer as a theologian and critic of Strauss   36
  VI. Bauerian Critique of the Gospels   45
 VII. Bruno Bauer as commentator on Hegel   62
VIII. Bauer's conception of religion and history   85
  IX. Bauer's political conception   109

PART TWO

KARL MARX AND BRUNO BAUER

    I. The personal relations and literary collaboration between
       Bauer and Marx   127
   II. Bauerian motifs in Marx's conception of religion   133
  III. Bauer's influence on Marx's dissertation   148
  IV. Bauerian motifs in Marx's conception of alienation   162
    V. The impact of Bauerian ideas on Marx's conception of ideology   180
  VI. Marx, Feuerbach, Bauer   202
 VII. The polemic between Marx and Bauer   223

Bibliography   241

Index   251

CONTENTS

Foreword

Abbreviations

PART ONE

BRUNO BAUER AS A YOUNG HEGELIAN
I. The problem
II. Literature on Bruno Bauer
III. Bauer's life until the publication of Strauss's *Leben Jesu*
IV. The split in the Hegelian school - emergence of The Young Hegelians
V. Bruno Bauer as a Hegelian and critic of Strauss
VI. Bauerian Critique of the Gospels
VII. Bruno Bauer as commentator on Hegel
VIII. Bauer's conception of religion and history
IX. Bauer's political conception

PART TWO

KARL MARX AND BRUNO BAUER
I. The personal relations and literary collaboration between Bauer and Marx
II. Bauerian motifs in Marx's conception of religion
III. Bauer's influence on Marx's dissertation
IV. Bauerian motifs in Marx's conception of alienation
V. The impact of Bauerian ideas on Marx's conception of ideology
VI. Marx's break with Bauer
VII. The polemic between Marx and Bauer

Bibliography

Index

FOREWORD

The present work is aimed at filling a hiatus in the literature dealing with the Young Hegelians and the early thought of Karl Marx. Despite the prevalent view in the past few decades that Bruno Bauer played an important part in the radical activity of Hegel's young disciples in the eighteen forties in Germany, no comprehensive work has so far been published on the relations between Bauer and Marx. In 1927 Ernst Barnikol promised to write a monograph on the subject, but he never did.

For the purpose of this study I perused material in numerous library collections and I would like to express my gratitude to the staff of the following institutions: Tel Aviv University Library, the Library and Archive of the International Institute of Social History in Amsterdam, the Heidelberg University Library, the Library of Göttingen University, the Tübingen University Library, Frankfurt University Library, the State Library at Marburg, the Manuscript Department of the State Archives in Berlin.

For research grants I am greatly indebted to the Tel Aviv University and Fritz Thyssen Stiftung. Their financial support enabled me to spend time abroad completing this work. My thanks to Leszek Kołakowski (All Souls College, Oxford), Eugène Fleischmann (University of Paris and Tel Aviv University) and Hans-Joachim Lieber (Cologne) for their helpful comments in the course of numerous conversations. I am grateful to H. P. Harstick of the International Institute of Social History, Amsterdam, for placing at my disposal the literary estate of the Dutch scholar, G. A. van den Bergh van Eysinga, and for giving me access to the proofs of Barnikol's recently-published book on Bauer. I am indebted to Mrs. Haia Galai who helped me in the preparation of the manuscript and to Charles B. Timmer who compiled the index.

Finally I owe a special debt of gratitude to the International Institute of Social History in Amsterdam and especially to its director, Frits de Jong Edz., and to Charles B. Timmer for making the publication of this work possible under the patronage of the Institute.

Z. R.

ABBREVIATIONS

The following abbreviations have been used for sources frequently cited in the text (see bibliography for details of edition):

Bruno Bauer

B — Bekenntnisse einer schwachen Seele.
BE — Briefwechsel zwischen Bruno Bauer und Edgar Bauer während der Jahre 1839–1842.
BR — Der Briefwechsel Bauers mit Arnold Ruge.
ChS — Der christliche Staat und unsere Zeit.
ECh — Das entdeckte Christentum.
Fae — Die Fähigkeit der heutigen Juden und Christen frei zu werden.
Fr — Die gute Sache der Freiheit und meine eigene Angelegenheit.
GK — Was ist jetzt Gegenstand der Kritik?
GM — Die Gattung und die Masse
H — Herr Dr. Hengstenberg. Kritische Briefe über den Gegensatz des Gesetzes und des Evangeliums.
HL — Hegels Lehre von der Religion und Kunst von dem Standpunkte des Glaubens aus beurteilt.
J — Kritik der evangelischen Geschichte des Johannes.
Jud — Die Judenfrage.
LF — Charakteristik Ludwig Feuerbachs.
LP — Die evangelische Landeskirche Preussens und die Wissenschaft.
Pos — Die Posaune des letzten Gerichts über Hegel den Atheisten und Antichristen.
RAT — Die Religion des Alten Testaments in der geschichtlichen Entwicklung dargestellt.
Syn — Kritik der evangelischen Geschichte der Synoptiker.
ThB — Leiden und Freuden des theologischen Bewusstseins.
ThS — Theologische Schamlosigkeiten.

Karl Marx

Cr — Critique of Hegel's Philosophy of Right.
Dif — The Difference between the Democritean and Epicurean Philosophy of Nature.
ET — Early Texts.

GI   – The German Ideology (Karl Marx and Friedrich Engels).
HF   – The Holy Family, or Critique of Critiqual Critique (Karl Marx and Friedrich Engels).
K   – Das Kapital. Kritik der politischen Ökonomie.
MEGA   – Karl Marx und Friedrich Engels. Historisch-kritische Gesamtausgabe. (In citations from this edition the large Roman numeral refers to the Section, the Arabic numeral that follows to the volume within that section, a small Roman numeral to the subvolume, and the final Arabic numeral to the page).
Ph   – Writings of the Young Marx on Philosophy and Society.
Pol   – Basic Writings on Politics and Philosophy.
R   – On Religion (Karl Marx and Friedrich Engels).

G.F.W. Hegel

BR   – Begriff der Religion.
BS   – Berliner Schriften.
HPh   – Lectures on the History of Philosophy.
Jen   – Jenenser Realphilosophie.
LH   – The Logic of Hegel.
Log   – Science of Logic.
Phen   – The Phenomenology of Mind.
PhH   – The Philosophy of History.
PhM   – Hegel's Philosophy of Mind.
PhR   – Lectures on the Philosophy of Religion.
PhRt   – Philosophy of Right.
ThJ   – Hegels theologische Jugendschriften.

Ludwig Feuerbach

E   – Essence of Christianity.
SW   – Ludwig Feuerbachs Sämtliche Werke.
SWr   – Selected Writings of Ludwig Feuerbach.

Periodicals and newspapers

ALZ   – Allgemeine Literaturzeitung.
An   – Anekdota zur neuesten deutschen Philosophie und Publizistik.
DJ   – Deutsche Jahrbücher für Wissenschaft und Kunst.
HJ   – Hallische Jahrbücher für deutsche Wissenschaft und Kunst.
JWK   – Jahrbücher für wissenschaftliche Kritik.
RhZ   – Rheinische Zeitung für Politik, Handel und Gewerbe.
ZspT   – Zeitschrift für spekulative Theologie.

PART ONE

BRUNO BAUER AS A YOUNG HEGELIAN

CHAPTER I

THE PROBLEM

Bruno Bauer (1809–1882), philosopher, scholar and publicist, wrote dozens of books and hundreds of articles on questions of religion, particularly Judaism and Christianity, German and French history, political subjects, and on various social and philosophical questions. He was the recognized leader of the Young Hegelians in Berlin and one of the leaders of this literary-intellectual movement in Germany as a whole. Bauer took part in the radical activities of the Young Hegelians for several years – between 1839–1843. After that, because of the policy of persecution, intimidation and suppression operated by the Prussian authorities, the movement began to disintegrate. The dismissal of university lecturers – an example of this was the expulsion of Bauer himself from Bonn University – the closing down of progressive newspapers, including the *Rheinische Zeitung*, (Marx served as its chief editor in its last year), the imposition of rigid and harsh censorship – all these prevented German radical circles from giving voice to their protest and their demands for change. In the light of the reaction then raging, the central personalities within the movement began to engage in a controversy as to the new path which should be followed in order to achieve their main objectives: democratization of government, separation of religion and state, abolition of privileges.

For those of them who tended to socialism, such as Moses Hess and Marx, the principles and demands of the movement had become invalid and they sought more radical framework for attainment of their social and political aims. This was the basis of the ideological campaign which Marx conducted against Bauer, which was expressed in three well-known essays: *On the Jewish Question, The Holy Family* and *The German Ideology*. Bauer, who had been Marx' close friend for four years, was depicted in these works as a nihilist of the worst type; a theologian who was incapable of dealing with any political, social or philosophical question without having recourse to arguments borrowed from religion or from the anti-religious, i.e. atheistic stand, as a speculative idealist totally detached from reality.

Whereas Marx's criticism in *On the Jewish Question* was sometimes harsh but generally pertinent, *The Holy Family*, published two years later (in 1845) was characterized both by use of various derogatory epithets and by an extremely selective method of picking Bauerian concepts for criticism. Marx, who deliberately disregards Bauer's views as expressed between 1840–43 and limits himself to presenting those views expounded in the *Allgemeine Literaturzeitung*, gives a caricaturized version of them. This enables Marx to state that Bauer's beliefs are "speculation reproducing itself as a caricature" and "the nonsense of German speculation in general",[1] "repetition of a *speculative* witticism" and "speculative theology".[2]

All this creates the impression that Bauer's views are empty of content and not worth studying, since there can be no point in discussing speculations which are detached from reality. But, despite the many statements in this spirit – this was not Marx's intention. Rather the contrary: Marx believes that *"real humanism* has no more dangerous enemy in Germany than *spiritualism* or *speculative* idealism, which substitutes 'self-consciousness' or the 'spirit' for the *real individual man."*[3]

There is an evident contradiction here. How could a conception which was "nonsense" and nothing but a "speculative witticism" endanger the status of the Marxian viewpoint and hinder its dissemination in Germany? One or the other: either Bauer's views are as described by Marx, in which case there is no point in discussing them or in going so far as to see them as the "dangerous enemy" or else they differ from Marx's characterization, in which case it is clear that all his descriptions of their superficiality, banality etc. are exaggerated, to say the least. This contradiction has previously been noticed and thus, for example, Gustav Mayer writes, in his biography of Engels: "Speculative idealism in its caricatured form, à la Bauer brothers, was not – in actual fact – an enemy which could endanger 'real humanism' as Marx and Engels wished to persuade others in the joint foreword to their book [...]. Even the Charlottenburg *Allgemeine Literaturzeitung*, whose articles aroused this criticism, eked out an existence far removed from the public, which paid it almost no heed."[4]

[1] HF 15.
[2] Ibid. 121, 138.
[3] Ibid. 15.
[4] Gustav Mayer: *Friedrich Engels. Eine Biographie*. Haag 1934, pp. 187–188.

In order to overcome the contradiction, Mayer selects from Marx's double system of arguments, which is self-contradictory, only the argument on Bauer's philosophical weaknesses. But the problem is not so simple, since the fact remains that Marx wrote, in *The Holy Family*, more than three hundred pages against Bruno Bauer and the group who cooperated with Bauer's paper. It is well-known that the excessive length of the Marxian text, which dealt in detail with secondary articles of no public importance whatsoever, astounded Engels, who, for his part, contended himself with a twenty-page text, and that this short and ironic response sufficed to reveal Bauer's true face to the public.[5]

Furthermore, the assumption of the superficial character of the Bauerian conception contradicts many of the statements which Marx himself had written not long previously regarding Bauer's good qualities and, in particular, his merits as a writer and scholar. It will suffice for our purposes to quote just a few of Marx's evaluations: "Bauer, with his profound commentaries, demonstrates their [i.e. the theologians'] ignorance";[6] "all this with dash, acuteness, wit and thoroughness in a style as precise as it is pregnant and energetic."[7]

It would seem that Marx's attitude to Bauer, as expressed in *The Holy Family* – which, as we have seen, was far from unequivocal – was the outcome of a complex causal connection and cannot be comprehended through one sole factor.

This dichotomy can be understood if we take into consideration the fact that Marx felt the need to engage in fatiguing polemics directed against Bauer, in order to detach himself from ideas which he himself had held for several years. No-one knew better than Marx how attractive Bauerian ideas had proved to German intellectuals only three years previously.

In August 1842, an Austrian secret police agent had written to his government: "Bauer's books [...] are owned by thousands [...] and what is worse [...] his ideas have penetrated to the heart of the educated world and become part of it."[8]

Hence there was no doubt as to the popularity of Bauer's ideas, and it did, in fact, constitute an obstacle to dissemination and absorption of Marx's ideas. But this was prior to the period in which Marx's essay

[5] Auguste Cornu: *Karl Marx und Friedrich Engels. Leben und Werk.* Vol. II, (Ost)Berlin Aufbau-Verlag, 1962, p. 274.
[6] Karl Marx: *Dr. Gruppe gegen Bruno Bauer.* MEGA I, 1, i 399.
[7] Ph 218.
[8] Karl Glossy: *Literarische Geheimberichte aus dem Vormärz.* Wien 1912. Erster Teil, p. 313.

appeared. This danger passed when Bauer returned to Berlin from Bonn, after his dismissal from the university. Bauer's disillusionment at the lack of widespread public support after his dismissal in the wake of his criticism of the Gospels and the Christian religion,[9] the lack of proportion between the fact that this appeared to Bauer a cosmic catastrophe[10] while the public remained indifferent – the protests of several journals, such as Ruge's *Deutsche Jahrbücher* and such papers as *Die Rheinische Zeitung* could not alter the situation – increasingly drew him towards criticism of mass passivity and to emphasize the pure nature of the theory he advocated. Under these circumstances, and particularly the atmosphere of intimidation then prevailing, Bauer forfeited much of his attraction for the progressive intelligentsia and their attachment to him was weakened. For this reason it is hard to believe that Marx, in his general evaluations, was referring to those Bauerian concepts which Bauer had advocated from 1844 onwards. He was referring to the whole range of Bauerian ideas, rich in intellectual content, the future revival of which would revive Bauer's popularity.[11]

Furthermore, Marx also wanted to prove, perhaps above all to himself, that there was no longer anything in common between Bauer's concepts and his own, or, to be more exact, that a chasm yawned between them – and hence the sharpness of the criticism, the desire to belittle the man as well as his work, the use of insulting terms and the tendency to caricaturize Bauer's theories. Thus the overcoming of his own philosophical past entailed, Marx believed, the total rejection of Bauer's basically critical approach as well as the endeavour to prove the superiority of Marxian humanism over the ideas of his former friend.

Marx's campaign against Bauer – to which we will return below in order to ascertain its ideological content – raises several questions: who was Bruno Bauer, what were his views and philosophical path, how did the close relationship between Bauer and Marx manifest itself and why did their paths eventually separate?

Before examining these problems, I would like to say something both about the existing literature on Bauer and on the attitude that scholars have taken towards him.

---

[9] B 70–90; Dieter Hertz-Eichenrode: *Der Junghegelianer Bruno Bauer im Vormärz*. Dissertation Berlin 1957, p. 89.

[10] Fr 20–40, 202–205.

[11] It is interesting to note that Engels thought at first that it was possible to get rid of Bauer by means of a short article ridiculing him, but changed his mind under the influence of Marx and wrote in the *New Moral World* that *"Bruno Bauer and Stirner are the sole serious enemies of Communism"*. (See Mayer *Friedrich Engels. Eine Biographie*, p. 227).

CHAPTER II

LITERATURE ON BRUNO BAUER

It is not easy to examine Bauer's views, not simply because of the wide range of subjects with which he dealt, but primarily because his scholarly and journalistic works are widely dispersed. A considerable number of his studies were published in journals with limited circulation, to which it is now hard to gain access. Other works, which were printed by publishing houses, are often hard to obtain since few copies remain, because of court orders against the publishers. Thus, for example, Bauer's book *Das entdeckte Christentum* was banned before distribution and was only republished many years later, in 1927, through the efforts of Ernst Barnikol, who found the text of the book in manuscript.[1]

Three additional facts undoubtedly discouraged scholarly interest in Bauer:

Firstly – Bauer's total rejection by Marx. The latter's claim that Bauer should be classified among the products of "the putrescence of the absolute spirit"[2] of Hegel, influenced, primarily, those scholars who accepted Marx's theories and thus accepted Marx's evaluation of Bauer treating him with a striking lack of respect and even contempt. But even among scholars who are not linked to Marx by a dogmatic attitude and even among those who disagree vehemently with his theories, it is accepted, because of the evaluation of Marx as well as their own lack of first hand acquaintance with Bauer's writings (this is actually the decisive point since almost all scholars rely on Marx in the Marx – Bauer polemics) – that Bauer was an imitator and compilator, who lived off the crumbs of Hegelian philosophy.

Secondly – Bauer held radical and critical views for a relatively short time, when he was active in literature, journalistic writing, the

---

[1] Ernst Barnikol: *Das entdeckte Christentum im Vormärz. Bruno Bauers Kampf gegen Religion und Christentum und Erstausgabe seiner Kampfschrift.* Jena 1927.
[2] GI 27.

study of Christianity, Hegelian philosophy and politics as a Young Hegelian. Before joining this movement he was an orthodox Protestant theologian, and even served as the editor of a journal of speculative theology. After the disintegration of Young Hegelianism he became a conservative and cooperated closely for many years with Hermann Wagener, editor of the *Staats- und Gesellschaftslexikon* and the *Kreuz-zeitung*, who was a notorious reactionary and antisemite.[3]

Because of ignorance, it may be said, many scholars preferred not to deal with Bauer's philosophical development, and thus the radical stage, during which Bauer developed original ideas and made a considerable contribution to the advancement of spiritual life in Germany has been almost totally neglected.

The third reason is not specifically related to Bauer but is more general. The view became prevalent that the views of the Young Hegelians, their concepts, thoughts and ideas, did not constitute an important chapter in the development of philosophical thought and that they belonged within the journalistic and political framework of Germany before the March 1848 revolution.

Thus, for example, Löwith wrote of them: "Their writings are manifestos, programmes, but never anything whole, important in itself. In their hand, their scientific demonstrations became sensational proclamations. [...] Whoever studies their writings will discover that, in spite of their inflammatory tone, they leave an impression of insipidity. They make immoderate demands with insufficient means and dilate Hegel's abstract dialectics to a piece of rhetoric."[4]

Bauer is referred to in the literature dealing with Marx's early philosophy, but only in a tangential fashion and the reason is clear: in studies of this type emphasis was placed on the evolution of Marx's ideas and concepts in the direction of communism and historical materialism, and Bauer was thus seen as a short episode in the life of Marx. Furthermore, a certain schematism became accepted in Marxology, according to which Feuerbach exerted considerable and sometimes even decisive influence on the development of Marx in the sphere of anthropology, critique of religion, society and state. This prevalent theory contains a great deal of exaggeration, and we will take the opportunity below of producing evidence of the fact that Bauer's role in crystallizing Marx's views has been unfairly underestimated.

---

[3] See on this point, Ernst Barnikol: *Bruno Bauer. Studien und Materialien*. Assen, Van Gorcum & Comp. 1972, pp. 349–353; Jürgen Gebhardt: *Politische Ordnung und menschliche Existenz*. In *Festgabe für Eric Voegelin*. München 1962, pp. 202–242.

[4] Karl Löwith: *From Hegel to Nietzsche*. Garden City, N.Y. Doubleday and Co. 1967, p. 64.

Studies devoted to the Young Hegelians have allotted a place to Bauer, but here too – apart from exceptional cases – we find no satisfactory analysis of Bauer's views. Stuke was right when he wrote: "Despite the considerable number of essays, articles and detailed comments, research on Bauer is still in the preliminary stage."[5]

But it would be a mistake to think that Bauer has been accorded only negative evaluations, such as that of Marx. Other views have also been expressed and I shall cite only a few examples. August Cieszkowski, who took part in the Young Hegelian movement and was known for his book, *Prolegomena zur Historiosophie*, in which he raised the problem of the praxis in a way reminiscent of Marx,[6] saw Bauer's importance as follows: "Anyone who claims that Bruno Bauer does not constitute an important scientific phenomenon is like someone who states that the Reformation has no historical significance. But this is no longer a query at all, but a fact: he resembles a radiant star, illuminating the horizons of science."[7]

Albert Schweitzer greatly admired Bauer's knowledge and his analysis of early Christianity and the New Testament and stressed that Bauer, in his critical studies, produced astonishingly profound ideas.[8] He believed that Bauerian critique of Gospel history was worth a dozen good essays on the life of Jesus, because it was the most brilliant and complete anthology of the difficulties entailed in understanding the life of Jesus which had ever been written.[9] Barnikol, who studied Bauer's writings for decades, saw him as the acutest critic of religion in modern times, surpassing even Nietzsche and Lenin as regards his "succinct knowledge and criticism" and noted that Bauer's humanism resulted from the removal of supernatural factors from human life and from his attempt to base understanding of man on spiritual motives, or, as Barnikol puts it: "As a scholar who was well acquainted with Hegelianism Bauer was the most consistent humanist of modern times, who consciously rejected Christianity and religion for the sake of a pure

[5] Horst Stuke: *Philosophie der Tat. Studien zur Verwirklichung der Philosophie bei den Junghegelianern.* Stuttgart, Ernst Klett Verlag 1963, p. 127.
[6] For Cieszkowski's concept of praxis, see Nicolas Lobkowicz: *Theory and Praxis: History of a Concept from Aristotle to Marx.* University of Notre Dame Press, Notre Dame-London 1967, pp. 193–206. See also: Horst Stuke *Philosophie der Tat.* Op cit. pp. 110–122; Shlomo Avineri: *The Social and Political Thought of Karl Marx.* Cambridge University Press 1970, pp. 124–128.
[7] August Cieszkowski: *Gott und Palingenese.* Berlin 1842, p. 93.
[8] Albert Schweitzer: *Geschichte der Leben-Jesu-Forschung.* Vol. 1, München und Hamburg, Siebenstern Taschenbuch Verlag 1966, p. 185.
[9] Ibid. 189.

spiritual approach."[10] Walter Nigg, author of the well-known book on religious liberalism, sees Bauer as follows: "Bauer's name was accompanied in the forties by a hint of threat and it appears cursorily in every work dealing with 19th century theology. But despite the constant use of the name, there is no clear picture related to this personality. The man is almost completely unknown. [...] He is enveloped in darkness and enigma. It is not clear why to this day no monograph on his life and work has appeared."[11] "The life and personality of Bauer resemble those of great figures of ancient times whose deeds were breathtaking."[12]

And what have the scholars to say about Bauer's ideological activity? Lukàcs sees Bauer as an extreme representative of the progressive Hegelian faction who, through the combination of subjectivist Fichtean motifs with Hegelian dialectics, crystallized a critical and activist approach to reality.[13] By placing emphasis on self-consciousness Bauer led to weakening of the link between the categories of dialectics and history.[14] The subjective factor, which played a central part in Bauer's concepts, precluded him from a correct view of the historical process and impelled him towards an aristocratic concept,[15] according to which the leader, aware of his mission and imbued with consciousness, faces the passive masses.[16]

Ernst Bloch attributes to Bauer limitless subjectivity, which approaches negation of the object, and sees his conception as spiritual arrogance. Bauer's subjectivism helps solve the problems of the world for those possessed of self-consciousness, but the world remains unchanged and does not feel this. Bauer combines contempt for the object with contempt for the masses.[17] Bloch, too, sees Bauer as a writer who transplants subjectivist motifs, originating in Fichte, into Hegel's idealistic-objectivistic method.[18]

Bloch and Lukàcs have nothing to add to Marxian criticism, which constitutes the basis and background for their view of Bauer. The

[10] *Religion in Geschichte und Gegenwart*[3], Vol. I, p. 923.
[11] Walter Nigg: *Geschichte des religiösen Liberalismus.* Zürich 1937, p. 166.
[12] Ibid. 166–167.
[13] Georg Lukàcs: *Schriften zur Ideologie und Politik.* Neuwied, Luchterhand 1967, pp. 205–206, 208; *Die Zerstörung der Vernunft*, Werke Bd IX, Luchterhand, pp. 230–232.
[14] *Schriften zur Ideologie und Politik*, p. 208.
[15] *Beiträge zur Geschichte der Ästhetik.* Berlin (Ost) 1956, p. 138. *Schriften zur Ideologie und Politik*, pp. 208, 518.
[16] *Schriften zur Ideologie und Politik*, pp. 217–218.
[17] Ernst Bloch: *Subjekt-Objekt. Erläuterungen zu Hegel.* Frankfurt/M., Suhrkamp 1962, p. 103; *Das Prinzip Hoffnung.* Frankfurt/M., Suhrkamp 1968, p. 315.
[18] *Das Prinzip Hoffnung*, p. 316.

same is true of Cornu, who, in his biography of Marx and Engels, gives numerous details on Bauer, his life and beliefs, but remains attached to Marx's viewpoint and evaluation – both as regards Bauer and the Young Hegelians in general.[19]

Koigen's book on the Young Hegelians is the first to deal systematically with this question.[20] He believes that Hegel's young disciples were the first to advocate a modern positivist social theory in place of the metaphysical system.[21] Metaphysical motifs dominated Hegel's thought, but these no longer exist in his radical interpreters, who moved away from the speculative approach and arrived at crystallization of a social theory, and this is particularly true of Marx.[22] Koigen cites many forgotten facts, from the eighteen forties, on the Young Hegelians, and some of these descriptions are still of service to scholars dealing with this group. At the same time the flaw in the work of Lukàcs and others is already fully apparent in his work: quotations by Marx serve as substitutes for the original text, *The Holy Family* sometimes takes the place of Bauer's critique of the Synoptic Gospels, and fact and fancy co-exist.

Extensive information on the political beliefs of the Young Hegelians appears in the articles of Mayer[23] which remain to this day a source of knowledge of the political nature of the movement, but the outline of Bauer's political theories was very lightly sketched.

[19] Cornu: *Karl Marx und Friedrich Engels. Leben und Werk.* Vol. I, pp. 97–98, 148–149, 208–211, 245–252, 357–359. Vol. II, pp. 24–29, 284–288, 325–332.

[20] David Koigen: *Zur Vorgeschichte des modernen philosophischen Sozialismus.* Bern 1901.

[21] Ibid. 308–319.

[22] A similar theory was advocated by Herbert Marcuse: "The transition from Hegel to Marx is, in all respects, a transition to an essentially different order of truth, not to be interpreted in terms of philosophy. We shall see that all the philosophical concepts of Marxian theory are social and economic categories, whereas Hegel's social and economic categories are all philosophical concepts. Even Marx's early writings are not philosophical." (*Reason and Revolution*, Boston, Mass., Beacon Press 1968[5], p. 258). Koigen's conclusions can be justified if we take into consideration that he had neither Marx's dissertation nor the *Manuscripts* at his disposal. But it is surprising that Marcuse fails to see the philosophical problems hidden in Marx's early writings. Even if one disregards the dissertation which deals with a specific philosophical topic, there remain the *Manuscripts* which also contain a philosophical debate which relates to the economic-social discussion. Anyone who fails to see this, has not grasped the Marxian conception that alienated life precides private property, that there exists a human essence, etc. From this point of view, the title *Economic and Philosophic Manuscripts* faithfully reflects Marx's objectives. Incidentally: Marcuse's interpretation, which denies the philosophical aspect of Marx's thought is in contradiction to the opinion he himself voiced at an earlier stage of his intellectual development. Cf. *Über die philosophischen Grundlagen des wirtschaftswissenschaftlichen Arbeitsbegriff.* In *Archiv für Sozialwissenschaft und Sozialpolitik*, Vol. 69, Part 3, 1933.

[23] Gustav Mayer: *Die Anfänge des politischen Radikalismus im vormärzlichen Preussen.* Zeitschrift für Politik. Vol. VI/1913. Recently published in: *Radikalismus, Sozialismus und bürgerliche Demokratie.* Frankfurt/M., Suhrkamp 1968, (all page references refer to this publication); *Die Junghegelianer und der preussische Staat.* Historische Zeitschrift. Vol. 121/1920.

There are a number of flaws and omissions in Hook's study of the Young Hegelians.[24] This work, the first edition of which appeared in 1936, discusses Marx as if the extensive problems of the early writings were non-existent. The facts discovered by Lukàcs four years before publication of the "early writings" by Ryazanov – the meaning of externalization and alienation in the thought of the young Marx – find no mention in Hook's book. The subtitle notes that it deals with the intellectual development of Marx, but, in actual fact, any connection between Hook's discussion and the development of Marxian thought is coincidence. He does not attempt to show how Marx's clash with Bauer, Hess, Ruge, Feuerbach, Stirner and others on the philosophical, historiosophical and political plane served as a stimulus for crystalliza-tion of his ideas. Hook presents the views of the Young Hegelians in contrast to those of Marx: he maintains constant confrontations be-tween Marx's views on 1844/6 and the theories of Hegel's young disciples. This method naturally enables him to depict Marx's theories as more clear and more convincing than those of his opponents.[25] Like Marx, Hook claims that Bauer's "pure critique" always character-ized his beliefs, although Marx knew only too well – and Hook should have known – that until 1844 Bauer held views clearly aimed at chang-ing reality. In order to prove his claim that Bauerian criticism was abstract and far from serving the interests of progress, Hook provided labels for Bauerian theories, describing them as solipsism, historical fatalism, anti-liberalism, adventurism, sentimental philantrophy etc. It is of no importance to him that these labels do not always find substantiation in Bauer's texts. When necessary, Hook quotes Edgar, Bruno Bauer's brother, and a number of other persons who wrote for Bauer's paper.[26]

Stuke's essay on the philosophy of praxis according to Cieszkowski, Bauer and Hess[27] is a valuable contribution to the study of the realiza-tion of philosophy through the unity of reason and reality. To start with, Bauer's philosophical theories – the theory of history and alienation, the relations between theory and praxis, the radical version of Hegelianism – are submitted to profound examination. At the same time there are a number of errors and omissions in the book, which cannot be disregarded. Stuke is actually following in Hook's footsteps

---

[24] Sidney Hook: *From Hegel to Marx. Studies in the Intellectual Development of Marx.* The University of Michigan Press 1968³.

[25] Ibid. pp. 152–164, 173–185, 205–223, 272–307.

[26] Ibid. pp. 98–125.

[27] Stuke: *Philosophie der Tat.* Op. cit.

in relying on Edgar Bauer in this case in order to substantiate the
theory that Bauer pinned his revolutionary hopes on bourgeois and
radical strata. Instead of quoting Bruno – who never clearly refers to
the social and class basis of the revolution, – Stuke prefers to quote
Edgar Bauer.[28] He does this even though it had already been demonstrated that such a method is inadvisable. I am referring to Marx and
Engels, who had much in common but who were divided on many
issues, so that there are at times more factors separating them than
uniting them. This is also true of the Bauer brothers. They agreed on
many points – such as critique of the state and, in particular, of religion,
– but Edgar's radicalism was much stronger than that of his brother,
especially on questions of society, property etc.[29] Many of Stuke's
arguments are, in fact, baseless assumptions. For example, his claim
that Bauer exerted considerable influence over Ruge, Engels, Marx
and Hess[30] is not based on evidence which justifies the statement,
though it is true in itself. A slight variation of the same phenomenon is
Stuke's attempt to attribute to Bauer's theory of the revolution the
characteristics of Marx's revolutionary theory.[31]

The recently published books by McLellan and Brazill[32] differ from
Hook's study which formerly represented English-language literature
on the Young Hegelians. The two authors display a critical attitude
to the sources. For reasons which are not clear, Brazill, who analyses
at length the ideas of six members of the group of radical Hegelians,
almost totally ignores Marx and, where Bauer is concerned, his
approach is routine.

McLellan devotes considerable space to Marx and to the relations
between Marx and Bruno Bauer. He is correct in his theory that Bauer
influenced the crystallization of Marx's concept of religion (in Marx's
dissertation). But, with the exception of the idea that the evidence
of the existence of God is actually evidence of the existence of human
self-consciousness, we find in McLellan's own work no justification for
his assumption. Again, when McLellan raises the question of theory-
praxis relations in the works of Bauer and Marx, he contents himself
with providing two quotations without going into a deeper analysis of

[28] Ibid. p. 173.
[29] See on this point: Edgar Bauer, *Der Streit der Kritik mit Kirche und Staat*. Bern 1844,
pp. 244, 255, 276, 278–279.
[30] *Philosophie der Tat*, p. 127.
[31] Ibid. pp. 172–179.
[32] William J. Brazill: *The Young Hegelians*. New Haven and London, Yale University
Press 1970; David McLellan: *The Young Hegelians and Karl Marx*. Macmillan, London 1969.

the problem. Thus, in place of a pertinent analysis, we have rather generalized evaluations.[33] But the very fact that Bauer's influence over Marx is discussed at all spells progress when compared to the commentary which sees Feuerbach alone as the source of inspiration for Marx's ideas, though Bauer's influence is clear and indubitable.

Hertz-Eichenrode's dissertation provides numerous biographical facts on Bauer and deals with his intellectual development up to 1843. The fact that this is a work of a biographer is evident: it is almost totally lacking in any analysis of Bauer's political ideas which are presented negatively through Löwith's negative prisma. There is almost no evaluation of the relations between Bauer and his associates in the movement, and the political and social background for his activity is lacking. The changes in Bauer's thinking are presented as if they occurred deus ex machina and the reader finds it hard to comprehend the intellectual motives for the evolution in his views. Eichenrode devoted considerable space to a discussion of self-consciousness, Bauer's main philosophical category, but fails to provide a plausible explanation for the various manifestations of self-consciousness in Bauer's thought, such as the general and individual self-consciousness, the natural self-consciousness etc.[34]

Another dissertation, that of Lothar Koch, tries to tackle the philosophical background of Bauer's concepts but in vain. The reason appears to lie in the author's lack of knowledge of the Hegelian texts and his acquaintance with them through interpretative literature alone.[35] This work has almost nothing new to offer and, as regards relations between Marx and Bauer, it repeats well-known facts.

Ernst Barnikol is the greatest of the scholars who have dealt with Bauer. He published several well-known essays on Bauer's life and ideas which revived interest in this forgotten philosopher. Barnikol deserves considerable credit for his studies – critical interpretation of the texts, comparative analysis of the view of Bauer and other Young Hegelians, perception of various ideological and political aspects of Bauer's philosophy, in contrast to others, who before the publication of *Das entdeckte Christentum* dealt with Bauer mainly from the viewpoint of his theories on religion. But despite all the above merits, Barnikol aimed his research in the wrong direction. The fact that he

---

[33] *The Young Hegelians and Karl Marx*, pp. 69–73.

[34] See Dieter Hertz-Eichenrode, *Der Junghegelianer Bruno Bauer im Vormärz.* Dissertation. Berlin 1959, especially pp. 41–47, 52–53, 70–73.

[35] Lothar Koch: *Bruno Bauers "kritische Kritik". Beitrag zum Problem eines humanistischen Atheismus.* Dissertation. Köln 1969, pp. 22–25, 27–33, 45, 51.

was a theologian left its stamp on his view of Bauer's ideas and the way in which he evaluated them. Because of Bauer's atheistic views, Barnikol depicted him as a destructive figure, criticizing religion and the state with acerbity and ability which are almost unparallelled among other critics, but without providing constructive solutions.

Barnikol regarded Bauerian atheism as "a dangerous example of where the concept which stifles man for the sake of a phantom can lead."[36] This is probably the greatest paradox in Barnikol's work: he did not restrict himself to analysis of Bauer's theological and anti-religious texts, but carefully examined his political and philosophical ideas as well, though always from the point of view of a religious man. As a result, all the discussions of various and diverse aspects of Bauer were transformed into theological questions. And we witness a fascinating phenomenon: Marx denounced Bauer because he saw in him a man incapable of casting off the theological approach ("for the theologian Bauer it is *self-evident* that criticism should, in the long term, be *speculative theology*, since *he*, the *critic* is a theologian by profession,"[37]) whereas Barnikol sharply criticizes Bauer from the opposite viewpoint, seeing him as a traitor to theology, engaged in its destruction.[38]

It should be pointed out in this context that the psychological factor, which appears in Barnikol's studies cannot, alone, explain Bauer's ideas; as a complementary methodological postulate it is not objectionable, but it becomes a serious obstacle when the objective is to examine ideological and cultural phenomena *mainly* by means of this method.[39] And this is exactly what Barnikol does, since he believes that religious psychology alone is capable of comprehending the essence of the concepts of "human" and "non-human" in Bauer's thought. According to this point of view, Bauer's basic concepts can be explained as being rooted in the subconscious of man, and this rule applies, above all, to the concept of divinity and Satan.[40]

It is impossible to refer to literature on Bauer without a brief mention of Engels; in the eulogy he wrote shortly after Bauer's death, he discussed Bauer's views on the origins of Christianity, and also referred to them in another article.[41] In these two essays Engels

[36] ECh, p. 74.
[37] HF 138.
[38] *Bruno Bauer. Studien und Materialien*, pp. 1–5, 25–30, 74–83.
[39] See on this point: Max Weber, *Methodologische Schriften*. Frankfurt/M., S. Fischer 1968, pp. 27–29.
[40] ECh, pp. 70–71.
[41] R 194–204, 324–325.

praised Bauer for his atheistic views and his opposition to the Christian version of the creation of this religion. Engels forgot, in 1882, what he had written about Bauer in *The Holy Family*, and was now willing to admit that the latter had once played an important part as a philosopher and religious scholar. According to Engels, Bauer had made a greater contribution to solving the Evangelical mystery than any other scholar. Bauer's atheism, long forgotten, was recalled thanks to Engels who, through this new approach, paved the way for the splitting of the Bauerian heritage into two: *a*) the philosophy of the self-consciousness as an invalid and contemptible speculative idealistic method, constituting a clear contradiction to the basic theses of historical materialism. Bauer's historiosophical approach, which contrasts those endowed with self-consciousness with the masses lacking this consciousness, belongs in this category. *b*) Bauer's critique of religion and, in particular, of Christianity, which can be exploited for conducting an ideological campaign against religious principles.

Engels' evaluation was accepted by German social-democracy which regarded him, after the death of Marx in 1883, as a great philosopher, the continuer of the Marxian tradition. Furthermore, Engels, through his renewed evaluation of Bauerian atheism, also determined a new behaviour pattern as regards religion, placing emphasis on an ideological system directed against religion and stressing the mythological elements of historical religions, in order to place them under attack and to show their anti-scientific and anti-humanistic nature.

A striking example of exploitation of Bauer's atheistic elements for anti-religious propaganda is the Soviet Union, where Bauer's theories took firm root. His mythological approach, which sees Jesus and the Apostles as the creation of the self-consciousness of the author of the Gospels, is regarded as scientific truth and any theory which recognizes the historical nature of the Jewish and Christian sacred writings is regarded as reactionary, and irreconcilable with the findings of history and with scientific achievement.[42]

---

[42] See for example: *Kratkij nauchno-ateisticheskij slovar'*, Moscow 1964, pp. 61–62, 587–592.

CHAPTER III

BAUER'S LIFE UNTIL THE PUBLICATION OF STRAUSS' *LEBEN JESU*

Bruno Bauer was born in Eisenberg, Thuringia in 1809. Thuringia was also the birthplace of Martin Luther and comparisons have often been drawn between the great 16th century German reformer and Bauer, who wanted to reform man and believed that it was necessary to abolish religion for this purpose.[1] In 1815 Bauer's family moved to Berlin and he lived there until his death in 1882. Only twice in the course of more than fifty years did he leave the city: between 1839–1842, when he served as a lecturer at Bonn University, and in 1855–1856, when he was in London. That he was particularly attracted to the study of languages, history and literature, we know from the curriculum vitae he wrote when he took up his teaching post at Bonn.[2]

Bauer spent four years studying at the Faculty of Theology of Berlin University. Theology was extremely developed in 19th-century Germany and played an important role in the intellectual and spiritual lives of the states – of which there were 35 after the Vienna Congress.[3]

Theology was very closely interlinked with philosophy: the language and methods of philosophical discourse served as the vehicle for the discussion of the concept of religious truths. Bauer studied under two great theologians: Neander and Schleiermacher. The latter was regarded as the greatest of Protestant theologians; he also published in the areas of philosophy, ancient and classical history and politics and for a period served as a priest.[4] But these two teachers failed to persuade Bauer. He was particularly disappointed with Schleiermacher's teachings, which were based on an attempt to find

[1] E. Schläger: *Bruno Bauer und seine Werke*. Internationale Monatsschrift. Zeitschrift für allgemeine und nationale Kultur. Vol. I. Chemnitz 1882, p. 378.
[2] Ernst Banikol: *Bruno Bauer. Studien und Materialien*, p. 6.
[3] Franz Schnabel: *Deutsche Geschichte im 19. Jahrhundert*. Vol. 3. Freiburg 1954, pp. 115–120.
[4] Ibid. p. 115.

a compromise between various conflicting schools of thought. To
Bauer's mind, this could only engender ambiguity and uncertainty.[5]

As he moved from the theological-orthodox approach, Bauer was
more and more drawn to Hegel. Under the influence of the latter, his
negative attitude to Schleiermacher was strengthened. Hegel was one
of Schleiermacher's sharpest critics, disagreeing with him on nearly
everything.[6] The sole Hegelian among the theologians – Marheineke –
became Bauer's spiritual patron. It is also possible that Bauer was,
for a time, influenced by Hengstenberg, who was not one of Hegel's
supporters, but this is not clear.[7] Bauer attended lectures given by
Hegel himself in the three years preceding the latter's death in 1831.[8]
At this time Hegel's influence in Germany was at its height.[9] As
Haym put it, in a well-known statement, German intellectuals "were
then either Hegelians or barbarians and idiots, contemptible and
retarded empiricists, and in the eyes of the authorities dealing with
education, it was almost a crime to be a non-Hegelian."[10]

Hotho's encyclopedic introduction and Hegel's lectures made a
forceful impression on Bauer; they made him feel at home and gave
him the sensation of encountering new ideas, which seemed to grow
naturally out of his own inner depths.[11] In 1829 the twenty-year-old
student won the Philosophy Faculty prize for a work on a subject
formulated by Hegel himself: "On the principle of beauty according
to Kantian philosophy."[12] Hegel took a very positive view of Bauer's
work, and lavished praise on it: "The lecture [...] develops most
convincingly [...] there is consistent development of the thought
and the author has also succeeded in exploiting the contradictions of
the Kantian principles, which are incompatible."[13]

Thus, during his studies, Bauer came into close contact with Hegelian ideas and even made use of them. The notes he took at Hegel's

[5] Hertz-Eichenrode: *Der Junghegelianer Bruno Bauer im Vormärz*, pp. 9–10.
[6] See: Walter Kaufmann: *Hegel. A Reinterpretation*. New York, Doubleday & Comp. 1965,
pp. 231–234.
[7] For this issue, see W. Nigg: *Geschichte des religiösen Liberalismus*, pp. 166–167; Hertz-
Eichenrode: *Der Junghegelianer Bruno Bauer im Vormärz*, p. 123.
[8] Bruno Bauer: *Die humanistische Bildung der Deutschen in der zweiten Hälfte des 18.
Jahrhunderts*. Vierteljahresschrift für Volkswirtschaft, Politik und Kulturgeschichte. Berlin
1876. Vol. 13/4, p. 45.
[9] Jürgen Gebhardt: *Politik und Eschatologie. Studien zur Geschichte der Hegelschen Schule
in den Jahren 1830–1840*. Münchener Studien zur Politik. I/1963, pp. 28–29.
[10] Rudolf Haym: *Hegel und seine Zeit*. Hildesheim 1962. Nachdruck der Ausgabe 1857, p. 4.
[11] Bruno Bauer: *Die humanistische Bildung der Deutschen in der zweiten Hälfte des 18.
Jahrhunderts*, pp. 60–61.
[12] Ernst Barnikol: *Bruno Bauer. Studien und Materialien*, p. 19.
[13] BS 670.

lectures were extremely well-ordered and were regarded as exempla-
ry; his notes on Hegel's aesthetics on 1823–28 were used by Hotho in
1835 for publication of the Aesthetics,[14] while his notes on the Hegelian lectures on the philosophy of religion constituted the basis of
the second edition. Bauer also helped Marheineke to edit the text, or
to be more exact, he himself edited the text and was paid for doing
so.[15]

After completing his studies Bauer was awarded the degree of
licenciate (equivalent to doctorate) and was appointed lecturer at
his alma mater. His doctoral thesis, which also served as the basis for
his appointment, was imbued with the spirit of conservative orthodoxy and pleased his two senior teachers – Marheineke and Hengstenberg. At the same time, it contained numerous Hegelian motifs, for
example on the Trinity, and particularly on the personality of Jesus.[16]

Bauer taught at Berlin from 1834–1839, delivering lectures on the
philosophy of religion, the Bible, the New Testament, history of the
Church and the history of dogma. There is no way of ascertaining the
degree of popularity of his lectures; the sole evaluation available is
that of Hengstenberg from 1843, i.e. at the time when Bauer was the
sworn enemy of theology and of Hengstenberg. According to the
latter's evidence, which is apparently slanted, few students attended
Bauer's lectures since "his dry abstractions tired and bored the
listeners."[17]

The suggestion that employment of Hegelian terminology and
concepts borrowed from Hegelian philosophy led to Bauer's alleged
failure, are not consistent with the facts, since the Hegelian system
of thought was well-known to philosophy students and the lectures
of the Hegelians were well attended (for example, those of Michelet,
Erdmann, Rosenkranz and Vatke).

Bauer commenced his career as a writer and scholar in the Hegelian journal *Jahrbücher für wissenschaftliche Kritik*, published from
1827 onwards. During his five years of teaching in Berlin he published
some 40 articles and reviews; most of the latter appeared in the *Jahrbücher*, while the articles mostly appeared in *Zeitschrift für spekulative
Theologie*[18] where he served as main editor. Both articles and reviews

---

[14] G. W. F. Hegel: *Vorlesungen über die Ästhetik*[3], vol. I, p. 7.
[15] BE 48–51.
[16] Ernst Barnikol: *Bruno Bauer. Studien und Materialien*, pp. 22–23.
[17] Evangelische Kirchenzeitung 6/1843, p. 43.
[18] Hertz-Eichenrode: *Der Junghegelianer Bruno Bauer im Vormärz*, VII–X.

reflected his conservative-orthodox approach. It is not surprising, therefore, that Bauer attacked D. F. Strauss's sensational book on the life of Jesus, which presaged the beginning of the process of splitting up of the Hegelians into groups hostile to one another.

CHAPTER IV

THE SPLIT IN THE HEGELIAN SCHOOL – EMERGENCE OF THE YOUNG HEGELIANS

Until the death of Hegel in 1831, there was a united front of Hegelians against other philosophical trends. Hegel supported, by various means, the establishment of a philosophical school and its bolstering against conceptions which differed from his own theories, and was aided in his endeavours by the Prussian Minister of Religion and Culture, von Altenstein. This did not escape the attention of von Humboldt, who wrote in 1828: "Hegel is maintaining a school and is doing this work deliberately."[1] But this unity, which lasted during the lifetime of the philosopher, came to an end shortly after his death. The speaker, who at his funeral cited the precedent of the dividing up of Alexander the Great's empire by the satraps,[2] could not have dreamed that the "war of the Diadochs" would break out so soon.

The disputes among the Hegelians and the split of the school into warring sectors occurred against the background of varying interpretations of Hegel's theory of religion, its essence and significance in the life of man and society. The crisis was triggered off by D. F. Strauss, who openly advocated Hegel's way of thinking, but interpreted both the Christological principles of Christianity and the process of crystallization of religion in a way which was not acceptable to many supporters of this philosophy. In order to understand the differences of opinion within the school, it is necessary first to examine Hegel's stand on religion.

In his conception of religion, as in his approach to other areas, Hegel did not see the empirical reality as the starting point. The dictate of logic determines that, as in other spheres of life: "If anything has truth, it has it through its idea; or something has truth

---

[1] Cited by Ludwig Noack: *Philosophie-geschichtliches Lexikon*. Leipzig 1879, p. 350.
[2] J. E. Erdmann: *Philosophie der Neuzeit*, vol. II, Berlin 1896, p. 641.

only insofar as it is idea",[3] or, as Hegel says elsewhere: "for the idea is one in all things; it is universal necessity; reality can be only the mirror of the idea, and for consciousness the idea can accordingly issue forth from everything, for it is always the idea that is in these infinitely many drops which reflect back the idea."[4]

The idea is a notion which realizes itself.[5] Religion is development of the notion and this development is nothing but determination of what is included in the notion. This determination fashions the reality of the notion.[6]

Within Hegel's general system, religion is the form of development of the absolute spirit, constituting a synthesis of the subjective spirit and the objective spirit. According to this concept, religion is a kind of attitude of the human consciousness towards God, or, to be more exact, the self-perception of God within the framework of the self-consciousness: "God is God only so far as he knows himself; his self-knowledge is, further, his self-consciousness in man, and man's knowledge of God, which proceeds to man's self-knowledge in God."[7]

The motifs present here are more clearly seen in the following remarks by Hegel: "God is also finite, while the self is infinite. God returns to himself within the self to cancel finiteness, and is God only within this return. *Without the world, God is not God.*"[8]

It transpires, therefore, that from Hegel's point of view God is a kind of process of the absolute and the absolute is a process of the divine spirit which, at the end of this process, is what it is: a God who comes to himself. And all this occurs in the sphere of the human consciousness, wherein, in the stages of his development, God knows and conceives of himself.

Whereas in pre-Christian religions the notion of religion is realized in specific and partial fashion,[9] in Christianity the notion arrives at completion of its development. Its emergence was a decisive turning point in human history, since this is the absolute and complete religion.[10] Christianity is a religion of revelation as well as a revealed religion, since it contains no mystery or secrets but the truth alone.[11]

---

[3] Log II, 395.
[4] PhR III, 114.
[5] Log II, 396–398.
[6] BR 63.
[7] PhM § 564.
[8] BR 148.
[9] PhR I, 148.
[10] Ibid. pp. 327–348; PhH 333.
[11] Phen 759–760; PhH 15.

The founder of the religion, Jesus Christ, is identical with the divinity or, according to another definition in Christianity, the divine spirit knows and conceives itself, makes itself into an object.[12] The process of consciousness of identity does not end with the appearence of Jesus, but reaches the height of its development within the framework of the Christian community, where identification of the individual self-consciousness of the Christian Messiah with God yields place to identification of the general consciousness with God.[13]

Following on the elevation of the Christian consciousness to the level of divinity and communion with it, man's subjugation is abolished and the declared principle is that men are free and equal before God.[14] Christianity, particularly in its Protestant form, should be regarded as the culmination of the process of development of religion, but it does not constitute the final stage in the development of human consciousness. From this point of view, philosophy has precedence over religion. In this context Hegel developed his well-known theory that, as regards its content, religion does not differ from philosophy since they have a common object: the absolute spirit, which is identical with God and with the eternal truth. "The object of religion, as well as of philosophy is eternal truth in its objectivity, God and nothing but God and the explication of God [...] philosophy only unfolds itself when it unfolds religion, and in unfolding itself it unfolds religion."[15] The difference between them results from the fact that religion knows the absolute spirit through representation and philosophy through thought.[16]

There are two reasons why philosophy is much more important than religion: philosophy knows the absolute concretely while religion knows it only in an abstract fashion. While philosophical thought both conceives and explain religion, religion is incapable of conceiving and understanding philosophy.[17]

Preference for the logical factor and the conception and understanding of the religious content as mainly spiritual-intellectual are responsible for the fact that the historical fails to play an important part in the philosophy of religion: "The truth is just that which has been called the mysteries of religion. These constitute the speculative element in religion [...]"[18] Accordingly, Jesus, for example, is understood as a

[12] Hph I, 73.
[13] Phen 760–761.
[14] PhH 416–417.
[15] PhR I, 19.
[16] Ibid. pp. 21–23; HPh I, 63–64.
[17] Ibid. pp. 21–22; HPh I, 64–81.
[18] HPh I, 79.

spirit, or as the general self-consciousness,[19] while the historical image
of Jesus as a concrete and individual personality does not appear within
Hegel's field of vision. The author of the *Phenomenology* was conscious
of the christological principles he advocated, when he claimed that the
personality of Jesus and the external conditions within which he operated did not pertain to religion, but to the natural world, while the
spirit of truth which filled him and his reconciliation with God belonged
to the sphere of religion and as such should interest the philosopher of
religion.[20] The speculative idea in religion also finds expression in the
concept of the Trinity which was defined by Hegel as follows: "The
abstract God, the Father, is the Universal, the eternal all-embracing
total particularity. We have reached the stage of spirit; here the Universal includes everything within itself; the Other, the Son, is infinite
particularity, manifestation; the third, the Spirit, is individuality as
such. The Universal, however, as totality is itself Spirit; all three are
Spirit."[21]

The idea of the Trinity is not merely a matter of the three images
of the Christian God; this category is exploited by Hegel mainly in
order to demonstrate his own philosophical method. Hegel is saying
something explicit here, whereas he claimed that the Church regarded
the Trinity as the relation between the three forms of the Christian
God – the Father, the Son and the Holy Spirit, but "this is a childlike
relation, a childlike natural form."[22] Hegel understands the above idea
as the basic principle of the logical-onthological self movement of the
spirit, which is in a permanent state of externalization for the sake of
realization within reality, but, despite this, exists eternally within
itself, since it always returns to itself and overcomes the externalization.[23]

On the philosophical-religious plane the idea of the Trinity expresses
the eternal unity, the dialectical intermediary between God and man.
For Hegel, Christianity represents the absolute stage of religion since
it has succeeded in understanding the meaning of this idea unequivocally.[24] But there is no doubt that the principle of the Trinity is of
universal importance just because of its great significance within the

---

[19] PhR III, 33–45.
[20] *Vorlesung über die Philosophie der Weltgeschichte.* Edited by Georg Lasson, Leipzig
1919, pp. 735–740.
[21] PhR III, 25.
[22] Idem.
[23] Phen 755–769.
[24] PhR III, 11–12.

framework of the Hegelian system. Herein lies the explanation of Hegel's view that "God is thus recognized as Spirit, only when known as the Triune. This new principle is the axis on which the history of the world turns [...] This is the *goal* and the *starting point* of history."[25] As we have noted, philosophy has priority over religion and there is no doubt as to its priority where Hegel is concerned. He deduced from this, consistently, that philosophy, and not the Church, conducts the authentic worship of God.[26] Philosophers are the true priests, it is they who know the secret of the divinity. The sacred writings without correct interpretation, that is to say philosophical interpretation based on the Hegelian interpretation[27] are nothing but dead letters.[28] On the other hand, proliferation of interpretations made the sacred writings into "what may be called a nose of wax: this man finds this thing, the other man that."[29]

Hegel believed that if Christianity was based on the Bible "it is brought down to the level of unspirituality."[30] He regarded himself as a Protestant and, on every occasion, highlighted his affiliation to this religion and the importance of the Lutheran-Evangelical faith to his beliefs and his life.[31] There is no reason to doubt the sincerity of his declarations. But there is a considerable discrepancy between his view of himself and the main points of his theory. In his view of religion as the relation of the consciousness to God, in his conception of God as a spirit, an absolute substance and eternal truth, and of the historical religions as developing in accordance with developmental dynamics of the notion, – Hegel interprets all these problems mostly in panlogical and intellectuel terms. In Hegel's philosophy God is not endowed with Christian qualities: personal, merciful, redeemer etc. Furthermore, and this is perhaps the central category casting doubts on the Christianity of the system–Hegel's philosophy is characterized by the immanency of God in the world and in man and hence by man's presence within God. The principle of obtaining absolute knowledge of the eternal truth, "science", according to Hegel – also overcame the limitations of the Christian faith. This faith is no longer evidence of something hidden, as Paul wrote in his Epistle to the Hebrews, but the absolute knowl-

---

[25] PhH 319.
[26] PhR I, 20.
[27] See on this point Nicolai Hartmann: *Die Philosophie des deutschen Idealismus*. Vol. II. *Hegel*. Berlin-Leipzig 1929, p. 38; see also PhR I, 21, 24–26.
[28] BR 39; HPh III, 12–13.
[29] Ibid. 38; HPh III, 13.
[30] HPh III, 13.
[31] See for example HPh I, 73.

edge of the self-understanding spirit. One cannot, therefore, but agree with the conclusions of Iljin, who understood Hegel on this point as follows: "This 'new revelation' – and Hegel saw himself as its representative and interpreter – can, under no circumstances, be identified with Christianity – for one sole reason at least: Jesus' teaching has nothing in common with pantheism and panlogism and it opens the way for man to a personal God, a merciful father, a redeeming son of God . . ."[32] And then: "Hegel *learned* his best things [. . .] in Christ's Gospel; but what he *taught* was not Christianity."[33]

Any scholar who sees but this apect of Hegel's philosophy, which is alien to the spirit of the Gospels and to traditional Christian teachings, is taking a onesided view. Hegel's system, as a giant synthesis, created by superb intellectuel forces, of all of Western thought, from Aristotle to Schelling and from Jesus to Jacob Böhme, neither rejected religion in general nor Christianity in particular. It coopted them and integrated them within its framework. Religion was absorbed in the Hegelian sub-framework according to Hegel's dialectical concept and, in particular, in accordance with the principle of *Aufhebung*, i.e. elevation to a higher level of reason. This is attested to by the general attitude to religion, which was basically positive from Hegel's early writings until the day of his death. Even when he was directing harsh criticism at various manifestatons of politicization and exploitaton of religion for purposes which may be denoted ideological, and fighting prejudice, he nevertheless held a positive view both of religion in general and Jesus' teaching in particular, both as regards the moral level and the positive function it fulfilled.[34]

Hegel's stand on religious matters was far removed from the spirit of the Gospels and alien to the principles of Christianity in general but, in the end, Hegel combined Jesus' principles with the creative logos, and thus transformed man into a collaborator with God, both in his redemption and in the process of development of the divine spirit.

There can be no doubt that a widespread philosophical-theoretical system which aspired to revealing the rational contents of religious images and dogmas could not arrive at unequivocal solutions. And this, in fact, is what happened. Hegel himself did not differentiate suffi-

---

[32] Iwan Iljin: *Die Philosophie Hegels als kontemplative Gotteslehre.* Bern 1946, p. 381.
[33] Ibid. p. 418.
[34] For this point see: *Hegel's theologische Jugendschriften.* Edited by Hermann Nohl, Tübingen 1907, pp. 3, 5, 112–150, 175, 347–348; BR 34, 69, 177, 311; HPh I, 62–63, III, 5–6, 10–12, 21–23; PhR 333–335, 416–417; *Vorlesungen über die Ästhetik.* Edited by Fr. Bassenge. (Ost)Berlin, Aufbau Verlag 1955, p. 250.

ciently clearly between principles of faith and dogmas, as D. F. Strauss noted.[35] Those who tended to accept the orthodox interpretation, or those philosophers who advocated an independent approach to religious faith could rely on the Hegelian conception. The former based themselves on Hegel in order to explain the rational nature of the Protestant faith, while the latter treated the system as a model for evaluating various principles of Christianity, and of Lutheranism in particular. At the same time, the reconciliation of faith and philosophy aroused protest in two groups hostile to Hegel – among the extreme orthodoxists and the uncompromising rationalists.

Sharp criticism was already directed against Hegel in his lifetime. It was argued that in Hegel's system of thought religious-dogmatic principles had forfeited their original meaning, since they had become philosophical terms, aimed at proving the truth of the system and nothing more. It was argued that God, as conceived by Hegel, had nothing in common with the Christian God, who punished sinners and granted his mercy to those who did good, and that it was easy to reduce this God to a rational entity, operating in accordance with the rules of Hegelian logic and that this absolute entity could not be separated from the rest of the world and arrived at self-recognition through man's consciousness, Hegel was accused of having abolished the distance between man and God, of intending to create identity between them, of being a pantheist or even an atheist.

Hegel was also attacked on another point – the question of the immortality of the soul. It was argued against him that his abolition of the personification of God also led to the vanishing of the individual believing human being with his eternal soul, which rose up to Heaven after the death of the body, and it was further said that Hegel had replaced the principle of the immortality of the soul by the theory of the absorption of the soul by the absolute.[36]

The jurist Göschel, who responded to Hegel's critics, understood the concepts of philosophy as compatible with the words of God[37] and as the fruit of Christianity.[38] He regarded Christian symbolism as the justification of speculative philosophy.[39] He believed that Hegelian

[35] *Streitschriften zur Verteidigung meiner Schrift über das Leben Jesu und zur Charakteristik der gegenwärtigen Theologie.* Tübingen 1837, pp. 95–96.
[36] Erdmann: *Philosophie der Neuzeit*, vol. II, pp. 642–659; Gebhardt: *Politik und Eschatologie*, pp. 66–68.
[37] *Aphorismen über Nichtwissen und absolutes Wissen im Verhältnis zum christlichen Glaubenserkenntnis.* Berlin 1829, p. 97.
[38] Ibid. p. 2.
[39] Ibid. pp. 63–67, 160.

philosophy was based on revelation, since only within the framework
of the revelation and through the Christian Messiah could man recognize God.[40] Göschel even argued that this philosophy advocated the
personalization of God and the immortality of the soul. Hegel himself
set the seal of approval on these opinions.[41] And essays were written by
Hegelians such as Gabler, Marheineke, Daub, Konradi and others in
the spirit of Göschel's views.[42]

As against Göschel's theories, Ludwig Feuerbach, in his anonymously published 1830 essay on death and immortality, represented the
opposite viewpoint. The idea of individual immortality is the product
of Protestantism and modern individualism, since both place emphasis
on the individual and assume that his perfection leads to immortality,
while philosophy proves that only reason and the spiritual life of mankind are unlimited and included within the concept of immortality.
Human life is finite and limited to the period of time and the place in
which man lives under earthly conditions. The sole significance of immortality for the finite man is related to the affiliation of man to the
species which is, as noted, characterized by the quality of immortality
in the spiritual sense.[43] Feuerbach's book met with almost no response
among the Hegelians for several reasons: his contempt for Marheineke,
whom they respected; certain expressions which could be interpreted
as a disguised attack on Hegel himself; and in particular the basing of
the essay on the conflict between the finite and the infinite, the essence
and the phenomenon etc., which, according to Hegel, are categories
which only the abstract understanding cannot overcome.[44]

But, after a relatively short time, in 1833, two years after the death
of Hegel, the Hegelians found themselves the focus of a stormy dispute
on the question of the immortality of the soul. It was sparked off by
an essay by Friedrich Richter, who denied the continuity of human
life after the death of the body and claimed that the dogmatic-Christian
principles were totally irrelevant to Hegelian philosophy. He even suggested that only egoistic people were interested in this belief, since they
were unwilling to give up their lives, even within the gloomy framework of the baptism of fire according to Christian concepts of sin and
punishment etc. He believed that philosophy should move away from

[40] Ibid. pp. 63, 65.
[41] BS 353–389.
[42] Erdmann: *Philosophie der Neuzeit*, vol. II, § 239.
[43] *Gedanken über Tod und Unsterblichkeit*. Ed. W. Bolin and Fr. Jodl. Stuttgart 1903,
(SW, I), pp. 6–15, 44, 68–73, 80–82.
[44] Erdmann: *Philosophie der Neuzeit*, vol. II, p. 688.

the idea of redemption after death and transplant eschatology from the Judgment Day to the sphere of philosophical speculation. The necessary conclusions drawn from this theory should later be realized in historical existence.[45]

But it was Strauss and not Richter who caused the split among the Hegelians, or, to put it more exactly: the trends previously evident found such extreme expression as a result of Strauss's literary activity that the split became inescapable.

Strauss was a graduate of the famed Tübingen Theological Seminary. He was an admirer of Hegel and even went to Berlin in order to study under him, but arrived shortly before Hegel's death in time to attend his funeral. His renowned essay on the life of Jesus appeared in 1835 and this work, together with others, put an end to attempts at reconciliation of philosophy and theology. According to Strauss, the vision of eternal peace and harmony between philosophy and religion was groundless, and those scholars who could not reconcile themselves to the imaginary harmony and who simply exposed the distortions and twofacedness of religion more than others were the Hegelians.[46] Although religion is widely regarded as the wisdom of the world, in actual fact it is, said Strauss, incompatible with both understanding and justice. To prove this point he cites the fact that religious institutions persecuted scholars and scientists, mentioning explicitely the cruel deaths of Bruno and Vanini and the torturing of Galileo.[47]

Strauss acknowledged that, despite the errors in Hegel's conception of religion (the reconciliation of religion and philosophy, the apologetics for religion), the Hegelian philosophy of religion provides a correct explanation of religion as the product of human consciousness. "According to Hegel's concept, religion was representation and feeling, but these two were but the form of religion; the content was mental, intellectual and the right of thought and science to decide matters relating to themselves and to their relations with religion, were recognized.[48]

As assumed that religion is the product of human consciousness, Strauss rejects the existence of supernatural entities. He even criticized dogmas common to all trends of Christianity, such as divine revelation, supernatural inspiration of the Holy Scriptures, the Trinity, prophesy

[45] Friedrich Richter: *Die Lehre von den letzten Dingen*. Breslau 1833.
[46] D. F. Strauss: *Die christliche Glaubenslehre in ihrer Entwicklung und im Kampf mit der modernen Wissenschaft*. Tübingen 1840, p. 2.
[47] Ibid. p. 6.
[48] Ibid. p. 11.

etc.[49] Using the Hegelian assumptions, Strauss integrated the absolute spirit within the process of development of nature and society and disagreed with the dogma concerning the Creation: "If God is not a transcendent entity, then the creation of the world is no longer related to an arbitrary act by God, which could happen but did not *have* to happen. The creation of the world should be regarded as a necessary stage in the development of the absolute idea."[50]

Strauss views the history of religions, including the Christianity, as the embodiment of ideas,[51] i.e. as the process of development in which religious ideas take on historical form.[52] He identifies these ideas with myth, which to his mind, is the product of unconscious creation of religious sects. "[...] The myth of the New Testament", he wrote, "is nothing but early Christian ideas which have taken on historical guise, created as an unconscious narrated legend."[53] The concept of myth, employed by some theologians and philosophers before Strauss – for example Gabler and Schelling – to clarify certain religious phenomena, was considerably expanded by the author of *Das Leben Jesu*, who applied it to most of the New Testament texts. The stories of the Immaculate Conception, Jesus' family background, the healing of the sick, the crucifixion, the resurrection of Jesus[54] etc., are the products of the unrestrained imaginary consciousness of the Christian sects.

The main problem which preoccupied Strauss in his attack on orthodox-theological circles was the dogma of the embodiment of God in Jesus. This dogma was particularly hard to decipher from the standpoint of the Hegelian philosophy. The identification of God with the infinite absolute, which through self-cognition is embodied in limited beings made extremely difficult to accept the theory that the absolute can fully express itself in an individual who is finite as regards time and space. It is logically inconsistent, for the infinite to find complete expression in something finite,[55] Strauss argued, referring to the fact that the infinite and unlimited absolute was embodied in Jesus. In contrast to Karl Rosenkranz, who believed that "Jesus is not a complex of definitions relating to the human spirit, but simply their concrete uni-

[49] Ibid. pp. 156–158, 205–210, 246–267, 462–465, 583–585.
[50] Ibid. pp. 66–67.
[51] *Das Leben Jesu, kritisch bearbeitet*, vol. I, Tübingen 1835, p. 2.
[52] Ibid. p. 74.
[53] Ibid. p. 75.
[54] Ibid. 115–129, 173–180, 232–233, 288–294, 417–429. Vol. II (1836), 24–31, 527–557, 645–664.
[55] D. F. Strauss: *Streitschriften zur Verteidigung meiner Schrift über das Leben Jesu und zur Charakteristik der gegenwärtigen Theologie*, Heft 1, Tübingen 1837, pp. 69–72, 76–80.

fication" and "the essence of the idea also contains within it the recognition of its embodiment in the image of the individual or, to be more
precise, in the image of this individual",[56] Strauss, in his renowned
summary in *Das Leben Jesu* presented the theory that God the absolute is constantly embodied within the human race and thus realizes
his infinite essence. "The idea does not realize itself through transplanting its content to one individual and thus preventing others from receiving it. To the contrary: it tends to bestow its riches on many, who
complement one another, and in incessant change replace one another."[57] This is the key to all the Straussian Christology, that in place
of one sole object it sets up all humanity. Mankind is a kind of unity of
the two natures: the divine and the human, and thus, the humanization
of God (*Menschwerdung Gottes*) is attributed to the human race as a
whole and not to the individual.

The fact that in the Roman world, it was believed that Jesus was
the embodiment of God is explained by Strauss with the aid of psychology: at a time of profound breach, of physical and spiritual plight,
the Christians conceived of an entity symbolizing the divine element
struggling with suffering and death, and within a brief period there
emerged belief in its resurrection, which was to serve as the guarantee
for general resurrection. In other words – the individual fate of Jesus
was transformed into an expression of the imaginary general consciousness.[58]

Strauss's concept brought Christianity down from the peak of the
pyramid – it ceased to be the absolute religion, for the simple reason
that the incessant embodiment of the absolute within all mankind
transformed Christianity into one of the levels, and not even a particularly high level, of the manifestation of the absolute. At the same time,
in contrast to the prevalent view, Strauss did not deny the historical
existence of Jesus.[59] He assumed the existence of a historical nucleus
within the Gospel stories, around which the myth had crystallized,
created unconsciously by members of the early Christian community
who lived later and were not acquainted with Jesus. Strauss does not
clearly delineate the borders between the authentic material and the
mythological element. His attitude towards this problem is hesitant.
In the first edition of *Das Leben Jesu* the historical nucleus is reasonably

[56] Karl Rosenkranz: *Enzyklopädie der theologischen Wissenschaft.* Halle 1831, p. XVII;
Kritik der Schleiermacherschen Glaubenslehre. Königsberg 1837, p. XVI.
[57] *Das Leben Jesu*, vol. II, p. 734.
[58] Ibid. pp. 635–636. See also *Streitschriften*... pp. 74–75.
[59] Ibid. vol. I, pp. 104, 191, 389–390, 544, 553.

limited, but under pressure of conservative-orthodox circles he introduced considerable concessions into the third edition in favour of the
traditional view of the origins of Christianity. In the fourth edition,
on the other hand, he returned to his original theory.[60]

Strauss made a valuable contribution to the formulation of a radical
stand on religion. There were two reasons for this: 1) critique of the
Jewish and Christian holy writings, and of the orthodox version of
Christianity, its essence, origins and development, and what is related
to this: negation of Christian dogmatism; 2) rejection of the theory
that existing reality is an expression of the full realization of the idea
and the absolute. In accordance with Strauss's historiosophical concept
the infinite should not be reduced to a finite being, realization of the
idea is an continuous process. Strauss deduced from the fact that the
idea is not fully expressed in existing reality that the future stages of
its development are more important than the existing ones, and that
it is then that the idea will be realized in more complete form within
actual historical events.

The tendency to emphasize the future, which was already evident
in Richter, is consciously developed in Strauss's conception, as on the
basis of Hegel, he formulates the idea if realization in the future. This
idea, which was adopted by all the radical Hegelians, did not fit in
with the postulate that Hegel and his immediate pupils advocated:
that philosophy can only comprehend its own times, the reality which
encompasses it or, as Hegel put it: "Whatever happens, every individual is a child of his time; so philosophy too is its own time appre-
hended in thoughts. It is just as absurd to fancy that a philosophy can
transcend its contemporary word as it is to fancy that an individual
can leap beyond his own age."[61]

The transplanting of emphasis from the present to the future had
one very important implication: the present situation was seen as
limited, fragmentary and incomplete. Within the framework of this
conception, lack of approval of the existing situation was self-evident.
Christianity ceased to be the perfect expression of the religious idea,
just as Hegelian philosophy ceased to fulfil the function of absolute
philosophy and became a springboard for the search of those with
radical orientation for a new path. This is valid both for Strauss and
for the other Young Hegelians, such as Cieszkowski, Ruge, Bruno
Bauer, Hess, the young Marx etc.

[60] Albert Schweitzer: *Geschichte der Leben-Jesu-Forschung*, vol. I, p. 154.
[61] PhRt 11.

In addition to the historiosophical approach, emanating from an infinitist interpretation of Hegel's philosophy or from consistent application of Hegel's dialectical methodology to all the phenomena of the history of mankind, there is an additional factor which constituted a link between the critique of religion commenced by Strauss and other Young Hegelians, such as Feuerbach and Bauer, and criticism of other manifestations of human life, and above all, political ones: the destruction of faith in Jesus as a redeemer or in religious redemption, inevitably created a new vision of salvation achieved on earth. The negation of religious eschatology raised, in its stead, belief in politics as a means of redemption or, to employ a secular phrase, a means of liberating man from subjugation to earthly powers. The Young Hegelian movement would seem to confirm Camus's theory that only two worlds exist for the human spirit: sanctity and revolt. A being who anticipates divine mercy is incapable of rebelling against the mundane order. The disappearance of the world of sanctity brings in its wake the creation of the world of rebellion.[62]

The eschatological category, which at first was linked to religion, takes on human-earthly flavour, to a large extent, in Strauss's works since man takes upon himself the work of Jesus or, as Gebhardt says: "Strauss consciously attributes to himself the task of Jesus."[63] But changes occurred on this plane as well. Though Strauss still preserved the rational nucleus of religion, the religious-theological content of eschatology soon yielded place, in the fullest meaning of the term, to the secular and anthropological. Strauss's rational and immanent religion was replaced by critique of religion in general and by Bauer's atheism, and the hope of rational improvement of the existing Prussian political institutions was succeeded by criticism of the existing state. But there is continuity of motifs in both cases – the liberation of man, and creation of conditions enabling people to live free lives without oppression and humiliation.

The term Young Hegelians (*Junghegelianer*) calls for clarification. At first it was employed to denote both the young generation of pupils

---

[62] Albert Camus: *L'Homme révolté*. Paris 1951, p. 34.

[63] Gebhardt: *Politik und Eschatologie*, p. 93. In his work Gebhardt expounds the theory that the Hegelians, and particularly the radicals among them, regarded politics as the eschatology of this world. Incidentally: an eschatological tone was already evident in the young Hegel. This tendency was expressed in those sections of the early theological writings (the inapt title Nohl gave to those essays which contain abundant antitheological motifs) in which Hegel analyzes positive institutionalized and authoritative Christianity and arrives at the conclusion that present-day Christianity had reached the same stage as Judaism at the time of Jesus when it was in need of basic reform. Hegel's "folk religion" should fulfil the functions of Jesus' religion of centuries earlier.

of Hegel, who knew him for only a brief period to his death (Feuerbach, Bruno Bauer etc.) and those who never met him, (Hess, Marx,
for example), and studied his theories through his writings. But the
term soon lost its original significance and increasingly symbolized an
oppositionary attitude towards the ideological, political and even
social conditions then prevailing. Criticism of certain phenomena in
intellectual and social life derived at first radical interpretation of
Hegel's philosophy. But, in due course, there was increased detachment from Hegel, accompanied, in many cases, by sharp attacks on
his methodology. In both the cases cited the Young Hegelians were in
opposition to the Old Hegelians (*Althegelianer*), i.e., the older generation of Hegel's pupils who generally tended towards reconciliation of
Christianity and Hegelian philosophy and to preservation of the latter's
framework.[64]

But, in addition to the term Young Hegelians, we find, in literature
on the subject, that the title Left Hegelians (*Linkshegelianer*) is also
employed; it originated with Strauss who divided the Hegelians, like
the political currents of the French Revolution, into left, centre, and
right. His criteria for classification are religious – the attitude towards
unity of human and divine nature, the nature of God, the problem of
immortality etc.[65] Strauss classified himself alone in the leftwing group
and located his sworn opponents, such as Gabler, Göschel, Bruno
Bauer and others on the right. Rosenkranz, who represented a more
moderate stand, was classified at belonging to the centre.

As new spheres, such as cultural institutions, education, the state
etc. – were added to the subjects of criticism such as religion and church
institutions – the term Left Hegelians was considerably expanded.[66]
But employment of the term "left", which is essentially political, does
not appear relevant where the Young Hegelians are concerned, for
several reasons:

1) The radical group of Hegelians never arrived at crystallization of
an organizational framework and was never united. The sole sphere of
cooperation of members of the group was literature – participation in
a limited number of journals, particularly those edited by Ruge. The
lack of cohesion resulted from the conditions then prevailing in Prussia

---

[64] K. Löwith: *From Hegel to Nietzsche*, pp. 50–62.
[65] D. F. Strauss: *Streitschriften...*, pp. 95–110.
[66] Wilhelm R. Beyer: *Hegel-Bilder. Kritik der Hegel-Deutungen.* (Ost)Berlin 1970[3], pp. 51–
64.

– absence of freedom of association and of expression.[67] This was the direct cause of the speedy closing down of radical journals.[68]

2) Not all the Old Hegelians, who disagreed with their juniors, represented conservative political tendencies. Thus, for example, Gans, the well-known jurist from Berlin University, who was Marx's teacher, disseminated progressive ideas, on both the political and the social plane.[69] And even if we reject Lübbe's theory that the right represented a characteristically liberal political line,[70] because of its general, abstract far-reaching nature, it is still clear that liberal trends remained within the group which fought the Young Hegelians.

3) Hence the employment of political criteria obscures the essence and borderlines of intellectual activity and obstructs understanding of it. And, in general, it seems that political concepts are irrelevant to a *Weltanschauung*, a philosophical standpoint, views on religion, culture, education etc. The utilization of political-party concepts as regards philosophy and religion took root among orthodox-dogmatist Marxists as a result of Lenin's ideas, as presented in his article on *The Significance of Militant Materialism*.[71] Lenin differentiated between idealism, religion and a political and social standpoint that was hostile to the proletariat, progress and communism on the one hand, – and materialism, atheism and the interests of the proletariat and of progress on the other. There is no substantiation for this differentiation – there have been materialists and atheists who represented a reactionary standpoint and vice versa: quite a few idealists and supporters of religious ideas held leftwing political views.

The use of the term Young Hegelians is therefore preferable to the term Left Hegelians or the Hegelian Left.

---

[67] Reinhart Koselleck: *Staat und Gesellschaft in Preussen 1815–1848*. In *Staat und Gesellschaft im deutschen Vormärz 1815–1848*. Stuttgart 1952, pp. 79–112.

[68] See Fritz Schlawe: *Die junghegelische Publizistik*. Die Welt als Geschichte 11/1960, pp. 30–46; Hans Rosenberg: *Arnold Ruge und die "Hallischen Jahrbücher"*. Archiv für Kulturgeschichte, vol. 20, pp. 292–308.

[69] On Gans see Cornu: *Karl Marx und Friedrich Engels. Leben und Werk*, vol. I, pp. 74–76. Stuke (*Die Philosophie der Tat*, pp. 32–33) rightly points to Gans as a serious obstacle to identify the Old Hegelians with the right. But doubt should be cast on another of his theses, namely that there were Young Hegelians who supported right-wing ideas, since Kierkegaard, despite his classification in this group by Löwith, was never a Young Hegelian.

[70] Hermann Lübbe: *Die politische Theorie der Hegelschen Rechte*. Archiv für Philosophie. Stuttgart 1960, p. 175 ff.; *Die Hegelsche Rechte. Texte*. Stuttgart 1962, p. 10.

[71] W. I. Lenin: *O znachenii woinstwoyushchego materializma*. Sochineniya, Izd. IV, tom 33, Moscow 1953, pp. 202–203.

CHAPTER V

BRUNO BAUER AS A THEOLOGIAN AND CRITIC OF STRAUSS

The response to Strauss's *Leben Jesu* on the part of the orthodox-conservative Hegelians was penned by Bruno Bauer. This came as a complete surprise to intellectual circles in Germany which had expected Göschel, Marheineke or Gabler, i.e. a well-known personality, to launch the anti-Strauss polemic in writing. The editorial board of the *Jahrbücher für wissenschaftliche Kritik* took an unconventional step in accepting Bauer's critical article for publication, before it had received the reactions of the more famous Hegelians. But, at the same time, there was justification for the decision: Bauer was regarded as a rising star in the academic world, as a result of several articles he had published. His critique of Strauss's book made the young lecturer famous throughout Germany overnight, and increased his prestige in the eyes of the conservative Hegelians.

On the other hand, radical elements among the Hegelians began to regard Bauer with reservation, suspicion and even anger. In 1839 Ruge had classified Bauer among the conservatives together with "the camels, Göschel and Erdmann."[1] Bauer's attack on Strauss aroused the hostility of the latter, and this attitude never changed while both lived. In 1842, seven years after their first controversy, Strauss informed Ruge that he felt obliged to cease contributing to the *Deutsche Jahrbücher* because it had published a favourable review of one of Bauer's books. Ruge wrote of this incident: "Strauss spits poison at Bauer and vice versa. Strauss cannot tolerate the changes which have occurred in Bauer's views nor his extremism [...] Bauer, for his part, seeks glory in condemning Strauss."[2]

Bauer did not attempt to disguise the fact that his radical criticism

---

[1] *Ruges Briefwechsel und Tagebuchblätter aus den Jahren 1825–1880.* Edited by P. Nerrlich. Vol. I. Berlin 1886, p. 181.
[2] Ibid. p. 260.

stemmed from his ideological conflict with Strauss's theories: "After Strauss's great achievement, criticism will never again face the danger involved in continued advocating of the categories of the old orthodox viewpoint."[3]

After his first critique in 1835, Bauer published four additional ones, in which he discussed the significance of the concept of myth and the essence of Strauss's attack on the Hegelian-conservative version of Christianity. He claimed that the struggle on this point was being conducted in two directions: rationalism, which sought a natural-scientific cause for every occurrence and clarified the events depicted in the Holy Scriptures, and mythological interpretation, which strove to represent sacred history as grounded in the human imagination, and thus to invalidate religious dogmas and, above all, the basic principles of Christianity. But what had appeared, before Strauss, as a limited approach to some of the bible stories, was transformed in Strauss's work into a frontal attack.[4]

It was Bauer's view that the concept of total rejection, through transformation of all sacred history into mythology could only benefit speculative theology, since it helped the latter to comprehend the nature of its enemy and his intentions. But, at the same time, Bauer was not trying to defend the historical nature of the events depicted in the Gospels, according to Hegel's postulate: "You may make of Jesus, from the interpretive, critical, historical viewpoint, what you will [...] the sole question which should be asked here is – what is the idea in itself and for itself."[5]

According to Bauer, Strauss's ideas were a continuation of the empirical analysis which had characterized the various rationalists who, on the basis of the contradiction between natural-historical findings and commonsense on the one hand, and the revelation, miracles etc. on the other, sought total rejection of the entire structure of religion.[6]

Before Strauss, critics had employed mythological arguments as regards the three Synoptic Gospels, whereas the author of *Das Leben Jesu* discussed the fourth Gospel as well. But the destruction of the religious framework only goes to prove that the mythological method is, by essence antithetical, destroying without building. This destructive viewpoint is typical of the modern world since the Enlightenment, basing

[3] Syn I, p. VIII.
[4] JWK 1835, No 109, p. 889.
[5] ZspT II, 2 (1837), pp. 411–412.
[6] JWK 1837, No 41, p. 323.

itself on history and empirical findings and totally indifferent towards
the idea underlying the various phenomena, including the phenomenon
of religion.[7] Bauer deduced from this the need for a new synthesis,
which does not negate the analytical-empirical methodology but, at the
same time, is capable of delving to the depths of problems and of
understanding the idea which constitutes the basis and essence of the
phenomenon. Bauer's objections to Strauss's approach are aimed at
proving that *Das Leben Jesu* does not solve the central problem of
Hegelian philosophy: history and the speculative method confront one
another without any real contact between them. The idea does not
appear in integral fashion within the historical events. As a result, the
spirit utilizes an unconscious myth, in order to realize itself within the
consciousness of the Christian sects. If it were possible to substantiate
this theory speculatively, it could be deduced that the idea of the
Christian faith is not, in fact, dependent on the events in the Gospels.[8]
In this case it is necessary to clarify another problem: is the concept of
myth understood by Strauss in so pure a fashion that "its absolute
content [...] constitutes the moving force behind its creation?"[9]
Bauer's answer is negative. Strauss cannot apply his theory to many of
the New Testament stories, since he believes that they displayed
tendentiousness, for example as regards the adaptation of the image of
Jesus to the Jewish messianic tradition. This tendentiousness is in
contradiction to Strauss's approach and methodology because it is
based on the principle of consciousness and not on unconscious development of the myth in the consciousness of Christians. Strauss is
thus contradicting himself. But what is more important: Bauer arrived
at that time at the conclusion that every historical event commences
with the activity of the individual and within his self-consciousness.
How, therefore, is it possible to present the lack of consciousness as the
central problem and as a methodological postulate?

Bauer attacks the theory of totality, arguing that in order to comprehend any large scale historical event, it is always necessary to start
out from the individual, and that this is true in the case of Christianity
and other religions as well. Messianic predicates should not be understood exclusively, as if the individual – namely Jesus – acted instead
of mankind in carrying out the abolition of the finite within the infinite;
the question should be understood inclusively: the individual opened

---

[7] Ibid. No 109, p. 886.
[8] Ibid. No 41, p. 323.
[9] Ibid, No 109, p. 904.

a gate for the whole, for mankind, to enable each and every man, each "historical self" to enter in.[10] As against the theory of the myth based on lack of direction, and as against the Straussian idea, which constitutes a substance in itself, Bauer develops the theory that the self-consciousness guides the individual in all his activities.

For Bauer, the maturity of the self-consciousness was one of the characteristic traits of speculative theology, in contrast to rationalism and the mythological approach, which lack a sufficient degree of this consciousness. Self-consciousness, which is aware of its essence and mission, lies at the basis of history and all historical events. These are the first burgeonings of Bauer's historiosophical and methodological approach, which in due course engendered his atheism and individualism.

Bauer's book, *Kritik der Geschichte der Offenbarung*, published in 1838, marked a new stage in the evolution of his outlook, and contained a reasonably solid nucleus of subjectivism. In his analysis of the concept of religion he starts with the assumption that religion is the attitude of the subject towards God or, in his own words: "It [religion] is but the process of the subjective spirit which relates to God."[11]

The title which Bauer gave to the chapter dealing with this question – "The concept of religion in its subjective manifestation" – leaves no room for doubt that not only the starting point of the discussion but the entire debate is conducted from the subjective viewpoint. Bauer held that subjectivity was one of the characteristic traits of the modern Enlightenment in its outlook on religion.[12]

Where various theologians placed emphasis on the revelation and on the presence of God in the world, Bauer was only concerned with the understanding of God by the subjective spirit,[13] or, to be more exact: he saw man's attitude to God as intellectual.[14] We should note this fact which attests to the location of the relations between man and God in the domain of the human mind, as well as to the fact that, in the end, the stages of development of these relations correspond to the forms of human consciousness. Bauer enumerates three such stages: *a*) the religious attitude in the stage of feeling; *b*) contemplation as the second stage; *c*) representation – as the third stage. It is true that Bauer bases his arguments on this question on Hegel, but the stage of contempla-

---

[10] Ibid. No 86 (1836), pp. 681–682, 703–704; No 109, pp. 903–904.
[11] RAT, vol. I, p. XXX.
[12] Idem.
[13] Ibid. p. XXXI.
[14] Idem.

tion is lacking in Hegel, and Bauer has considerably amended the essence of the two remaining stages, again – tending to emphasize the
subjective element.

Thus, for example, it is known that Hegel fought all his life against
the theory that feeling was the main source of religion, as Jacobi and
Schleiermacher, for example, claimed, and against absolutization of
feeling in epistomology.[15] For him feeling is the primary expression
non-mediated, dialectically speaking, and therefore imperfect, of the
relations existing between subject and object, a kind of storehouse in
which there are heaped, without order, all the perceptions and experience which the subject has accumulated in his contacts with the objective world, and which have no independent existence.[16] Hegel also
emphasized that the content of feeling is often neither true nor correct[17]
and noted that feeling is subjectivity in the worst meaning of the
term.[18] On this point there are considerable variations between the
Bauerian and the Hegelian conceptions. Bauer believes that thought
is contained in feeling and thus is able to arrive at the conclusion, that
within the sphere of feeling God is grasped by the thinking self. "If
thought is the sphere of unity of subject and object", he wrote, "then
this thought is already contained in feeling or, to be more exact, feeling
is the direct manifestation of thought."[19] Elsewhere Bauer points to
the fact that "in the definition of feeling, God appears as the infinite
and unlimited extension of the self."[20]

The tendency to subjectivization of religion and to a view of human
intellectual activity as the source of religion is also evident in other
Bauerian ideas; he says, for example that "God or redemption are the
products of representation"[21] or that "man relates to himself as he relates to God."[22] These subjective motifs do not appear by accident,
since Bauer deviated from the Hegelian approach of unity of subject
and object, thought and experience – and emphasized almost exclusively the great, and sometimes decisive, significance of the subject.
But here, as in his polemical arguments against Strauss, Bauer knew
where to draw the line of his subjective theories. He gave expression

---

[15] See PhR I, 118–138; HPh III, 419–422; BR 97–100, *Jenaer Schriften*. Theorie-Ausgabe.
Frankfurt/M. 1970, pp. 333–393.
[16] PhM §§ 403–405, 447, 471.
[17] BR 100–101.
[18] Ibid. 102.
[19] RAT, vol. I, p. XXXII.
[20] Ibid. XXXIII.
[21] Ibid. XLII.
[22] Ibid. XLIX.

to his belief that God is a presupposition for his attitude towards the various religious issues,[23] and thus considerably moderated the tendency to show religion as the product of human intellectual activity. But the very use of the term "presupposition" is worth examining, since it is the nature of such a supposition that it is accepted without examination of its origins, essence etc., that is to say without explicit research into it. In other words: the self-consciousness of the absolute spirit of God remains, for Bauer, an abstract construction and the dialectics of the historical process do not apply to it. Historically speaking, only human consciousness or self-consciousness can be conceived and they play a central part in history.

In the light of the dynamics of development of Bauer's philosophy, the evolution towards radicalism and atheism is logical, and his acquaintance with the literature of the French Enlightenment inevitably turned him into an atheist. Only lack of knowledge of the source material can explain why certain scholars claim that Bauer suddenly became an atheist after holding orthodox views on religion for years.[24]

It should be noted that German intellectuals who followed Bauer's philosophical development in the eighteen thirties and forties, were of an entirely different opinion. This conclusion may be drawn from an anonymous article, published in the mid-forties, which stated that Bauer, when a theologian, conducted a campaign against rationalists and Hegelians of Strauss's type, inter alia, in order to prove that no pantheistic elements were to be found in Hegel's theories whereas they were anchored deep in the philosophy of this group. Surprisingly enough, the article went on, Bauer himself had adopted those views which he had previously criticized, in particular the concept of revelation as the internal movement of the self-consciousness; human consciousness as the creator of religious ideas and the view that the self-consciousness should be liberated from all restrictions.[25] The author of the article deduced from this that "Bauer was then already defending the principle of the free self-consciousness, and refused to recognize anything else. It is also clear that these assumptions were totally unacceptable to apologetic theology and that the affair had to end in war."[26]

Shortly afterwards, in 1839, Bauer clearly separated himself from

---

[23] Idem.

[24] William J. Brazill: *The Young Hegelians*, p. 179.

[25] *Bruno Bauer oder die Entwicklung des theologischen Humanismus unserer Tage*. Wigands Vierteljahresschrift. 1845. Vol. 3, pp. 56–62.

[26] Ibid. p. 58.

the orthodox-apologetic approach. He himself was later to point to his book against Hengstenberg[27] as the work in which he abandoned – for ever – the "sophism of the apologetic concept."[28] This was not the first time that Bauer attacked Hengstenberg; he had done so before[29] but it was his first concentrated attack on the standpoints of orthodox-apologetic theology. The reason for this onslaught lay in Hengstenberg's hostile attitude towards the principle of subjectivity, as Bauer notes in one of his articles.[30]

In this polemical essay directed against Hengstenberg, Bauer explicitly identifies religious self-consciousness in its absolute internality, i.e. the pure manifestation of the principle of subjectivity – with the Gospels,[31] while viewing Judaism as coercive and external law, restricting free subjectivity and preventing it from arriving at comprehension of itself and its mission. He writes of Judaism: "The religious spirit in its historical form has not yet arrived at realization of the concept – and is in conflict with it, since it grasps it as the otherness of itself, and not as its will but as the will of God, a will essentially differing from its own." Thus all the qualities of the law are seen as external and positive,[32] as "statutory".[33] He claims that form and inner content are connected, and accordingly Judaism does not only imply the subordination of the subject and the self-consciousness to hostile and alien factors, but also contains sparks of spirit struggling for the triumph of internality; these however are mere formal statements, and their aim is to demonstrate the existence of dialectical principles within the domain of religion. This view has no practical implication, particularly as regards the Bauerian historical analysis of Judaism. Analysis of the Old Testament and the historical development of Judaism reveals according to Bauer, that this religion totally lacks belief in individual immortality and the perpetuation of spiritual life in the next world,[35] that Jewish law, which is the essence of this religion, is particularist and opposed to the principle of universality,[35] that the Hebrews did not expect spiritual reward in the Kingdom of Heaven but rather aspired to immediate recompense on earth,[36] that Jewish law is coercive and

[27] H.
[28] Fr 23.
[29] RAT, I, pp. 140, 257, II, pp. 129, 147, 268–269, 304–305, 325, 361, 370, 429.
[30] ZspT II, 2 (1837), p. 466.
[31] H 32.
[32] Ibid. pp. 33–38, 56–60, 79–80.
[33] Ibid. p. 81.
[34] Ibid, pp. 9–28.
[35] Ibid. pp. 70–77.
[36] Ibid. pp. 29–53.

political, rather than moral and based on the dictates of conscience,[37] that the Jewish revelation was extremely limited and Christianity should not be regarded as the continuation of Judaism in this respect but as a religion endowed with new quality.[38]

Christianity is identified with subjectivity, the free will, self-consciousness. Judaism symbolizes the complete opposite of all these qualities and is therefore regarded by Bauer as contemptible and unacceptable. His hostility towards the Christian-orthodox theory of the origins of Jesus' teachings and their place in the development of the religious idea, is clearly evident. Christianity is not the direct continuation of Judaism and the Christian revelation is not a continuous process emanating from the Jewish revelation, since there is no possibility whatsoever of reconciling subjectivity and the dead letter, morality rooted in individual autonomy and external coercive law, the principle of spirituality and the principe of materialism, to reconcile altruism and egoism.

His reliance on the principle of free self-consciousness led Bauer to declare war on orthodox Christianity because of its concept of Judaism as preparation of the conditions which engendered Christianity and because of its view of Christianity as the continuation of Judaism.[39] But it is not hard to see that the philosophical principle of self-consciousness, which took on historical guise, was not necessarily connected with Christianity. It became increasingly clear that it was not Christianity which was guiding Bauer's philosophical footsteps, but the principle of free self-consciousness. As long as Bauer restrained himself by accepting the authority of the basic tenets of Christianity, there was no danger that he might represent an atheistic standpoint. But, as noted, his tendency to intellectual-subjective interpretation contained within it the seed of the possibility that he would be drawn into criticism of religion from an extreme point of view. As a pupil of Hegel, from whom he derived the principle of self-consciousness, Bauer could not disregard the fact noted above, that for Hegel philosophy was more important than religion. Absolutization of the theory of the supremacy of philosophy, like the absolutization of self-consciousness (which played an important part in Hegel's philosophy, but constituted only one aspect of subject-object relations) was one of the main causes of Bauer's rejection of theism.

[37] Ibid. pp. 78–97.
[38] Ibid. pp. 67–70, 102–109.
[39] For the anti-orthodox motifs in Bauer's work, see *Herr Dr. Hengstenberg. Kritische Briefe über den Gegensatz des Gesetzes und des Evangelium* (Rez.) HJ III (1840), pp. 972–976.

Not only the development of philosophical motifs already present in his concept, but also various events in his life exerted decisive influence on this issue. His fierce onslaught on Hengstenberg led to Bauer's transfer to Bonn university, due to the intervention of von Altenstein, who wanted to help Bauer to obtain an appointment as professor, this being out of the question in Berlin after his harsh criticism of a senior member of his own department.[40]

But more important in this context are the ideological and social contacts Bauer established in the Berlin "Doktorklub", before his transfer, with young people who held extreme views. The club was attended by lecturers, high-school teachers and writers, including people who were later to become famous, such as Rutenberg, Köppen and Karl Marx. Bauer was considered the moving spirit of this group, and it is obvious that he could only have won such a position thanks to the radical tone which was beginning to be evident in his writings on religion and politics.[41] His tendency to a critical approach to religion and the German intellectual scene in those days – based on his interpretation of Hegel – developed into a clear stand under the impact of his contacts with rationalist literature with its deist and atheist motifs, and his acquaintance with various antireligious trends, mainly French in origin.

---

[40] G. A. van den Bergh van Eysinga: *Aus einer unveröffentlichen Biographie von Bruno Bauer*. Annali. Anno Sesto 1963. Feltrinelli Milano, p. 329.

[41] For Bauer's central role in the *Doktorklub*, see Jürgen von Kempski: *Bruno Bauer. Eine Studie zum Ausgang des Hegelianismus*. Archiv für Philosophie. I/1962, p. 233; Cornu: *Karl Marx und Friedrich Engels. Leben und Werk*, I, pp. 97–98.

CHAPTER VI

BAUERIAN CRITIQUE OF THE GOSPELS

Engels wrote of Bauer that of all his intellectual and research activities, the most noteworthy was his valuable and significant contribution to understanding of the early days of Christianity.[1] Elsewhere Engels speaks of Bauer as the scholar who did more than any other to advance knowledge of the nature of the Gospels.[2]

It is, of course, possible to disagree with Engels' evaluation, which was based not so much on knowledge of New Testament texts and of the facts relating to the crystallization of Christianity, as on political and ideological considerations. But his opinion is important insofar as it is the evidence of a man who played an active part in the Young Hegelian movement and was closely acquainted with Bauer. The truth is that Bauer concentrated mainly on the study of early Christianity to which he devoted the bulk of his intellectual efforts, and his books aroused great interest among thousands of German intellectuals, many of whom regarded him as a trailblazer who had succeeded in uncovering some of the most hidden secrets of Christianity and mankind.

It should be noted that for scholars and students of the subject, the problem of the origins of Christianity was not merely an academic-historical issue. Schweitzer's view that the activity of those scholars who studied the life of Jesus was not inspired by historical and scholarly interests but rather by attempt to cast off dogmas[3] is valid where Bauer is concerned, more than as regards any other scholar. The link between the events which had occurred more than eighteen hundred years before in Palestine and the Roman Empire and the prevailing political and spiritual situation, was self-evident, however strange this may seem. Jesus, as depicted by historians, was obliged, in certain

---

[1] R 247.
[2] Ibid. 195.
[3] *Geschichte der Leben-Jesu-Forschung*, I, p. 47.

cases, to help people liberate themselves from the yoke of the Church. Other scholars go further and see Christianity, which led to the creation of the world of European culture, as the embodiment of false prophecy, which guided human development into the path of suppression of individuality and created a state of stagnation in Europe for many generations.[4] In his essays of the eighteen forties, Bauer tended increasingly towards total detachment from the traditional-orthodox theory on the evolvement of Christianity and all it entailed – and from the conservative-clerical regime which ruled the country and dominated the Theology Department in which he taught. Furthermore: Bauer, who was glad to leave Berlin where there were left-wing elements, more extreme than he was,[5] arrived himself at an extreme viewpoint after a very short time in Bonn. He began to regard Christianity (in *Das entdeckte Christentum*) as the factor bearing the blame for all the catastrophes which had been inflicted on mankind since the decline of the Roman Empire. And thus the circle was closed. Bauer, who had started out as a theologian, came naturally to deal with the Gospels and with early Christianity. He was no ordinary theologian, but rather a speculative, that is to say Hegelian one. His commentaries on Hegel's philosophy opened the way for his critique of Christianity and of religion in general. Within three years he became a most acerbic critic of theology and theism, perhaps the harshest in nineteenth century Germany.

It is interesting to note that in the first book he published after moving to Bonn: *Kritik der evangelischen Geschichte des Johannes*, Bauer denied that his research was guided by a philosophical approach and claimed that his critique was solely historical,[6] that is to say, based on empirical findings and on historical analysis of the text. His brother, Edgar, also noted that Bruno's critique was not based on presuppositions, which spell death to any scientific project.[7] Since these statements could mislead scholars, it would seem necessary to explain them. "Without presuppositions" – this was the slogan used by D. F. Strauss in *Das Leben Jesu*, and adopted by the Bauer brothers. But this phrase then held a totally different meaning from that which would be attributed to it today, and this was made very clear by

---

[4] Albert Camus: *L'Homme révolté*, pp. 52–53; Schnabel: *Deutsche Geschichte im 19. Jahrhundert*, III, pp. 510–511.

[5] Cf. Bruno Bauer's letter to his brother Edgar, 15 March 1840 (BE p. 50).

[6] J, p. XII.

[7] Edgar Bauer: *Der Streit der Kritik mit Kirche und Staat*, pp. 43–44; *Bruno Bauer und seine Gegner*. Berlin 1842, p. 21.

Strauss, who claimed that his study was free of presuppositions (*voraus-setzunglos*) because he accepted neither the assumption that the Gospels dealt with supernatural events nor the theory that they were based on historical happenings. His view was that it was necessary to examine whether the issue under study belonged to history.[8]

Bauer employs Straussian terminology, and there can be no doubt that on this specific question his position is close to that of Strauss. Secondly – it is untrue that Bauer was not guided by philosophy in his critique of the Gospels and of religious history, as he claimed. The motifs of Bauerian criticism change – particularly as regards the existence of the absolute spirit and the concept of Christianity as the supreme manifestation of the spirit – but the principle of self-consciousness endures and is even developed further. This fact is reflected in various statements by Bauer. Thus, for example, he noted that the New Testament writings are the expression of a process of historical development within the framework of which self-consciousness arrives at awareness, and said that it was the task of criticism, which is the product of thousands of years of development of this consciousness, to comprehend this process.[9] Hence Bauer's admission that "from the first the objective of the critique was to discover within the Gospels the remnants of self-consciousness."[10] And, more emphatically: "the descriptions in the Gospels are the necessary realization of categories of religion which transform the internal destiny of the consciousness into external historical events."[11]

In the foreword to *Kritik der evangelischen Geschichte der Synoptiker* Bauer, in contrast to what he had written previously, pointed out the close connection between his historical research and the philosophical system he advocated: "It is incumbent upon us to safeguard the principle of self-consciousness from the attack of substance [...] let us not conceal the fact that the correct concept of the history of the Gospels has a philosophical basis – the philosophy of self-consciousness."[12]

---

[8] D. F. Strauss: *Das Leben Jesu*, vol. I, p. V.

[9] J 183.

[10] Syn I, 183.

[11] Ibid. p. 24.

[12] Ibid. p. XV. With reference to Bauer's statement that he had employed a historical-empirical method, it was claimed in exegetic literature that on this point Bauer was deluding himself. See Martin Kegel: *Bruno Bauer und seine Theorien zur Entstehung des Christentums*. Leipzig 1908, p. 26. In actual fact, it was not self-delusion but rather a view of the philosophical method as an integral part of the research methodology. Under such circumstances the sense of the mixing of philosophy with historical analysis totally disappears.

It may be deduced from all this that Bauer's attempt to describe his method as historical-empirical has no basis in fact. The previous trend to classification of the historical material and its evaluation according to criteria of the dialectical development of the self-consciousness has not disappeared, and has, in fact, been expanded to encompass the entire critique of sacred history.

Bauer commenced his critique of the Gospels with the fourth book, the Gospel according to St.John, which many commentators before him believed to be the first of the Gospels. Strauss was also convinced of the seniority of this Gospel. But Bauer did not share this view; he raised the question of the historical pragmatism of the Gospel which must be exposed in order to arrive at the understanding of its trend.[13]

In his analysis of the introduction to the Gospel according to St.John, which relates to the Logos, Bauer found that the theory of the Logos, which had played so important a part in Greek and Hellenistic philosophy – as expressed in this Gospel, did not reflect the attitude of Jesus, nor was it directly connected with Jesus, but was rather the individual philosophy of the author.[14] According to Bauer, the author was, at the same time, obliged to take into consideration the patterns of consciousness of the Christian community of his time. Whereas in Filon's writings the qualities and image of the Logos are, in the end, absorbed by the pure divine entity, in Christian consciousness they merged with real and actual history and were related to the individualist presence of the Divinity on earth.[15] On the basis of this and other facts, such as the concept of the character of John the Baptist, understanding of the messianic nature of Jesus etc.,[16] Bauer arrived at the conclusion that John had written his work a long time after the Synoptics wrote their Gospels.[17]

John's stories create an artificial world. The impression after a reading of the Gospel is that it contains numerous facts regarding the period, places and people but, to Bauer's mind, these facts are undefined and problematic.[18] In an earlier article on this Gospel, Bauer had expressed the view that its content was historical and reflected actual events,[19] but in this book he argues that this Gospel is the pro-

---

[13] J, p. XII.
[14] Ibid. 3.
[15] Ibid. pp. 6–7.
[16] Ibid. pp. 10–17, 43–45, 191–195, 250–279.
[17] Ibid. p. 54.
[18] Ibid. pp. 50–51, 59.
[19] *Der Alt-Testamentliche Hintergrund im Evangelium des Johannes.* ZspT. Vol. I, 2. Berlin 1836, p. 158.

duct of reflective historical writing, which, in retrospective fashion, attributes views and concepts from later periods to the time of Jesus. Thus, for example, the rejection of the principles of the new religion by the Jews, the relations between the Father and the Son are grasped, in the contexts presented in this Gospel, only from the viewpoint of the relations prevailing in later Christian communities.[20]

Bauer explains in speculative fashion the theological idea of the inspiration of the Holy Spirit which allegedly guided the author of the Gospel: the Holy Spirit is, in fact, the inner agent of human experience, self-consciousness and the memory of this consciousness within the description of the ideal and historical events.[21] There is actually no difference between the externality of history and the internality of the witnesses contemplating it at this first stage of self-consciousness on the part of the spirit, or as Bauer puts it: "The elementary externality of the historical process and the internality of subjectivity are the same thing."[22] The writer and the historian who are at this stage are still in a state of subjectivity.

At the second stage of development of self-consciousness it differentiates consciously and voluntarily between the external and the internal, as history becomes the object of contemplation and literary description. This situation is typical of the activity of the inner spirit within the object as, through tremendous effort, it ascends to the level of self-consciousness.[23] The absolute spirit does not exist outside the finite and limited and goes through all the stages of this spiritual activity "in order to arrive at complete historical consciousness of itself."[24] Bauer still tends to underplay this idea and does not emphasize its significance and practical meaning – arrival at an atheistic approach – but in his letters to Ruge he expressed his hostility to the various manifestations of theism. Thus, for example, he wrote in his letter of 16.4.1841:

"I have realized the dialectic in reasonably precise fashion. There are many things which it is necessary to complete first in theory, before it is possible and permissible to express them through the words of the previous concept [...]. It is possible to do this when one arrives at the last battle and when the principle has triumphed to such an extent in reality that it has become a determining factor. From now on science

[20] J, 89–90, 99–101, 140, 209–212.
[21] Ibid. pp. 170–174.
[22] Ibid. p. 179.
[23] Idem.
[24] Ibid. p. 181.

must ensure that its categories and their development are free from contact with the previous concepts. The breach must be absolute [. . .]. I always suffer an attack of philosophical shock when I read the countless highflown phrases on the absolute spirit, spirit of the world etc. It is necessary to overcome substance completely (Strauss was too much enslaved to it). In the sphere of the Bible and religion I have finished with the substance and with the positive [. . .]. Apart from this, we must totally destroy theology and those who couple with it and bring forth children in such circumstances of shame and disgrace."[25]

After his determination of its dependence on the Synoptic Gospels and on the ideas of the Christian community, and after examining the text which revealed the author's original literary adaption, Bauer was in no doubt that the Gospel according to St. John was, to a large extent, a literary construction and an artistic project.[26] This Gospel should not be regarded as the product of arbitrariness, but, at the same time, it did not contain historical content. Bauer believed that the author of the Gospel lived many years after the events he described, and boasted in later years that he had produced countless pieces of evidence that the fourth Gospel was in entirety and in every detail the product of late pragmatism.[27]

In 1840 Bauer was still of the opinion that the three Synoptic Gospels related historical truths. He arrived at this conclusion on the basis of their harmony, the simplicity of their narrative, rich content etc.[28] He was also convinced of something else – that John had not distorted history, that he had had no intention of depicting events in untrue fashion. It was his opinion that the author of the fourth Gospel had believed that the events had really taken place as he described them. But shortly afterwards, at the beginning of 1842, Bauer wrote to Ruge: "It has been proved beyond all doubt that the fourth Evangelist is the greatest cheat in the world. Until now it was not known how far he had gone [. . .]. Christianity will decline when the true face of this exhibitionist is exposed."[29]

In none of his writings did Bauer take up such a stand, i.e. state that

---

[25] A microfilm of Bauer's letters to Ruge is extant in the International Institute of Social History in Amsterdam, and I was given the opportunity of perusing it. The letters themselves are located in Dresden, East Germany.

[26] J 52.

[27] HL 49–56.

[28] J 399.

[29] Cf. Bauer's letter to Ruge, 9 January 1842.

religion was the work of cheats, who were anxious to mislead others.
The facts known to us attest to the contrary. For example: Bauer
attacked the rationalist concept that religion was the invention of
priest and despotic rulers for the sake of realization of their own selfish
interests at the expense of the common people.[30] In his later writings,
such as *Die Posaune des jüngsten Gerichts über Hegel, den Atheisten und
Antichristen*, and *Das entdeckte Christentum* in which he criticized
Christianity with almost unparalled savagery, there is no trace of this
attitude. There is even record of Bauer's emphatic denial on this issue;
it was claimed against him that he had depicted the authors of the
Gospels as engaging in cheating, and Bauer vigorously rejected this
accusation.[31] It seems to us that, for all his deviations from the Hegelian concept and his subjectivist tendencies, Bauer never arrived at a
historiosophical conception according to which the course of history is
determined arbitrarily.

But here it is worth pointing out an interesting Bauerian theory. He
claimed that for a long period the formulators of religious principles,
authors of holy writings and various apologists believed in what they
disseminated. As far as Bauer was concerned, since he argued that he
had exposed the nature of religion as opposed to history and to truth,
this entire process was, of course, founded on self-delusion. This was
how religion operated at the best of times when it ruled in stable and
undisputed fashion. But the situation changed with the triumph of
the critical self-consciousness as the status of religion declined, its
security was undermined and its various parts beginning to absorb
ideas which were incompatible with its essence. In times of crisis and
deterioration the believers in and defenders of religion begin to understand its essence: that it is based on an incorrect description of phenomena in human life. The self-illusion is transformed into deliberate
falsehood or, as Bauer puts it: ,,Self-illusion, which at first has no
malicious intent behind it, turns into voluntary self-cheating; the
error becomes a lie, the defence – hypocrisy and cheating ...''[32]

In his book on the Synoptics Bauer analysed the content of the first
three Gospels. At first he assumed that, in contrast with the fourth,
they contained an authentic description of historical events, but further
perusal of these Gospels persuaded Bauer that there was no basic

[30] *Der Pantheismus innerhalb des Rationalismus und Suprarationalismus.* ZspT, I, 1
(1836), pp. 268–269.
[31] Syn I, 81–82, 268–269. See also Fae, 62.
[32] ThS 62.

difference between them and the Gospel according to St. John. Bauer
did not conceal the fact that negative conclusions as to the historical
nature of the latter had influenced his attitude to the Synoptics: "It is
the task of criticism [...] to examine whether, apart from the form,
the content is also of literary origin and the free creation of self-
consciousness and simultaneously, to recognize the criticism of the
latter regarding substance and the assumption that tradition is the
source of the Holy Scriptures."[33]

Since the Gospels were written by human beings, it was only natural
that they underwent a process of intellectual adaptation; but the central
problem, according to Bauer, was whether there was a gap between the
content, which was regarded as absolute and infinite, since it related to
sacred religious principles, and human consciousness, which was limited
and finite. The transplantation of the conclusions arrived at through
study of the fourth Gospel predetermined Bauer's objective on this
question – to prove that there is no such gap, that it is possible to
reduce the infinite to the finite and the absolute to the relative and
that outside the subject there is no factor which maintains autonomous
life. In this context Bauer tackled Strauss's viewpoint once again, this
time from a more extreme standpoint. Whereas Strauss held that the
Gospels were the product of the earliest Christian traditions, created
through the fusion of historical fact with various mythological elements
and evolved in accordance with ideas originating in the messianic
beliefs of the Jews and the Bible, Bauer denied that any tradition
whatsoever had played a part in shaping the Holy Scriptures. It was
his opinion that it made no difference "when, to the question of how
Gospel history and its description in the Gospels was created – the
answer is given that the authors wrote the Gospels under divine inspiration, or that Gospel history was shaped by tradition. These are
identical solutions, since both are transcendental and limit self-consciousness to an equal extent."[34]

In accordance with this concept which is based on the principle of
self-consciousness and endeavours to bestow on it preferential status in
human life and in the historical process of the development of human
society, Bauer produced various arguments to discount tradition. He

[33] Syn, I. p. XV.
[34] Ibid., pp. VII–VIII. Representation of tradition in Straussian style as transcendental
and as identical with the mystery of faith, was to become Bauer's central argument in his
polemic against Strauss. As a result Bauer was also to claim that Straussian criticism was
hesitant, compromising, ambivalent and semi-theological. For this issue see Bruno Bauer:
Das Leben Jesu, kritisch bearbeitet von D. F. Strauss (Rez.). DJ 105/1841, p. 417.

claimed that the latter had no hands with which to write, taste with which to formulate statements, judgment in order to reconcile contradictions and banish alien elements. Only a subject possessed of the above qualities could devote itself to universality and serve it.[35] Tradition as the continuity of creation and its preservation in numerous memories is identified by Bauer with the community as well: "The folk, the community can create nothing as a mysterious substance or from this substance. The subject alone – the individual self-consciousness – can arrive at form, image and definition of content [of the Holy Scriptures]."[36]

These statements by Bauer are, in the last analysis, based on philosophical argumentation from which he starts out and to which he returns at the end of the essay. But Bauer was aware of the fact that this was not sufficient to prove the correctness of his theories and that he was in need of arguments and facts from secular history. Two sets of arguments attest to his view that Strauss was in error and he himself was correct: a) before the appearance of Jesus and the crystallization of the Christian sect there was no clear concept of the Messiah, that is to say there was no Christology which the authors of the Gospels could adopt for their stories or even use as the basis for them. Messianic ideas emerged clearly only within the framework of the Christian community.[37] Bauer attributed considerable importance to this point, since he believed that his explanation of the roots and nature of Christology was prevailing over the Straussian conception and eradicating it once and for all. Thus, Bauer wrote to his brother: "In the appendix to the first volume [of Kritik der evangelischen Geschichte der Synoptiker]. I referred to the Messianic yearnings of the Jews and brought evidence against Strauss and the criticism prevalent till now. I fully completed the critique and freed it of any positive aspects."[38] This shows that Bauer drastically limited the chronological framework of the evolvement of Christianity. The historical background forfeited much of its importance, and analysis of the evangelical content was restricted to the relations between the authors of the various Gospels, and between the authors and the Christian community. b) Bauer adopted the assumption of Wilke and Weisse that the Gospel according to St.Mark was the first, while Luke and Matthew based themselves on this Gos-

---

[35] Syn I, pp. XVI, 71; see also Edgar Bauer: *Bruno Bauer und seine Gegner*, pp. 10–11.
[36] Syn I, 69.
[37] Ibid, pp. XVII, 407–416; Edgar Bauer: *Bruno Bauer und seine Gegner*, pp. 14–15.
[38] BE, p. 133.

pel,[39] thus creating literary dependence, and causing contradictions, vain attempts to reconcile anomalies, and mental acrobatics.[40] This viewpoint of Bauer's engendered two theories on the Gospels, which, at first sight, appear to contradict one another. On the one hand, the authenticity of the two Gospels which were traditionally first was refuted, while the third Gospel, now regarded as first, was the object of a fierce Bauerian onslaught. On the other hand, Bauer treats the texts with complete seriousness, perhaps more so than many theologians who believed that the Gospels were backed by tradition and myth and tried, through classification, to differentiate between them. From the point of view of Bauer, who rejects this version, no element outside these writings should be accepted. This is the reason why they are the sole object of his research. Hence, he did in fact deny the authenticity of the New Testament stories, but tackled the literary material in all seriousness and tried to find as many arguments as possible on which to base his theory.

An article signed "Berliner" in Ruge's journal, congratulated Bauer, who shortly before had been regarded as the number one enemy, on his triumph over Strauss. The anonymous author believed that Bauer's book on the Synoptics had relegated Strauss's *Das Leben Jesu* to the back-shelf. "Bruno Bauer", he wrote, "has brought Gospel criticism to the point where it is far distant from Strauss. The new criticism marks the revolutionary overthrowing of its predecessor. The new is extreme where the old was moderate and it is well-known that moderation is always the victim of revolution."[41] Elsewhere the "Berliner" asked: "In what way does Bauer's essay differ from that of Strauss?" and replied: "In a word – while Strauss assumes that many of the stories on the life of Jesus are historically true, while on vital points he believes that there is a historical kernel, and on others seeks the formation of mythical concepts in community tradition, – Bauer endeavours to prove that there is not a single kernel of historical truth in the Gospel, that it is entirely in the sphere of free literary invention of the authors."[42]

In contrast to Strauss, who specifically referred to Jesus and placed the figure of the Christian Messiah at the centre of his study, Bauer explicitly differentiates between Jesus and the authors of the Gospels.

---

[39] Syn I, pp. V–VI; see also Bruno Bauer: *Das alte neue Testament.* An 1843, pp. 188–193.
[40] Syn I, 87, 186, 193, 275; II, 25, 73, 115, 128; HL 41, 43, 56–59.
[41] *Vorläufiges über Bruno Bauer, Kritik der evangelischen Geschichte der Synoptiker.* DJ 105/1841, p. 417.
[42] Ibid. 418.

The self-consciousness of Jesus as depicted in the Gospels is one issue, and the self-consciousness of the authors of the Gospels is another. Even if the historical Jesus really existed, (something which Bauer once regarded as self-evident and later treated with reservation and eventually with great doubt bordering on denial of the historicity of the figure), the problem of which of the qualities attributed to him by the Gospel writers were truly his and which were invented so as to serve the pragmatic interests of early Christianity as these writers saw them, remains controversial, to say the least. In other words: whatever the historicity of Jesus, the issue for readers of the Gospels is the self-consciousness of the authors alone, and this was formulated to a large degree by early Christianity, or, as Bauer himself says: "To the question of whether Jesus was an authentic historical figure we replied that everything relating to the historical Jesus, all that we know of him, relates to the world of fancy, to be more exact – to Christian fancies. This has no connection with any man who lived in the real world. The question is answered by its elimination for the future."[43]

As regards the history of the Evangelists, Bauer believed that only when the Christian community had consolidated its principles and beliefs regarding Jesus, did the need arise for more exact details of historical-empirical conditions and various events in the life of the Christian redeemer. But at the time when this need arose, it was no longer possible to satisfy it. What trials and temptations could have faced Jesus in his struggle against the Jewish world, if not those of the Christian sect?! What subjects could he have broached and what could he have preached if not those subjects which caught the interest of Christian community? In short, it was within the self-consciousness of the Christian community that the struggles related to evolvement of the historical image of Jesus raged.[44] It is necessary to understand Bauer in order to comprehend the significance of self-consciousness on this point. He is not referring to the individual who acts arbitrarily when he makes use of the category of self-consciousness: "When we employ the category of self-consciousness we are not referring to the empirical self, as if he were able to formulate these views according to his concepts or arbitrary combinations – if he were to try and do such a thing, he would rapidly become convinced that is impossible and would abandon such a scheme."[45] Bauer also excludes the possibility of anoth-

[43] Syn III, 308.
[44] Ibid. II, 45–46.
[45] Ibid. I, 81.

er category of people when referring to realization of the aims of the
community and formulation of its ideals – i.e. those endowed with
critical self-consciousness (he himself is an example of this category),
who have arrived at understanding of true universality, whose authentic interests are opposed to those of religion.[46] In contrast to this type
of consciousness, creative religious consciousness contains universality
only in elementary fashion. People of this category of self-consciousness
are motivated by the vital need to transplant the content of their
consciousness beyond themselves. Without this act of creativity they
are unable to realize their essence and to survive. After projection of
the content of self-consciousness, they believe that it has status of its
own, independent of them or, as Bauer says: "As religious self-consciousness it [creative self-consciousness] sees itself in temporary conflict with its essential content, but after developing and depicting this
content, it sees it as existing outside it, as absolute and as history."[47]
The drive for development of this content and for its depiction comes
from outside, from the Christian community and even the material
utilized by people endowed with creative self-consciousness is anchored
in the beliefs of the religious community. The historical figures which
this consciousness provides, appear real in every way, since the consciousness does not exist in a vacuum, has strong links with the large
group of believers organized within the framework of the community
and is acquainted with its needs. Therefore Bauer believed that it
was incorrect to attribute to the Gospels the characteristics of free art,
like that of Greece, for example,[48] since the authors of the Gospels did
not aspire to exalted ideals, free of all interests, but were prosaic
pragmatists.[49]

The link between the individualist creative self-consciousness of the
author of the Gospels on the one hand, and the community on the other
is confirmed – *inter alia* – by the story of Jesus' temptation in the
desert. This story is nothing but the transplantation of the struggles
and experiences of the community to its leader and representative –
Jesus, who is regarded as its embodiment within the individual. This
story is a description of the struggle for evolving Christian principles.[50]
Thus, to depict Bauer as an extreme individualist, who places maximum
emphasis on the significance of the individual and to regard his

[46] Ibid. 81–82.
[47] Ibid. 82.
[48] Ibid. 83.
[49] HL 66.
[50] Syn I, 239–244.

historiosophical approach as extremely subjectivistic and heroic is not consistent with the true facts.[51] Bauer was indeed a subjectivist – this fact has already been noted – but he did not lean towards the theory that history is formulated by great men, without taking into consideration facts and situations outside the sphere of self-consciousness. It is not true to say that, according to Bauer's concept, several people who, in the seclusion of their homes, wrote the history of the ideals of early Christianity, shaped the image of Christianity.

It is, on the other hand, true that, by his various kinds of phrasing, Bauer misled scholars, particularly when he drew conclusions which did not derive directly from his outlook and did not fit in with it. One example of this is the following statement by Bauer: "The more profound the creation and the greater success it achieves, the more reasonable it is to assume that the author was far from reflecting universality and worked without prejudices, the influence of his life's substance being reflected in the intensity he invested in his work."[52] Many years later Bauer was to formulate this idea more sharply: "Only one man, only an individual is capable of creating a project which can dominate a nation or community or – as in the case before us – the entire world. Such a project was created by Homer some 900 years B. C. [...] a similar task was carried out by the first person to draw the picture of the struggle of the Messiah against the Torah, his death and resurrection."[53] This way of thinking is in contrast to Bauer's general outlook which places stress on the fact that the self-consciousness, in its creative activity, does not behave like the isolated self and creates nothing out of its direct subjectivity and particularly not in the case "where its project has been accepted by the nation or community, recognized by them and regarded for hundreds of years as their own outlook. Self-consciousness, without knowing of its ties with the surrounding world, or of the tension between it and substance, accepts its drives from the latter and is influenced by it."[54]

It is clear from this that the thought and volition of the individual do not draw their content from themselves alone, but are influenced to no small extent by the environment. The practical meaning of this

[51] See, for example, Koigen's statement: "[Bauerian] critique makes no concessions, and this is true both of tradition, of the human consciousness and of the existing actual world". (*Zur Vorgeschichte des modernen philosophischen Sozialismus*, p. 51).
[52] Syn I, 69.
[53] *Christus und die Cäsaren*. Berlin 1880, pp. 23–24.
[54] Syn I, 69.

phenomenon is that the Evangelists relied mainly on ideas which were known to the first Christian sects.

On the other hand it is, of course, impossible to disregard Bauer's tendency to highlight the contribution of the individual. Bauer's theory that individuals with talents and power of attraction play a vital part in history and, within its framework, in the history of Christianity, was explicitly presented in order to provide proper breathing space for great historical figures. The concrete significance of this theory, as regards evangelical history, is reflected in the idea of free formulation of ideas which had existed previously, by the authors of the Gospels.

We observe Bauer's attempt to present the relations between subject and object in history as existing in a system of reciprocal ties, but with clear and declared preference for action emanating from the developed self-consciousness. It is thus possible to decipher Bauer's statement that man formulates his own history or, to use his own words: "...Criticism must create history. History does not come to us, but rather our own actions must lead us to it."[55]

Bauer's criticism regarded the Gospels as documents attesting to the interests, objectives and aspirations of the Christian sects and reflecting those aspects of Christian activity which had undergone a process of literary adaptation by the authors of the Gospels. As a result the Gospels had entirely forfeited their historical nature and had been deposed from their eminent position. They had become relative documents, a kind of reflection of religious phenomena which had occurred many generations previously, and did not serve the interests of those living in a totally different reality. Bauer believed that by exposing the nature of the Gospels as a literary product and uncovering their pragmatic content he was doing a service to science and to humanity and making a great contribution to the liberation of man from religious outlooks.[56]

Edgar Bauer claimed, in this context – on the basis of his brother's outlook, – that the attitude towards Christianity was based to a large extent on belief in the divine nature of the Holy Scriptures. Anyone who undermined this belief was endangering the status of Christianity as a whole, since it would lose its main prop.[57] After the publication of the *Kritik der evangelischen Geschichte der Synoptiker*, Bauer became

[55] Fr 4.
[56] Syn III, 312–313.
[57] Edgar Bauer: *Bruno Bauer und seine Gegner*, p. 22.

the hero of the radical Hegelians. It was claimed in the *Deutsche Jahrbücher* that before the publication of this book, there had been no real criticism of the life of Jesus. Bauer's book was evaluated as equal in importance to Feuerbach's *Essence of Christianity*, which appeared in the same year (1841). Bauer was praised in particular for his consistent use of the postulate of rationalism, with the aid of which he succeeded in proving the irrational character of Christianity, which had long constituted an obstacle preventing man from attaining autonomy of thought and the free life. The expressions: "opens up a new era", "deeply penetrating", "most praiseworthy" were clear signs of the esteem in which the journal of the Young Hegelians held Bauer.[58]

The well-known writer and poet, Robert Prutz was enchanted by Bauer's "sharpness of outlook" and "erudition". He regarded the book as of "great" importance and believed that it would have "protracted influence."[59]

The enthusiasm of radical critics was in inverse proportion to that of the authorities – both of the university and of Prussia – towards Bauer. After von Altenstein transferred him to Bonn, Bauer encountered increasing difficulties at the local university. Before his arrival he had already been known as a Hegelian and an acerbic critic, and most members of the university faculty were anti-Hegelians who took a dim view of his critique of Hengstenberg and of theology in general. When Bauer proposed a course entitled "Critique of the Fourth Gospel" he was requested by the Dean to omit the world "critique". But these difficulties did not hinder Bauer's literary and scholarly work; rather the contrary – they stimulated him to prove that he and not the orthodox theologians, represented science and the correct approach to science.

"I cannot rest", he wrote to his brother, "until I have completely cleaned out the stable. I am engaged in preparatory work for the critique of the Synoptics. Victory will be mine in the end. I have found the point at which I must pull the strings in order to arrive at the solution."[60]

After the death of von Altenstein and the ascension of Friedrich Wilhelm IV to the throne (both events took place in 1840), Bauer's situation worsened considerably. He was forced to renounce the hope of

[58] D. Rhenius: *Kritik der evangelischen Geschichte der Synoptiker von Bruno Bauer.* DJ 219/1842, pp. 875–876; 220, pp. 877–884.
[59] R. Prutz: *Geschichte der neuesten Zeit. 1840–1850.* Vol. II, Leipzig 1850, p. 60.
[60] Cf. Bruno Bauer's letter to Edgar, 7 August 1840. (BE, 104).

rapidly attaining a professorship, and he fought for his right to remain a university teacher. After the publication of *Kritik der evangelischen Geschichte des Johannes* his position became intolerable and the Prussian Ministry of Culture offered him an annual grant to enable him to engage in research on the explicit condition that he agree to give up his teaching post. He rejected this proposal. The tendency to extremism which he himself had recognized[61] drove him to submit the first volume of the work on the Synoptics to the new Minister of Education, Eichhorn, who was known as a supporter of orthodoxy and conservatism. Bauer wrote to Ruge of this step: "It [the Faculty of Theology] has secretly oppressed me: now I have taken it to court [...] and have brought the matter before the Ministry so that it can decide whether the Faculty has a serious case for silencing me. I want to force both the Faculty and the State to arrive at a decision regarding the destruction of criticsm by the state. I naturally expect nothing of this court case, but there must be a decision, which will determine the matter once and for all."[62]

And, in fact, the decision was taken soon after. Eichhorn approached the faculties of Theology of various Prussian universities and asked them for their opinion of the nature of the Bauerian critique of the Gospels as reflected in his book on the Synoptics, and for their view on Bauer's continued employment at Bonn after his criticism of "the essential content of Christian truth."[63] The answers received were not uniform and there were quite a number of responses which recommended that Bauer's employment continue, lest the future of academic freedom be imperilled. But Eichhorn was adamant; at the end of March 1842 it was decided to terminate Bauer's employment and to deprive him of his *licentia docendi* – the practical implication being denial of the possibility of teaching theology at any Prussian university.

The theological-intellectual trial was accompanied by a political trial. Bauer was questioned by the police about his presence at a reception for the well-known South German liberal Welcker in Berlin and about his speech in the course of which he had praised Hegel as a thinker who "in his political outlook far surpassed the South German views as regards courage, liberalism and purposefulness."[64]

61 "The day will come, when I will stand resolutely against the entire theological world. Only then, so I believe, will I be in my right place, to which I have been persistently impelled by pressures and struggles during the past six years." Letter dated 31 March 1840. (BE, 60).
62 Cf. Bauer's letter, 10 February 1842.
63 Barnikol: *Bruno Bauer. Studien und Materialien*, 151.
64 Cf. Bruno Bauer's letter to Edgar, 9 December 1841 (BE 87, 161–163).

As a result of this event Bauer was admonished by the university authorities who noted that his dismissal had precluded the taking of further steps.[65]

Prutz wrote in this context: "To engage in polemics with the book [*Kritik der Synoptiker*] from the scientific point of view was difficult. It was more convenient and safe to call the police [. . .] Just as in Strauss's day the cry was again heard that religion was in danger, that anyone who undermined the dignity of the Bible was threatening religion; the undermining of religion endangered the state, all civil society, the family, morality, in short – everything which mankind regards as deserving to be sanctified and honoured."[66]

After his dismissal from Bonn University, Bauer returned to Berlin in order to support himself as a freelance writer and continue his scholarly work.[67]

[65] Ernst Barnikol: *Bruno Bauer. Studien und Materialien.* p. 155.
[66] Prutz: *Geschichte der neuesten Zeit. 1840–1850*, vol. II, p. 60.
[67] Cf. Bruno Bauer's letter to Edgar, 3 March 1842 (BE 179–182); see also G. A. van den Bergh van Eysinga: *Aus einer unveröffentlichen Biographie von Bruno Bauer*, pp. 329–333, 336–338, 364–373.

BRUNO BAUER AS COMMENTATOR ON HEGEL

During his stay in Bonn Bauer wrote two essays on Hegel's philosophy, its significance und purport: *Die Posaune des jüngsten Gerichts über Hegel, den Atheisten und Antichristen* (1841), and *Hegel's Lehre über Religion und Kunst* (1843). Bauer had been closely acquainted with Hegel's thought since he edited the second edition of the *Philosophy of Religion*. The first edition had been edited by Marheineke, and the second was also published under his name, but in the introduction Marheineke admitted that he had been too busy to engage in this work and that it would never have been published but for "the praiseworthy cooperation and support of my young friend, Mr. Bauer of Bonn [...] whose erudition, as demonstrated in his own writings, speculative talent and wise behaviour [...] constituted a worthy contribution to this work."[1]

Eduard Zeller wrote a critical article in which he praised highly Bauer's work on the Hegelian text, noting the many improvements, elaboration of the text, improved organization of contents, and expressing the view that Bauer's edition was markedly superior to the first edition.[2]

Weisse thought that Bauer had done an excellent job and produced a text "which, as regards content and form, cannot be faulted. It is in no way inferior to and possibly surpasses Hotho's excellent edition of *The Philosophy of Fine Art*."[3]

Critical notes were also sounded, for example in an article, the author of which claimed that Bauer had tendentiously altered the Hegelian text, but this evaluation cannot be taken seriously. The reason is simple: this author believed that Bauer still represented an orthodox-

---

[1] G. W. F. Hegel's *Vorlesungen über die Philosophie der Religion*. Zweite verbesserte Auflage, 1840, p. VI.
[2] HJ, No 50/1841, p. 198.
[3] ZspT, vol. VI (1840) p. 271.

conservative approach, which accounts for the assumption that Bauer had altered the Hegelian text in accordance with right wing interests. Bauer commented on this that in those days he had already gone over to the Young Hegelians and was as remote from apologetic elements as Heaven is remote from earth: "These people could have claimed, with a large degree of justification, that I edited the new edition in accordance with leftwing interests, but the sole truth is that I did this job out of total indifference and without practical interests [...] and party sympathies; if we must speak of interests, then the sole interest which guided me was purely theoretical."[4]

Eighty years later Lasson, the editor of a new edition of Hegel's writings, expressed certain reservations, some of them quite grave, as to Bauer's editing of the text of the *Philosophy of Religion*.[5] But he did not accuse Bauer of tendentiousness.[6]

In the two above-noted essays on Hegel, which he published anonymously, Bauer posed as an orthodox believer and this is attested to by the subtitle of the second work: "From the point of view of faith." At first his pretence at attack on Hegel and his supposed attempt to expose the true nature of Hegel as the enemy of apologetics, deceived both conservative circles and several of the Young Hegelians. Thus, for example, Hengstenberg's church journal congratulated the anonymous author of the *Posaune* as a "brother in faith"[7] while Ruge saw him as a "pietist" and claimed that his approach was "totally unashamed", though "this fellow understands Hegel better than many others."[8]

Bauer's aim was to depict Hegel as an atheist who had done everything possible to abolish Christianity and religion in general, and himself as holding the key to the secret of this philosophy, as Hegel's loyal and consistent pupil. In order to achieve this objective he starts by quoting the *Philosophy of Religion* so as to prove that Hegel recognized the substance of objectivity. These quotations mostly relate to Hegel's polemic against the above-noted subjectivist approach of Schleiermacher and Jacobi. Hegel countered this approach by demanding recognition of the objective. The following remarks should be classified in this category of Hegelian arguments: "It is onesidedness

---

[4] See Bruno Bauer's letter to Edgar, 15 March 1840 (BE 49–50).
[5] *Vorlesungen über die Philosophie der Religion*, vol. I, 1925, pp. 318–320.
[6] Van den Bergh van Eysinga: *Aus einer unveröffentlichen Biographie von Bruno Bauer*, p. 399.
[7] Dr. Modus: *Der Posaunist und das Centrum der Hegelschen Philosophie.* DJ 136–138/1842, p. 543.
[8] *Ruges Briefwechsel und Tagebuchblätter aus den Jahren 1825–1880*, p. 247.

to see religion as something *subjective* and to represent the subjective
aspect as the sole one. According to this concept, ritual becomes totally
empty, its action is like a movement without mobility and its relationship to God is a relationship to nothing."[9] Bauer cites this statement[10]
as he cites other examples from Hegel to demonstrate the necessity for
the subject, the finite, to rise above himself and sacrifice himself for
the substance. As long as the subject does not do this, he himself is the
sole yardstick for the worldly order, or as Hegel says: "all the objective
content, law, truth, duty disappear for me, I do not recognize the objective, the truth: God, the infinite are for me another world, entirely
separate from me."[11]

Bauer exploits Hegelian criticism of Schleiermacher's point of view,
in order to prove that Hegel deposed theology from its position and
exposed its non-scientific character.[12]

On the other hand, it is clear that Bauer took Hegel's opinion into
consideration when he quoted him verbatim, but his intentions are
clear from the beginning of the chapter, which deals with the religious
relationship as a substantial one. The fact that Hegel criticized theology deriving from feeling created, in his opinion, "the illusion
that, apart from the self-consciousness, there exists a universality,
a substance."[13] The truth is, according to Bauer, that for Hegel
the finite not only does not submit to substance, but maintains itself as such and, at the same time, transforms itself into the active
infinite, that is to say attributes to itself forces, importance and activity of the infinite.[14]

In order to illustrate this theory, Bauer relies on two sets of arguments set forth in Hegel's *Philosophy of Religion*. The first relates to
the subject who negates his temporal, brief and particular existence
through the act of thinking of the universal, the substance. Hegel made
it clear that thinking on the universal removed the subjective element
from thought: "I have renounced myself as a particularity; this re-
nunciation is identical with thought, i.e. the universal is an object";[15]
"this universal is but the point of view of the thinking reason."[16]

[9] BR 230.
[10] Pos 153–154.
[11] BR 137.
[12] Pos 155–156.
[13] Ibid. 153; see also *Einleitung in die Dogmengeschichte von Theodor Kliefoth* (Rez.). An,
vol. II/1838, p. 140.
[14] Pos 156–157.
[15] BR 143.
[16] Ibid. p. 142.

The second set of arguments derives from the well-known Hegelian idea that the finite is an essential quality of the infinite. Since Hegel identifies the infinite also with God, then he, as God, cannot lack the quality of finiteness.[17] Hegel deducted from this that "God is also finite, while the self is infinite; God returns to himself within the self to cancel finiteness, and is God only within this return. Without the world, God is not God."[18] He also deduced that the religious relationship is the relationship of the spirit to the absolute spirit or *"the self-consciousness of the absolute spirit."*[19] Thus the tables are turned: if at first the self, the subject sacrifices himself for the substance, subsequently the substance becomes the self, the subject. Bauer therefore arrived at the following conclusion: "It is clear that Hegel recognizes the validity of the substantial relationschip only for a moment, as the moment of movement alone, in which the self-consciousness appears as finite: the substance is the momentary flame to which the self sacrifices its finiteness and limitation. But the end of the movement is not substance, but the self-consciousness, which has set itself up as infinite and adapted the universality of substance as *its own essence.*"[20] It would be an understatement to say that Bauer is imprecise on this point. Hegel, who was interested in highlighting the organic links between the substance and the subject, between reality and thought, wrote on this question: "It is in fact true – subjectivity, ideality is the absolute flame which consumes all forms of being, the moment of speculativeness; but this moment is only *one* aspect and, as a result, incomplete negation."[21] Bauer cancels the first link in the substance-self consciousness relationship and thus leaves only the self-consciousness. He does this in contradiction of Hegel's proclaimed views, after himself citing Hegel's remarks on the onesidedness of the subjectivist approach. It is evident that Bauer has been selective in his choice of Hegelian texts and in linking them to contexts which create the impression that he, Bauer, understands Hegel while others are incapable of fully comprehending the views of the author of the *Philosophy of Religion*. Heine, in his essay *Geschichte der Religion und Philosophie in Deutschland* (1834) had already distinguished between the exoteric and the esoteric Hegel. Bauer discusses the Hegelian texts on the basis of the same conception,

---

[17] Ibid. pp. 146–147.
[18] Ibid. p. 148; see also p. 22.
[19] Ibid. p. 150.
[20] Pos 161–162.
[21] BR 139.

but in more pragmatic fashion. His interpretations of Hegel serve his aims, constitute a kind of philosophical basis for his atheism and for understanding of Gospel history. This fact was noted by many of Bauer's contemporaries, such as Marheineke for example, who argued that his ex-pupil had detached Hegel's statements from their original context and thus created a portrait of Hegel which did not fit in with the facts.[22] At this point – against the background of Marheineke's evaluation – let us break off our discussion of the Bauerian interpretation of Hegel's views and turn to Hegel himself.

In source, content and trend Hegel's philosophy is absolute idealism, that is to say integration of subjective and objective idealism (and therefore Hegel sees the two forms, when presented separately, non-dialectically, as incomplete and incorrect concepts). The principle of Hegel's methodology is above all, the subject, but this subject is not human; it exists objectively, it is independent of the individual man and his consciousness. Furthermore: it is both subject and object. Hegel's subject differs from the Kantian and Fichtean subject. For Kant the subject is not individual, but transcendental, but nevertheless persists as human consciousness.

For Fichte as well the subject is understood subjectively. It should have appeared in his method as the subject-object, but what emerges is a ,,subjective subject-object'', as Hegel put it. In Hegel's philosophy the subject – in contrast to Fichte's subject – is seen as an "objective subject-object" which existed before human consciousness and "before nature and the finite spirit were created." According to Hegel, Kant and Fichte tried to find the object in the subject while he himself – on the contrary – finds the subject in the object.[23] Both Kant and Fichte did not succeed in breaking through the standpoint of the subjective consciousness and the subjective spirit. "Both systems have clearly not reached the intelligible unity or the mind as it actually and essentially is, but only as it is in reference to something else."[24]

And to what subject is Hegel referring? In the most general fashion, we might say that the subject is being-endowed thought. Hegel is not only concerned with human thought. Thought exists independent of us, and is characterized by objective realism. Furthermore, if anything exists concretely and objectively, it is thought. In contrast to the common employment of the term "thought", which endows it with

[22] Fr 193–194.
[23] For all of this, see HPh III, 427–428, 488–495; LH §§ 24, 40, 60; PhM § 415; *Jenaer Schriften*, pp. 52–115.
[24] PhM §415.

subjective significance, Hegel stressed its objective nature: in accordance with this viewpoint "thoughts may be termed objective thoughts, among which are also to be included the forms which are more especially discussed in common logic, where they are usually treated as forms of conscious thought only. *Logic therefore coincides with metaphysics.* [...] To say that Reason or understanding is in the world is equivalent in its import to the phrase 'objective thought'."[25]

At the same time the expressions "objective thought" or "thought as the heart and soul of the world" are not suitable since they could constitute a hint that things in nature are characterized by some kind of consciousness, a theory which Hegel, of course, rejected, since he saw the ability to think as characterizing man alone. "The signification thus attached to thought and its characteristic forms may be illustrated by the ancient saying that '*nous* rules the world' or by our own phrase that 'reason is in the world' which means that reason is the soul of the world it inhabits, its immanent principle, its most proper and inward nature, its universal."[26]

Hegel's ontologization of thought does not mean that the subject is gifted with the capacity for thought, but that the subject *is* thought, The term "thinking subject" (if we dismiss the reference to the trivial phenomenon of the thinking finite spirit) means that the subject is no other than thought, makes himself into the object of thought on himself as thought and thinks of thought as of himself. This does not mean that the subject is endowed with the ability to think – the subject is thought itself while thought is the subject itself. The subject-thought is the principle of the entire system. As we noted as regards Hegel's attitude to religion, the spirit, the idea is the substance. To view the substance as a subject is an essential clarification of understanding of the nature of this substance. "In my view, a view which the developed exposition of the system itself alone can justify, everything depends on grasping and expressing the ultimate truth not as substance but as subject as well."[27] And elsewhere he writes: "The living substance is that being which is truly subject ..."[28] All the *Phenomenology* and to a certain degree the entire system deals with the evolvement and realization of the subject from a state of 'in itself' (*an sich*) to a state

[25] LH § 24.
[26] Idem. Zusatz 1.
[27] Phen 80.
[28] Idem. Cf. Hegel's expression: "That the truth is only realized in the form of system, that substance is essentially subject, is expressed in the idea which represents the Absolute as Spirit (*Geist*) – the grandest conception of all, and one due to modern times and its religion." (Phen 85–86).

"for itself" (*für sich*), or, as Hegel says in the last section which sums up the *Phenomenology*, "But this substance, which is spirit, is the development of itself explicitly to what it is inherently and implicitly and only as this process of reflecting itself into itself is it essentially and in truth spirit. It is inherently the movement which is the process of knowledge – the transforming of that inherent nature into explicitness, of substance into subject."[29] Hegel criticizes Spinoza from this point of view, for having started out from substance but proved incapable of attaining to understanding of the concept of subject. In confrontation with Spinoza's concept, Hegel argues that not only substance is truth but also the subject, while the notion of subject is grasped as "free" substance, "endowed with self-consciousness", "independent".[30]

So much for the concept of substance and the subject as notion, but Hegel was influenced by a strong current of philosophical tradition, which knew what is known in philosophical terminology as "the absolute" by other names as well:[31] the absolute which is the truth, and the truth existing as a whole, as a subject and as God.[32] God also appears in Hegel's thought by other names: subject, notion, absolute spirit, idea etc. These concepts are not always congruent with one another, and emphasis was usually placed in them on some aspect of level of development, as with the notion of God which is also only one of the aspects of the absolute. But the absolute – without relation to the name it is given – is always identified with all of reality, its essence. It is the sole reality, the subject as a creative force, which through self-realization creates nature and the finite spirit. When logic describes various categories, such as being, essence, notion, it is actually describing various stages in the development of God. Thus also philosophy, which endeavours to expose the essence of non-organic and organic nature but, in actual fact, investigates the nature of God, of the absolute operating in these spheres. This rule is also valid for the philosophy of the spirit, which deals with the essence of reason and self-consciousness, and the nature of law, morality, history, art, religion and philosophy which are all manifestations of divine activity. Two quotations serve to illustrate Hegel's stand on this question:

a) "God is the *absolute substance*, the sole true reality (*die allein wahrhafte Wirklichkeit*). Of the rest, that which is actual is not so for

[29] Ibid. 801.
[30] Log II, pp. 214–232; BR 191.
[31] For this issue, see Theodor Litt: *Hegel. Versuch einer kritischen Erneuerung*[2]. Heidelberg 1961, p. 78.
[32] Phen 80–82; Log II 221–227.

itself, does not exist in its own right; the sole absolute reality is God and God alone. He therefore is the sole substance."[33]

b) "Logic is to be understood as the system of pure reason, as the realm of pure thought. *This realm is the truth, as it is, without husk in and for itself.* One may therefore express it thus: that his content *shows forth God as he is in his eternal essence before the creation of nature and of a finite spirit.*"[34]

Hegel was able, with clear conscience, to reject the accusation of the merging of theology and philosophy and vice versa, since he held, as has been mentioned above, that both deal with the same object. At the same time he invested tremendous intellectual effort in defence of the theory of the existence of God and even supported all evidence of the existence of God: cosmological, teleological and ontological.[35] Furthermore: Hegel attempted to adapt the theory of the substance as subject, or the subject as God, which is anchored not in religion but in his philosophical system, to Christianity. This is the root of his argument that the God of this religion is spirit and truth. But his interpretations of this category attest to the philosophical nature of God, which develops through processes of alienation and their negation.

Hegel believes that this theory finds expression in theology as follows: "theology expresses this process in representation by saying that God the Father (this simple universal or being within itself), putting aside his solitariness, creates nature (the being that is external to itself, outside of itself), begets a Son (his other "I") but in the power of his love beholds in this other – himself; recognizes his likeness therein and in it returns to unity with himself."[36]

As noted above, substance is the subject, and the subject is – in actual fact – God. In order to better understand this problem, we must return to Hegel's anti-Spinoza polemic. Hegel regarded Spinoza's system as onesided, because of his concept of substance. The latter is in a state of immobility identical with itself, lacking self-consciousness, or to be more exact: does not aspire to self-consciousness, to freedom. In Hegel's thought, substance is identical with itself, but also different from itself, its "otherness". Substance is not dead, it is a process, an activity with an objective: to become the subject, to reveal within itself that which is different, to eliminate this difference and to be identical with itself and with the difference revealed and thus to attain

[33] BR 191.
[34] Log I, 60.
[35] BR 207–225; PhR III, 155–367.
[36] PhM § 381, Zusatz.

to supreme reality.[37] The absolute becomes the subject only with discovery of the otherness within itself, when this difference becomes the
object of the consciousness, and recognizes the way in which it contains self-identification with it. Through thus conscious act, the absolute is realized and achieves freedom.[38] This self-recognition is the
basic quality of the absolute. The object of recognition is, of course,
the absolute itself. But here the one is split into conflicting elements –
subject and object. At this point there is revealed the difference between the absolute in itself and what it should be for itself, the difference between the absolute and its concept. But in contrast to external
nature, which is destroyed by such a profound contradiction ("as for
external nature it arrives at its end through the contradiction"), the
spirit is capable of maintaining itself despite contradictions, and even
overcoming them. The consequence of the dialectical process of creation of contradictions and their negation through *Aufhebung* is absolute knowledge. Absolute knowledge is the last stage in development
of the absolute, when it arrives at recognition of itself.

The absolute spirit strives to recognize itself, – this is its objective.
But this objective is not transcendent – the spirit constitutes an objective in itself. By realizing its aim it realizes itself. Before this self-
cognition the spirit is not real – realization is identical with knowledge,
with philosophy. But the absolute is not endowed with consciousness
and therefore cannot be endowed with self-consciousness. Consciousness is created only in conflict with something, it is always consciousness of something. The splitting of the absolute into consciousness and
object is possible only on condition that the finite spirit, i.e. man exists,
since only human beings are endowed with consciousness. Hegel describes the development of the absolute in his logic as belonging to the
sphere of pure thought but this process is not realistic:

"For the cognition already contained in the simple *logical* idea is
only the notion of cognition thought by us, not cognition existing on
its own account, not actual mind but merely its possibility."[39] Hence
a pure logical idea does not conduct real life, but exists in theory and
possibility alone, in a world of shadows.

The development of the absolute in the sphere of pure thought is
carried out before consciousness and outside it. It commences in the
being which is the idea and ends in the idea which is being. Nature is

---

[37] Ibid. § 382, Zusatz.
[38] Idem.
[39] Ibid. § 281, Zusatz.

the first form of real existence on the part of the absolute. In nature man is created and with him the spirit. But, in nature the idea is still impotent, lacking consciousness or with latent consciousness. Yet it liberates itself from externality, alienness and returns to itself, to the source of its strength and life – the spirit. Through the act of cognition the spirit awakes, transforms nature into its object and appears as conscious spirit.[40]

The absolute is realized in nature and in the human consciousness, and through this consciousness is realized in morality, in the state, in history, art, religion and philosophy. All these forms of existence of the absolute are implemented through and within human consciousness. Knowledge and information can only find real expression through this consciousness and within its framework, since no other consciousness exists. Human consciousness is a kind of finite spirit; but the spirit is, by essence, infinite. But true infinity is not unilaterally opposed to the finite, but rather contains the finite within itself, as an element. "Mind *qua* mind *is* not finite, it *has* finitude within itself ... Mind is *as well* infinite *as* finite, and neither merely the one *nor* merely the other."[41] It is incumbent upon philosophy to prove the necessity of evolvement of the finite spirit, since there is no cognition outside the spirit, or, to be more exact outside self-cognition. Self-cognition of the absolute spirit through human consciousness – this is a theory with far-reaching conclusions. It transpires from this, on the one hand, that the absolute, the subject, God, the absolute spirit is *real* only in human consciousness and as human consciousness, and on the other hand, that it can arrive at this condition only in the finite spirit, in man, in mankind. Outside consciousness the absolute it is not real. But human consciousness is not only finite. Manifestations of the absolute in man are identical with manifestations of the human and finite in the absolute, in other words the absolute is finite to the same extent that man is infinite and absolute. In order to recognize infinity and its absolute nature, the absolute must be turned into the finite, into man or to use religious terminology – God must become man. Hegel was relying here on the Christian doctrine of humanization of God who, in his earthly revelation, took on the image of his Son. In the act of revelation God revealed that his nature was inextricably bound up with his Son, namely that he was obliged to stand apart from himself, to take on finite nature but, at the same time, despite this difference, God

[40] Idem.
[41] Ibid. § 386, Zusatz.

remains in himself, regarding his Son as himself. Thus unity with the Son, in order to be for himself in another, means that the Son is not the simple instrument of revelation but himself constitutes the preparation of the revelation.[42]

To return to Bauer – Hegel's polemic against theology based on feeling was understood by Bauer as a clear sign that Hegel saw substance as the sole factor in reality. God as objective universality is the substance which contains all being (including man). Bauer attributes to Hegel the Spinozian conception of the identity of reality with substance, in order to declare: "This is it: only this pantheism and this concept of the substantial relationship are the basis of Hegel's conception of the notion of religion."[43]

There is no basis for this conclusion, since we already know that Hegel disagreed profoundly with Spinoza's concept of substance, which disregarded the subject and the self-consciousness striving for cognition and freedom. We are faced with the same secret of Hegelian philosophy, which Bauer discussed extensively, the secret of dialectics, of the integral connection between the subject and the objective reality, between thought and being. Hegel wants organic unity of these two elements. Bauer acts non-dialectically in presenting substance as the opposite of the subject. Hegel's secret is to a large extent the secret of the Bauerian concept as well: to sever the existing link in Hegel's system between subject and object, subjectivity and substance. In this way Bauer could claim that Hegel started out as a pantheist, and moved over to a specifically atheistic approach. Bauer's way of thinking on this issue is as follows: the implications of the substantial relationship are such that the subject is the accidens while the substance (God) is the essence. As a result all of man's activity is in fact activity of the substance, of God and the subject does not exist in its own right but only as a factor of substance.[44] Hence human thought is neither incidental nor arbitrary, but identical with Divine thought. This thought is directed towards an aim: self-cognition of God as universality or as substance through finite human consciousness, as mediated cognition. On the other hand, human consciousness also attains more noble character thanks to its mediated task on this issue, since it is in the role of consciousness of substance. As Bauer sees it: "This is one act, one movement when universality knows itself in finite conscious-

---

[42] Ibid. § 381, Zusatz.
[43] Pos 157.
[44] Ibid. pp. 158–159.

ness and finite spirit, and the finite spirit grasps its essence in this universality. This is the same self-consciousness of substance."[45]

Whereas formerly Bauer detached the subject from the substance and transformed the latter momentarily into the sole absolute, thus enabling himself to interpret Hegel as a pantheist like Spinoza, he later transplants the emphasis from the substance to the subject and totally eliminates the former. Thus pantheism gives place to atheism. According to Bauer's view, the subject first submits to substance, but it later transpires that the substance without the subject remains without consciousness and thus the substance can negate its essence only in the subject and its consciousness. "Substance offers itself up as a sacrifice for the self and is absorbed by it."[46] "Man's self-consciousness becomes all and is the universal force, to which is attributed universality which was allegedly attributed to substance."[47] This thought was more clearly formulated by Bauer when he noted that "self-consciousness is the sole force of the world and history, and history has no significance other than evolvement and development of self-consciousness."[48] As the result of negation of substance and the crowning of the self, which is identified with self-consciousness as a monopolistic force in the world, God became the product of the self and forfeits his right to existence: "God is dead for philosophy and only the self as self-consciousness lives, creates, acts and is everything."[49] While the believer thinks that in religion he is dealing with a personal God, the philosopher knows that God is only the other self, that man is dealing with himself. The fulfilled self-consciousness is like a conjuring trick, where on the one hand, the self is split in two, like a reflection in a mirror, and on the other hand – after man has for thousands of years seen his image in the mirror as God, he suddenly discovers that he is looking at himself.[50]

It is impossible to say that Bauer finds no substantiation in Hegel's system, when he tries to base his views on the authority of the author of the *Phenomenology*, and this has already been noted.[51] Bauer made particular use of two Hegelian ideas: the primacy of philosophy in comparison to religion and the lack of consciousness in the absolute. Reliance on these views and on other elements of the Hegelian theories enabled Bauer to create the illusion that there was congruence between

[45] Ibid. p. 158.
[46] Ibid. p. 160.
[47] Ibid. p. 161.
[48] Ibid. p. 164.
[49] Ibid. p. 169.
[50] Ibid. p. 212.
[51] Stuke: *Philosophie der Tat*, p. 181.

his views and Hegel's teachings, when he claimed, for example, that philosophy understands religion but the latter cannot understand philosophy,[52] or when he emphasizes the fact that the substance should be regarded as subject.[53]

Bauer's interpretation would appear to have committed its first transgression – and this is the root of all the errors – when it split Hegel's thought into two components: substance and subject.

Several years later, in 1845, Bauer wrote: "Hegel combined Spinoza's substance and Fichte's self. The unification of these two, the bridging of the gap between opposed spheres, the incessant transition from one direction to another [. . .] giving preference to the first factor at the expense of the second, and the second as against the first – these constitute the crux of Hegelian philosophy, and they created a new era in philosophy but, at the same time, determine the weaknesses and finiteness of this philosophy [. . .] this contradiction, that the absolute is the noble and elevated, the perfect, the truth for man, a yardstick, essence, substance and end of man; and on the other hand that man is substance, that self-consciousness is the product of man's activity and exists thanks to his deeds and historical struggle, this contradiction, in the framework of which the Hegelian system exists and from which it could not liberate itself, should have been abolished once and for all."[54]

It may be deduced from Bauer's clarifications that of the two paths he could have chosen on this issue – to put an end to substance or to negate self-consciousness, he chose the former alternative, since he wished to emphasize the importance of personality. Herein lies the key to understanding of the phenomenon that the self-consciousness which, in Hegel, is bound up with reality, as we have seen above – conducts independent life in Bauer's philosophy, independent of any substantial factor, that it creates all wordly phenomena; without it there is no freedom, no society, no nature.[55] Substance is understood as objectivization of self-consciousness, when man transplants the content of his consciousness beyond himself, or as a moment in the development of the self-consciousness.[56] Bauer does not hesitate to draw the obvious conclusion: if substance does not have a sphere of its own and is a manifestation of self-consciousness or – at worst – an illusion and nothing more, then, in the end, the relationship of substance to self-

[52] Pos. 181.
[53] Ibid. p. 159; *Einleitung in die Dogmengeschichte von Theodor Kliefoth*, pp. 140–141.
[54] LF 86–87.
[55] Pos. 216; HL 162.
[56] Pos 151, 161–162.

consciousness should be regarded as the relationship of self-consciousness to itself.[57]

According to Bauer's evaluation self-consciousness has no place outside the intellectual activity of human beings. It is rooted in this activity and constitutes its beginning, basis and conclusion. It is not surprising therefore that, in accordance with this concept, Bauer sees the self as the true substance or, as he puts it, the substance which has been cancelled. The self, i.e., man, the standard bearer of self-consciousness, is the true content and material of spiritual and natural life.

In the light of this approach it is not difficult to comprehend why Hegel's struggle with the problems of substance, the problem of the organic link between subject and object was overlooked by Bauer, who was sufficiently alert to see substance transformed into subject, but was blind to the objective dimension of the activity of the spirit and the true relations between the subjective and the objective in Hegel.

It has been noted that Hegel identifies substance with God. Through cancelling substance Bauer achieved his longed-for objective – the negation of God and religion. In three chapters entitled: "Hatred of God", "Destruction of religion" and "Religion as the product of self-consciousness", Bauer tries to prove that Hegel was of the opinion that religion exists only in human consciousness, has no objective basis in reality and constitutes a destructive and harmful element.

Bauer simplified matters for himself in this issue. He grasped God as thought: "What is God? Absolute truth, Hegel replies, the universal in itself and for itself. But this universal, which is God, is nothing but thought."[58]

Since thought is a quality of the self, the product of man, then for Bauer the conclusion is obvious: the existence of the universal, of God is conditional to man, anchored in human consciousness: "We learn from this that the content of thought is also its product and is the being. But this being characterizes the object only in the consciousness of the self."[59]

This is a clear disregard for the objective character of thought in Hegel's philosophy, and for the comparison between thought of subjective dimension and the *nous*.

The objective element of the spirit disappears as if it had never existed. In pointing to thought as the source of philosophy and in

[57] Ibid. pp. 158, 161–162.
[58] Ibid. p. 204.
[59] Ibid. p. 205.

proclaiming the disappearence of God and the basis of religious faith as the result of the abolition of substance, Bauer forgot, apparently, that philosophy and religion have the same object, and that they differ only in the means they employ. To rely on the idea that the absolute has no self-consciousness of its own and understands itself through the finite self-consciousness, in order to prove that Hegel was an atheist, is a paradoxical step in the light of the fact that the selfsame idea appears in Hegel's writings as an argument in support of the theory of the truth of the Christian religion (humanization of God, Jesus as a God and man together).

The erroneous and misleading Bauerian interpretation derives from Hegel's antithetic interpretation. In place of the integration of substance and subject, self-consciousness and the absolute, Bauer preferred, because of his pragmatic considerations, to proclaim the existence of only one side and to treat it as an all-powerful force. In Hegel, as we have noted, the discovery of the human element in the absolute is identical with revelation of the absolute, i.e., divine, in the finite spirit and vice versa. Bauer, on the other hand, who reduces the substantial, the divine to man and sees in him the product of self-consciousness, sees the entire spectrum of relationships as the relation of the "I" to himself. As a result religion becomes an intellectual issue and Bauer also failed to see various aspects of the Hegelian theory of religion. For example – in Hegel's thinking love played an important part from the early writings onwards as a means of reconciling man and the absolute and this matter is also represented in the *Philosophy of Religion*, with which Bauer was closely acquainted. In referring to the Holy Trinity, Hegel notes that the term "love" is the most appropriate for definition of the network of relationships between an abstract God or eternal totality and its revelation in man, namely the finite spirit. God himself is seen in this context as love: "When we say God is love, we are expressing a very great and true thought."[60] Love serves as the expression of a living fabric of relationships between man and God, containing both respect and the sense that God lives and exists.[61]

Bauer paid no regard whatsoever to this Hegelian concept, because of the absolutization of the subjective-intellectual aspect.

Hegel's attitude towards Christianity was not unequivocal and contained a large degree of criticism; he also voiced ideas which only with

[60] PhR III, 10.
[61] Ibid. p. 11.

great difficulty could be reconciled with the various currents of Christianity, but the awarding of the status of "absolute religion" to Christianity attests to his attempt to preserve Christianity within the framework of the "Fifth Gospel" of his own founding. Bauer, for whom reason was in militant opposition to religion, proclaimed the superiority of philosophy to religion in order to remove the latter from the life of man, endowed as he is with self-consciousness. Guided by this tendency, he declares the Christian Trinity to be an illusory religious image, its source the self-consciousness: "It would be foolishness on our part to imagine that Hegel was actually referring to the Trinity of Christian faith when he spoke of the Kingdom of the Father and the mission of the Father, the Son and the Holy Ghost. Did he not clearly express his opinion that God, the representation of religion, is but the totality of self-consciousness, nothing but thought which is aware of this totality [. . .]?"[62]

Bauer translated the "absolute religion" into his own language. Christianity is the absolute religion since it is a pure representation of the self-consciousness and its development. In his opinion, Hegelian divine reason should be understood as externalization of human reason. Such an interpretation makes it possible to understand that realization of human consciousness cannot be reconciled with the existence of Christianity, which exists thanks to the transplantation of the contents of self-consciousness outside and beyond man and their attribution to an alien entity. Their restoration to man is identical with triumph of the idea that the world is not the fruit of the labours of the gods, or, in the case of Christianity – the action of one God, but of the self-consciousness, which is "the all-powerful magician, who creates the world and all its differences." The act of cancelling alienation (we will return to the question of alienation further on) implies liberation of man from religion and the cancellation of Christianity.[63]

The separation of man from the logical-ontological Hegelian framework, departure from the typically Hegelian view that man is a factor in process of the absolute – these caused Bauer to represent man on another plane. The absolute is related to man only in the sphere of the specific Bauerian logic, and it is within this framework that the conscious processes which bring man to see the totality of his self-consciousness as God, should be investigated. Bauer advocates a human-

---

[62] Pos 213.
[63] Ibid. pp. 214–220; *Einleitung in die Dogmengeschichte von Theodor Kliefoth*, pp. 139, 141, 147–153.

istic approach: man is seen as the arbiter of his fate and creator of history. Transcendental forces such as substance, God, the spirit of the world etc. – have no place in this conception.

In the *Posaune* Bauer devotes a special chapter to the ghost known as the world spirit, and tries to depict this Hegelian category as a phantom, an illusion. According to Bauer, Hegel himself was convinced that this term should only be utilized for immediate needs and that the self-consciousness is concealed behind this concept.[64]

Despite the cancellation of substance and the reliance on self-consciousness, Bauer does not offer the postulate of negation of universality. He had learned from Hegel that history is not shaped by the arbitrary deeds of human beings and he therefore tries to endow his conception of Gospel history with a theoretical-philosophical dimension. In his view, it is necessary to distinguish clearly between the particular and the universal.

The particular is related to fleeting moods, the foolishness and caprices of human beings, views which serve as the expression of intimate and personal situations. All this is to be found in the individual self-consciousness, which is the moving force behind the behaviour if human beings as individuals. Many remain in this state, outside science and philosophy, which are related to the universal self-consciousness.[65] Only a minority, brought up in the spirit of science and aware of the authentic needs of human society, are capable of rising above petty-mindedness and selfishness, and understanding – with the help of philosophy – the nature of the universal self-consciousness.

Only on the face of it is the universal self-consciousness "simple expansion and projection of the self on the world around it."[66] But closer perusal reveals that the subjective truth is not, in many cases, consistent with objectivity.[67] On the basis of analysis of Hegelian texts Bauer attempts to prove that the universal self-consciousness is a process which terminates in the attainment of two things: truth and liberty.[68] In several places Bauer explicitly identifies the universal self-consciousness with liberty and humanity.[69]

---

[64] Pos 162–165.
[65] *Bremisches Magazin für evangelische Wahrheit gegenüber dem modernen Pietismus (Rez.).* An, vol. II, pp. 126–127.
[66] Idem.; Pos 205–206.
[67] Pos 206–210.
[68] *Einleitung in die Dogmengeschichte von Theodor Kliefoth*, pp. 140–142.
[69] Ibid. pp. 140–141, 148–149; ChS 7; Jud 80–82.

This combination shows that humanity, in this context, is free of the chains of spiritual and political servitude.[70]

The basic elements of the universal self-consciousness appear in the conception of Christianity, for example in the writings of the authors of the Gospels, but these are only preliminary burgeonings, since religion is incapable of arriving at understanding of the nature of humanity and its needs.[71] From this point of view, Christianity could only grope in the dark, but was completely incapable of solving problems.

The problem of freedom, which for Hegel was related to substance realizing itself in the subject or in the subject-substance, and which was i.e. attributed to the self-conceiving spirit, underwent a metamorphosis in Bauer, as did the concept of self-consciousness. This consciousness was understood as both personal and individual and as a universal category, in whose framework all of human history is represented as development of self-consciousness. Self-consciousness constitutes the basis for historical conflicts, since it is "unity of the laws and the movement of the natural and spiritual cosmos." It is the power "which, in the end became sovereignty and makes history into its own free creation.[72]

It transpires therefore that Bauer endows the self-consciousness with metaphysical status. Whereas in the case of the individual self-consciousness we are dealing with the self-consciousness of a person, a subject, when it comes to the universal self-consciousness Bauer represents a totally different standpoint. This is self-consciousness which exists in its own right, it is sovereign and rules the world, or, as Bauer says: "The self-consciousness is the sole force of the world and of history, and history has no significance other than the evolvement and development of self-consciousness."[73]

On this point the Bauerian conception is undoubtedly torn between two tendencies: on the one hand he presents the subject as the creator of art, of religious and political projects etc., and explicitly attributes to the subject qualities of freedom, referring to a free and creative self-consciousness; on the other hand, he limits the individual, endowed with free self-consciousness, in various ways, which have been enumerated in the chapter on Gospel history: no man can break out of the cultural and historical framework within which he lives and

---

[70] ChS 8–9, 25–27, 32; B 86.
[71] Syn I, 241.
[72] *Die christliche Glaubenslehre in ihrer Entwicklung und im Kampf mit der modernen Wissenschaft* (Rez.). DJ 1842; *Feldzüge der reinen Kritik*, p. 86.
[73] Cf. ch. VII, n. 48.

operates; he cannot arbitrarily shape the various spheres of reality; he must take into consideration the ideas existing and rooted in the consciousness in the sphere of universality. It is surprising that Bauer employed the terminology of self-consciousness for the universal and objective. It is reasonable to assume that he wanted, in this way, to note that the universal – culture, religion, science, politics and the existing institutions of human society – is the fruit of the endeavour of human beings and that nothing exists in the human world which has not passed through the consciousness of human beings. But the term "self-consciousness" is deceptive, since it creates the impression that we are dealing with a quality or state of the subjective spirit. In actual fact, transplanting of the emphasis from the substance to the self-consciousness did lead to deviations from the Hegelian conception (with all its implications, such as proclaimed atheism, a radical view of reality etc.) but contents which existed in Hegel's world spirit, such as reasonability, the march to freedom etc., were preserved in the universality of the self-consciousness. In addition, those endowed with critical self-consciousness, who are guided by reason comprehend the tendencies of the universal self-consciousness and see its historical and social manifestations.[74] There is a clear link between the processes occurring in the two forms of consciousness – the subjective and the objective, as with the relations between the absolute and the finite spirit in Hegel.

As noted, the selfish human being is incapable of rising above individual interests and therefore cannot grasp the principles of the universal self-consciousness. This calls for clarification. For Bauer egoism is identified, above all, with religion. The religious man is an egoistic creature, because he prefers the redemption of his soul to anything else. His main attention is given to the problem of Divine mercy and his own individual fate. And for this reason he is incapable of liberating intellectual potential so as to solve other problems, which are the authentic problems of humanity, such as the furthering of liberty, organic ties with others, the development of science and the arts etc.[75] The existence of religion attests to man's defect; as a result of his dependence on an alien external force, he sees himself as a poor and weak creature. Thus a vitally significant contradiction is created between the human essence and the religious man, who is the common

[74] ECh 156–157.
[75] Ibid. pp. 131, 134–135.

empirical man. The essence of man is liberty, and the entire development of human history is the realization of this essence.

"Man is not the product of nature but of his own freedom", says Bauer.[76] Religion also raises the issue of individual freedom, but in a way which offers no practical solution of the problem: on the one hand it claims that man is free, and on the other it stresses, particularly in Christianity, the rule of God over man. And, in short, the entire network of views of religion is based on anomalies, on contradictions, such as God and man, spirit and matter, mercy and freedom. These views and the entire network of practical relations of Christianity prevent man from casting off his husk and his narrow world and from comprehending his own essence and the essence of universal self-consciousness.[77]

As against subjugation and the unability to understand the authentic processes occurring in history, Bauer presents those individuals who have liberated themselves from contradictions, alienation and passivity. They cooperate with one another for the sake of advancement of the state and of mankind, and it is they who are in the front line of the struggle for freedom. This combination of individual and universal objectives, the harmony between the aim of the individual struggle and the tasks of humanity is a conditio sine qua non for the attainment of liberty. Bauer was explicit on this point: "Without self-love, love of humanity is impossible, without self-respect there can be no respect for mankind, without enthusiasm for realization of individual liberty there can be no fulfilment of the freedom of human beings."[78]

If this is so, then the Bauerian conception depicts two processes which occur – in identical form and content – in parallel fashion: on the one hand, development of the individual self-consciousness, on the other the evolution which characterizes universal self-consciousness. In both forms of consciousness changes take place in the direction of liberation from the chains of religion, spiritual and political subjugation. Freedom is the objective of both. There is no explicit explanation of the link between them and therefore the impression may be gained that a dualist approach is being presented. But this would be a hasty conclusion. What emerges from Bauer's phrasing is that there is a connection between these two forms of self-consciousness. When

[76] Ibid. p. 138.
[77] Ibid. pp. 111–112, 138–139.
[78] ECh 135.

the individual self-consciousness is consistent with the metaphysical principle of historical development, it undoubtedly influences it – and vice versa – self-consciousness which encourages action on behalf of freedom is consistent with the demands for historical development which are raised by the universal and infinite self-consciousness.

Two things appear to lie outside human consciousness: the metaphysical principles which are the basis of history – reasonability and freedom and those products of human consciousness which are the fruit of human endeavour, such as political and religious institutions etc.[79] Since Bauer represents a negative attitude towards philosophy which recognizes substance and attributes various qualities to it, he refrains, insofar as possible from clear characterization of the self-consciousness which is related to universality, as if he had sensed that his views on the universal and all-powerful nature of human self-consciousness are not easily reconciled with this historiosophical approach.

It is also hard to say that Bauer solved the problem of the relations between man (the individual self-consciousness) and the world around him, a world which is grasped as necessity. There is conflict between the trends of free will and creation on the one hand and necessity on the other, a shift of standpoint from indeterminism to determinism and vice versa.

Hence Bauer did not overcome the difficulties which, to his mind, arise out of the Hegelian conception, which he saw as composed of two elements: the objectivist and substantialist Spinozian and the subjectivist Fichtean. Bauer clearly leaned towards Fichte, and this is understandable since the "I", that is to say man, the standard-bearer of self-consciousness, is the true content of spiritual and natural life – and in fact this component of Bauer's thought brings him close to Fichte. And what is more interesting: Bauer never concealed the fact that the objective of his interpretations of Hegel was to amend his mentor's theories through the Fichtean system, which he regarded as an essential complement of Hegel's thought.[80]

Like Fichte, Bauer attributes to spiritual activity absolute value and sees in the spirit the self-consciousness (both individual and infinite), the sole being; and the entire world is seen as the changing ex-

---

[79] For Bauer's concept of individual and general self-consciousness, see: *Einleitung in die Dogmengeschichte*..., pp. 148–152; *Bremisches Magazin*..., pp. 117, 120, 123; *Die christliche Glaubenslehre*..., p. 87; Syn I, 25, 69–70, 81–83.
[80] Pos 32, 168–169.

pression of the spirit, the means employed by the spirit in order to bring about change and to change itself dialectically. According to Bauer there is constant contradiction between the self-consciousness and reality, an assumption which, with certain modifications of style – is a repetition of the Fichtean conception on the contrast between what should be and what is. Whenever the self-consciousness transplants its content beyond itself and is realized in whatsoever fashion in a given reality, a contradiction emerges in due course between the perspectives of development of the self-consciousness and the product of its activities or, to be more precise: between the unlimited ability of the general consciousness to develop, and the level of development it has reached.[81]

It may be deduced from this that all existing phenomena are, as it were, stages in the development of the self-consciousness and are fated to disappear and to yield place to new forms. Hence Bauer's radical conclusions on this issue – religious, political and cultural institutions and currents had the right to exist in the past, when they were congruent with the level of development of the self-consciousness, but since then consciousness has advanced – and the best expression of this is the critical consciousness of Bauer himself – they are doomed to vanish from the historical arena sooner or later.

If Bauer had examined Hegel's theories on the philosophy of nature and history more closely, he would have realized that Hegel was advocating absolute idealism, where there was rooom for two elements–the subjective and the objective, but subjectivism in the style of Fichte was alien to the spirit of his thought. Hegel's attitude towards subjectivism can be ascertained in the chapter of the *Phenomenology* in which he criticizes empty idealism. Hegel attributes emptiness to subjectivism because its declarations concerning the relation of being to consciousness are completely abstract and empty of true content: "Reason knowing itself in this sense in its object", he wrote in this context, "is what finds expression in abstract empty idealism; it merely takes reason as reason appears at first, and by its pointing out that in all being there is this bare consciousness of a 'mine', and by expressing thing as sensations or ideas, it fancies it has shown that abstract 'mine' of consciousness to be complete reality."[82]

In addition to moving over to subjectivism, Bauer also attempted to give Hegel's thought an intellectual-atheistic character like that

[81] Ibid. pp. 205–206, 209, 211; Syn I, 82–83.
[82] Phen 279.

of Voltaire and Holbach. The atheism derives from his specific understanding of Hegel's thought, but it is no accident that he sees this
philosophy as atheism in the French style. Bauer was known for his
studies on French philosophy and history and we will return to these
spheres of interest which exerted tremendous influence on his political
ideas. These studies apparently also influenced the consolidation of his
atheistic views.

Bauer believed that "Hegel held views identical to those of the
French atheists",[83] that he wanted "to depose religion and rejected
no measure which could accelerate the collapse of religion,"[84] that
Hegel "pursued the French"[85] where critique of religion and exposure
of its inhuman and reactionary nature was concerned. In his conclusions Bauer claimed that, essentially speaking, Hegel's stand was almost identical with that of various French rationalists, with slight
modifications deriving more from a certain caution in formulating
statements than from a viewpoint differing from that of the representatives of the two main currents of Enlightenment towards the religious
life.

Bauer appears to have arrived at an atheistic standpoint as a result
of his interpretation of Hegel, and not as a result of his acquaintance
with Fichte's writings. This is why his universal and infinite self-
consciousness has many elements in common with Hegel's *Weltgeist*.
But as noted above, there is in Bauer's interpretation of Hegel's
thought a trend to subjectivization, and, as a result, dismantling of
the Hegelian system into the substantial and the conscious elements,
with emphasis on the latter. Hence Hegelian theory served as the
basis and springboard for consolidation of Bauer's own views and to
regard Fichteanism as the decisive factor in evolving Bauer's atheism
and subjectivism is incredible.

[83] HL 70.
[84] Idem.
[85] Ibid. p. 90.

CHAPTER VIII

BAUER'S CONCEPTION OF RELIGION AND HISTORY

On the face of it, this is a somewhat surprising title. What is the point in classifying these two phenomena – religion and history – together? Religion is the fragmentary expression of man's being and experience, while the history of mankind contains within it many additional components. But the truth is that for Bauer, religion, until it is abolished and replaced by atheism, plays a central role in the life of men and nation. "The truth is", Bauer wrote, "that religion shapes the essence of the state, art, etc.; but it is the imperfect and chimeric essence of the imperfect and chimeric state and the unfree essence of unfree art. As the state and art improve, religion ceases to constitute their soul or their principle."[1]

There is an additional factor which links religion and history: alienation. For Bauer the religious individual is a representative sample of the alienated man in general, just as the confessional era is characterized above all by alienation. At the same time, there is no total correspondence of religiosity and alienation since, apart from religion, other factors affected the alienation situations and among these the political factor plays a not inconsiderable part. It is worth noting this fact in this context in order to preclude misunderstandings, which are prevalent in exegetic literature, particularly that which draws inspiration from Marx.

The initial stage of known history is defined by Bauer as the life of nature and the folk[2] and he is referring to the dependence of man on nature and on the folk to which he belongs. This was reflected in ancient religions in which the forces of nature and social, familial and popular forces played a decisive part. Natural forces were seen as supernatural, influencing human lives and promising salvation. Because of the dependence of the individual on the community and

[1] ECh III.
[2] Syn III, 309.

emphasizing the importance of the category of the nation for individual life, Bauer sees the spirit of the folk (*Volksgeist*) as the foundation of the historical process at this stage in the development of human society.[3] For Bauer, this spirit forfeited its universal significance (this is obvious in the light of his proclaimed aim to reject the substantial element, expressed in his attacks on the folk spirit in the *Posaune*) and comes synonymous with natural consciousness. The latter sees in nature the essence of man and accordingly natural objects such as: fire, water, mountains etc., are seen as manifestations of this essence.[4] In other words: nature is the principle directing all the phenonomena of human life and this is, in actual fact, the old Hegelian thought in a new metamorphosis. Hegel believed that the primeval religion is the religion of nature, within the framework of which man merges with nature to the point of obscuring the specific human element.[5]

Bauer clearly deviates from Hegel when he imposes the framework of natural religion to a large extent on Judaism as well, since, for Hegel, Judaism as the religion of sublimity (*Religion der Erhabenheit*) is classified among the religions of free individuality, in which the spirit overcomes nature and detaches itself from dependence on the natural surroundings. As against this concept, Bauer claims that "Judaism supplies only the needs of that man who is interested in the external world, in nature."[6]

Bauer sees a distinct trait of the life of nature and the folk in the fact that man is not free but attached to "natural" institutions based on ties of blood and origin, such as family, parental home, tribe and nation. This rule also applies to the division of this kind of society into castes and estates which are seen as natural institutions.

Almost all of Bauer's clarifications relate to Judaism: "Only one of various ways of strengthening the spirit of the Jewish people was the hierarchy, the caste system. The hierarchy exists wherever the spirit of the people is incapable – for lack of force, liberality or development abilities – of activating all the limbs of the folk."[7] "It is the religious duty of the Jew, as Jew, to belong to a family, a tribe, a nation, i.e. to live for the sake of certain human interests; but this is only a seeming advantage, based on a deficiency. Man in his universal essence, man as

[3] Ibid. pp. 309–310; *Bremisches Magazin...*, p. 122.
[4] *Die christliche Glaubenslehre...*, p. 93; Cf. also: Jud 33, 36.
[5] PhR I, 265, 270–273.
[6] Fae 58.
[7] Jud 38.

more than a member of a family, tribe or nation was still unknown to Judaism."[8]

In the Greek and Roman religions the natural element was, of course, far stronger than in Judaism. Hence the deification of certain natural forces and factors. On the other hand Bauer sees these religions as integrated in a patriotic political framework and in human interests.[9]

Ancient man and all the generations since who have lived "a life of nature and folk" were not aware of the fact that the world in which they lived was their own world, shaped by themselves. Rather the contrary: it seemed to them to be something alien, imposing its way of life upon them. Thus the roles were exchanged: the world and its various objects were understood as a sovereign ruling force and man as totally dependent on it and on the gods, the personification of natural forces. It is not surprising that under these circumstances man saw himself as a weak creature, lacking the talents needed to change reality and make men free.

Thus this Bauerian conception sees alienation as the characteristic trait of prehistoric society and the early cultures. This fact is worth noting since it leads to the conclusion that since the very beginning human society had existed in a constant regime of alienation, lack of sovereignty and freedom. Incidentally: this conception is understandable in the light of Bauer's attitude towards religion, since, for him, religion is the symbol and expression of man's weakness, both as regards his lack of free self-consciousness and his dependence on objects, which are the fruit of his activity. Since man has been living from the first within a religious framework, it was clear to Bauer that alienation has accompanied human society since its creation. But this alienation was not overt, or, as Bauer says: "In ancient religions essential interests concealed the profundity of the alienation and its full horror: the view of nature is attractive, the family tie is pleasant, the interest of the folk augments the enthusiasm of the religious spirit as regards the adored worshipped forces; the chains which bound the human spirit in the service of these religions were decorated with flowers."[10]

[8] Fae 61.
[9] Syn III, 309.
[10] Idem. The expression *Blumen an der Kette* is very frequently used by Bauer in characterizing religious alienation. This phrase was taken up by Marx and appears in the well-known section of the *Introduction to Critique of Hegel's Philosophy of Right,* in which Marx refers to the critique of religion and its consequences (Cf. MEGA I, 1, i, p. 608).

As time passed the flowers faded – this is the fate of all plants – and there was increasing resistance to the dependence of human beings on nature and the objective world. Bauer's explanation of the existence of oppositionary forces is dialectical: the conflicts and contradictions are the rule and an immanent phenomenon in history,[11] and without them there can be no development whatsoever.

The opposition to the life of nature and the people which maintained human beings in spiritual and social slavery derived from the philosophy which regards the self-consciousness as its homeland.[12] Epicurism, stoicism and scepticism revealed to man his internality, demanded his self-definition, demanded that he be awarded rights and made him aware of the principle of self-consciousness. All these postulates and their realization were related to the struggle with existing institutions and their cancellation, to the casting of doubt on deeply-rooted habits and to the elevation of man to the level of a yardstick for all reality. It was in accordance with this view that the modern principle of individuality and personality was crystallized in the Roman world.[13]

Another factor operating against the life of nature and the nation was the worldwide rule of Rome, which severed the old familial and folk ties, put an end to "natural" institutions and also, for its own part, introduced the principle of personality, as displayed by the tyrannical all-powerful ruler.[14]

The worldwide rule of Rome and philosophy were – according to this conception – "movements of universal force, which tried to rise above limitations through nature and the people – mankind and its consciousness."[15]

But religion then constituted a universal force and, as a result, the liberation of self-consciousness could not occur outside it. The philosophy of the self-consciousness and the universal rule of Rome prepared the ground for a new outlook and for a new order, which were utterly opposed to the worship of nature and to a regime based on the folk and its religion. We are referring to Christianity, which liberated man from the rule of the folk and of nature and inculcated in him awareness of the principle of internality, subjectivism and infinity. Despite the shattering of the rule of nature and transplantation of emphasis to the "I", the alienation which had afflicted man did not weaken. On the

---

[11] *Einleitung in die Dogmengeschichte...*, p. 156.
[12] Pos 168.
[13] Syn II, 46.
[14] Idem.; Cf. also: Ibid. III, p. 309.
[15] Ibid. III, p. 309.

contrary: Christianity exacerbated alienation and made it total or, as Bauer says: "Within the sphere of the self-alienated spirit the existing limitations of universal life had to be abolished – if the liberation was to be basic and on behalf of mankind, i.e., alienation had to become total and to encompass all of human life."[16]

Thus there collapsed the natural and concealed forms of alienation, in which there was almost no sense of dependence on the creations of man, and a world was created based on transfer of power to the self, but not the human self, i.e., not to the many peoples composing humanity, but to the sole "I", the embodiment of all mankind and its representative before God – Jesus Christ. The following is the best known of all Bauer's statements:

"When the flowers faded in the course of history, and the chains were broken by Roman power, the vampire of spiritual abstraction completed its project. It sucked from humanity all its vital juices, blood and life to the last drop: nature and art, family, folk and state – of all these only shadows were left and on the ruins of the dying world perched the exhausted self, sucked-dry, lonely but at the same time the sole force. After the tremendous defeat, the self could not create out of its own depths and universality the lost patterns of life – nature and art, folk and state – at least not at once. The sole thing of interest to it was the absorption of all those things which existed in the old world. The self was now everything and at the same time utterly empty; it became a universal force and at the same time sat on the ruins of the world, gripped with terror of itself and sorrow at its defeat; this self, which was empty, despite its absorption of everything, did not have sufficient courage to see itself as a universal force, that is to say, it still remained in the category of religious spirit and completed the alienation through the act of setting up its universal forces in opposition to itself, seeing them as strange and alien powers which should be served in fear and trembling so that they would act for its existence and redemption. It saw the guarantee of this existence in the Messiah, who represented those same qualities which were actually its own qualities: universal power as the force in which were invested all the natural views and moral distinctions of the moral spirit, the popular spirit, the life of the state and views of the various arts."[17]

Because of his fears and his plight, deriving from the necessity to be independent and at the same time to render his self and his hopes

[16] Idem.
[17] Ibid. pp. 309–310.

dependent on something outside himself, man retreated in his internality and saw the solution to his problems in negation of the world and its earthly institutions. He turned his back on the world, from which he could not hope for fulfilment of his anticipations, and built a new conceptual world located beyond mundane reality, on which he pinned his hopes for peace, security, tranquility, prosperity etc.

The transcendental force towards which yearnings are directed, God or Son of God, is the self elevated to Heaven, the self become God. [18]

It transpires therefore that man, having detached himself from dependence on the natural world and the natural order became a slave to ideal forces which he created by his own powers: through his imagination, ideological conceptions, emotions. This world was transplanted outwards, and in the eyes of believers was accorded the status of objective existence and increasingly played the role of supreme authority, the guide not only in matters of the soul, salvation and redemption but also in material and mundane affairs.

Bauer devoted special attention, in this context, to the sources of religion. On this point there are clear and admitted connections with the ideas of the French Enlightenment, and particularly with Holbach, but Bauer's view is much wider and does not overlook various factors which the rationalists tended to disregard. The common denominator of Bauer and the rationalists is the lack of intellectual ability of human beings to comprehend conditions of their life – as the root of religion. Bauer sees in the absence of knowledge, the opposition to science, the intellectual limitations of man and his foolishness the reasons for the adherence to religious belief[19] which explains natural phenomena, social and cultural life in a simple manner and through supernatural factors.

At the same time Bauer outdoes many of the critics of religion among his contemporaries in his anti-evolutionary view of religion and religiosity. In contrast to the conception which draws a line between the development of science and technology and the narrowing of the basis of religion, which is supposedly grounded on lack of knowledge and ignorance, Bauer saw that there was no constant and direct connection between these phenomena. The vision of dissemination of knowledge which will lead to the almost automatic abolition of religion, was far removed from Bauer. Thus, for example, Bauer declared with intellectual integrity that "church decrees have never been as strictly

18 ECh 94–104; see also: ThB 153–155.
19 ECh 127–129; ThS 46.

observed as in our day when industry is conquering nature and man is nevertheless not sufficiently courageous to admit that he is the master of the world."[20]

The reason for the gap between Bauer and the various rationalists lies in a wide spectrum of Bauerian explanations of the roots and tasks of religion in modern society. Bauer points to fear of family and personal catastrophes, fear of death, man's sufferings in this world, poverty and other plights, which impel people to believe in future reward and in a better fate.[21] Religion lulls the believers and helps reconcile them to existing reality through its visions of heavenly mercy and the joys of the next world. Religion is compared to a dream, an illusion, alcohol, a state of sleep etc.[22] Bauer also employs, at least twice, the word *opium*, which enjoyed such great success in antireligious literature. In the light of the importance of the subject, it is worth giving the statements in Bauer's own words:

"After fulfilling its destructive urge towards everything that is noble and good on earth, it [religion] sketches, in its opium intoxication, a picture of the future situation, which differs drastically from the order of this world, since everything changes and is renewed."[23] "The pure Christian state is a state in which theological law prevails. This law attains to real power or, to be more exact, absolute power, when, through its results which are identical with those of opium, it puts all parts of mankind to sleep and if some occasionally awake – they carry out crimes which horrify mankind, which has not yet become Christian in the full sense of the word or has already abandoned the Christian framework."[24]

In order to understand the task of religion as opium it is necessary to see the connection between this issue and Bauer's view of the existing world as "inverted" (*verkehrte Welt*). According to this view religion sees reality in distorted fashion since religious consciousness is basically torn and divided. The representative sample of this miserable consciousness, on the basis of Hegel's terminology in the *Phenomenology*, is Christianity, whose theological consciousness is seen by Bauer as split within itself and self-alienating; it does not know that it shapes its own fate – at least in general fashion – but transplants its mission to a celestial sphere and believes that it is dependent on the forces ruling

[20] Fr 216.
[21] ECh 94.
[22] B 70–71.
[23] Fr 212.
[24] ChS 9–10.

this imaginary sphere. Unlike the free consciousness which knows it is able to recognize and control its living conditions, the miserable Christian consciousness "has detached its mission from the human entity, transferred it to the celestial world and caused the confused and pathetic individual self to arrive at a total breach with the real universal self, namely with the individual self, worthy of being called man."[25]

There is an additional reason to view the world as inverted. Such a viewpoint is consistent with the aim of the ruling religion, whose founder turned water into wine and carried out many miracles.[26] The distorted essence of religion derives from its very nature, based as it is on deeds opposed to the worldly structure. Bauer also believed that because religion ruled the world and thanks to the cooperation between it and the state, the illusion of relations between man and the heavenly and earthly gods was commonly accepted: "Christianity is mankind's illusion at this particular stage on itself and its general mission. [...] Since this state, this law, this viewpoint of mankind cannot maintain themselves for fear of the vengeance of the free universality of the self-consciousness, they concluded that the state, constitution and society should obliterate themselves in the face of a higher universality of the spirit. This delusion, this vain conclusion, this murderous universality is the religious consciousness."[27]

As a result of this approach, which is influenced by irrationality as regards man's needs in this world, when man is understood as a dependent and contemptible creature and the celestial forces as a demiurge shaping the course of events in the world, the relations in the state and society are also grasped incorrectly. "Faith [...] had tremendous force as regards the transformation of the worldly order."[28] "It is as one of the wonders of the power of faith that we should regard the creation of an inverted world, which is the act of the consciousness, or, to be more exact, of lack of consciousness."[29] Elsewhere he writes: "The contradiction, the distraction and the alienation return in the objective world, shaped by the undefined religious consciousness."[30]

25 ThB 156. Elsewhere Bauer comments that the mission of man, who should be free, was grasped falsely and distortedly by Christianity, which claims that man should submit to the supreme forces, obey them and regard all manifestations of human history as the dictates of heaven. (ECh 141–142).
26 Cf. the chapter "The inverted world" in *Das entdeckte Christentum* (ECh 139–140).
27 Ibid. pp. 141–142.
28 Ibid. p. 143.
29 Idem.
30 ThB 157.

Bauer sees the world as distorted because of its numerous deviations from the rational pattern determined by him: the state, instead of liberating man, enslaves him to authority, above all to the church and to religious patterns of life. Man is persecuted by the police and by reaction, there is stringent censorship of the press and of literature, the regime withholds from citizens freedom of expression and conscience and other freedoms. Man, instead of being active and determining his own destiny, endowed with a diverse and rich personality, is passive, miserable, poverty-stricken and pathetic.[31]

Bauer was aware that he was attributing to religion qualities of ideology. As he understood it, religion defends the existing political and social regime, lends it justification and legitimation and at the same time its defects and flaws are related to the flawed and non-human worldly order.

There is a two-way relationship here to the problem of the relations between the religious consciousness and the objective world. On the one hand, religion transplants beyond itself – to the objective world – its tendencies and thus, torn and alienated, creates a world of similar character, and on the other hand, it is seen as "the expression, isolated manifestation and sanction of the omission and disease of existing relations. It is the general essence of all relation and tendencies, but a distorted essence, an essence which has been detached from them, that is to say, as a distorted essence it constitutes expression of lack of essence and of distortion."[32]

According to Bauer's point of view, religion as ideology is distorted consciousness of a distorted reality. It is not the true consciousness of a distorted reality nor is it distorted or false consciousness of an authentic world. The distortion is twofold and as such is immanent to both religion and the world. Bauer deduced from this consistently that the mundane reality must be changed as must the human consciousness, imbued as it was with religion, in order to redeem mankind and bring it the message of freedom.

Bauer believed that the Christian state had adopted all the patterns of religious subjugation and was utilizing religion to defend its very existence. This was why he regarded it as essential to commence changing the reality of the state: "It is not the church which constitutes a burden for us – just as we are not a burden in its eyes – but the Christian state burdens us through its Christian demands. [...] The Church does

---

[31] ECh 93–96, 112, 128–129, 134–135, 138, 143, 162–163.
[32] Fr 217.

not constitute something in its own right, since it is the isolated expression of the essence of the state."[33]

There is an open and obvious contradiction here between the theory that religion is the essence of the state and of society, as presented above, and Bauer's view that the state is responsible for the spiritual, social and political plight of mankind. But the contradiction is more illusory than real. It may be deduced from Bauer's explanations that the state he denotes Christian, has adopted all the qualities and principles of religion: "We cannot be born, graduate from school, marry without the state forcing upon us religious ceremonies which we did not request, cannot request and will never recognize."[34]

Bauer longs for change, radical transformation of the political reality, making the state free and at the same time deposing religion from its position of influence and rendering it a personal issue alone.[35]

In order to understand better Bauer's conception of Christianity and the Church of his day, it is necessary to attempt to comprehend the nature of Christianity. Unlike natural religion, which values ties with nature, emphasizes man's ties with mundane institutions, with science and art, and does not disregard man's material needs and aspirations, Christianity esteems the supernatural world, distinguishes between the spirit and the flesh, heaven and earth, the soul and the body, takes a positive view of the former and a negative view of the latter. Christianity turns its back on science and art, man's authentic creation, and its interest in God and the redemption of the soul. Hence Christianity's hatred of mankind as it strives for solutions other than those proposed by the Christian religion. It is not so relevant, in this context, that Christianity as depicted by Bauer is not the same Christianity existing in his day, but an ascetic-abstenious religion characteristic of the Middle Ages or, to be more exact, certain trends of the practical Christian thought of medieval times.[36] It is more important to note that Christianity sets itself at a distance from all human conceptions, from the authentic human world, and transplants its interest beyond this world – to a fictitious and illusory sphere. All Bauer's views on this point are aimed at proving one sole thing – that Christianity causes total dehumanization of man and the forfeiting of his human qualities. Bauer was convinced that it was no accident that Christianity was

---

[33] Ibid. p. 218.
[34] Idem.
[35] Ibid. pp. 214–219.
[36] For this issue, see Reinhart Seeger, *Friedrich Engels. Die religiöse Entwicklung eines Spätpietisten und Frühsozialisten*. Halle 1935, pp. 116–117.

hostile towards science; this attitude derived from the very nature of science, which demanded of man that he concentrate on cognition of nature and on mundane-human issues, whereas Christianity demanded of its believers that they direct their attention to questions of salvation and life in the next world, i.e. turn to "the emptying of their internality and lack of humanity."[37]

The artificial contradictions contained in Christianity, i.e. between God and man, mercy and liberty are in total conflict with the nature of man and eventually cause man to arrive at self-contradiction and to see himself as the slave of an imaginary alien entity, which is but the product of his own intellectual and emotional activity. The result is that "in religion he himself became an inhuman entity and he adores this entity which lacks humanity as his own essence."[38]

When Bauer compares the Christian world with the future society, based on his proposed pattern, he determines:

"It is clear that the slave fears freedom, the non-human entity (Unmensch) fears humanity, the madman fears reason, the inhabitant of the inverted world fears the world of truth, order, morality."[39] This context derives logically from the view of the existing world as inverted, distorted, and the view of the common man as religious, namely admiring a non-human entity. Therefore life becomes irrational and dependent on acts of relevation and on the miracles of religion, and as such, of course, is in conflict with reason, just as dependence on God is in conflict with the ideals of human liberty. But the main question has not yet been answered: what impels Bauer to claim that in religion man understands the product of his activity as a non-human entity and what are the characteristics of this non-human situation? Bauer's answer would appear to have been provided in the following sentence:

"We have come so far that the 'animal' has become man's ideal, the animal state man's normal situation."[40] The theme of "religion of animals"[41] is prevalent in Bauer's work and it means: the conditions under which man lives cause constant tension between him and the world around him, which is non-rational, imperfect, inverted and distorted, or, in other words: Man cannot realize himself under the given conditions of a miserable afflicted world, and therefore he opposes

---

[37] ECh 129.
[38] Ibid. p. 138.
[39] ThS 44.
[40] B 77.
[41] Ibid. p. 78; ThS 44.

it and protests against it. This protest finds expression in the transplantation of practical life to the celestial sphere. But a vitally significant transformation takes place in the process of externalization of
human essence and its conception as independent of man and ruling
his life. Man's humanity is lost. The adored entity attests to a widespread network of flaws, shadows and defects: the sense of fear, submission to authority, lack of autonomous reason, sacrifice of man's
personality to a greater force, passivity, spiritual predicament, foolishness, man's nothingness, his self-seclusion etc.[42] These are not authentic
human qualities, they characterize animals. Man must be guided by
autonomous reason, engage in the affairs of mankind, and help it break
free of servitude, dedicate his life to mundane affairs, for the state,
society, art and science. Courage, intellectual daring, intensive activity
and belief in man as man – all these qualities are demanded of him for
fulfilment of these objectives.[43] The trouble is – according to Bauer –
that man does not believe in himself and in his powers within the
framework of religion, but rather displays qualities which conflict with
his humanity. This is also the reason why Bauer sees the essence of
"theology" in "the animal spirit"[44] and the religious man at the level
of a "dumb animal."[45]

There is a basic difference here between Bauer's and Feuerbach's
conceptions of alienation, in contrast to the view of those scholars who
have dealt with the issue and believe that there is affinity if not
identity between them. Thus, for example, Arthur Drews wrote: "In
his views Bauer arrived at a standpoint identical with that represented
by Feuerbach in *The Essence of Christianity*."[46] In actual fact the
similarity between the views of Bauer and Feuerbach was external and
merely formal; for both Christianity and religion in general are the
creation of man, who transplants beyond himself his qualities, feelings
and aspirations and sees them as belonging to another entity. In Feuerbach, however, and in this he is poles apart from Bauer, there is no
difference between man and God as a projection of man and of human
qualities: "I show that the true sense of theology is anthropology, that
there is no distinction between the predicates of the divine and human
nature, and consequently no distinction between the divine and human

---

[42] ECh 91–101, 104–110, 116–117, 128–131, 134–135; ThS 44–49.
[43] ThS 44; B 70–73.
[44] Fr 232.
[45] ECh 96.
[46] Arthur Drews: *Die Leugnung der Geschichtlichkeit Jesus in Vergangenheit und Gegenwart.* Karlsruhe in Baden 1926, p. 41.

subject."[47] Hence also Feuerbach's well-known statement that "the secret of theology is anthropology."[48]

Unlike Bauer, Feuerbach sees religion as characterizing man, who has set out on a search in order to comprehend the world and himself in relation to the world, but because of the limitations of his life cannot understand correctly the essence of religion and of his own self. It was therefore clear to Feuerbach that there was a tremendous difference between the world of man and the animal world, or, as he puts it: "The essence of man, which sets him apart from animals, is not only a foundation of religion but also its object."[49]

When Feuerbach relates to the divine essence as to the essence of man he is not, of course, referring to empirical man but to a man free of limitations,[50] who, by respecting the personality of God, is actually seeing himself as supernatural, immortal, sovereign and unlimited.[51]

From this point of view it is clear that negation of man equals negation of religion.[52] Feuerbach believed that love plays a vital role in relations between man and the religious essence which he worships, and at the same time serves as a characteristic of the fact that in religion man relates to himself or, as he himself says: "The clearest, most irrefragable proof that man in religion contemplates himself as the object of the Divine Being, as the end of the divine activity, that thus in religion he has relation only to his own nature, only to himself [...] is the love of God to man, the basis and central point of religion."[53]

It is not surprising, therefore, that according to this approach, the God of religion wishes to bestow on man joy and his mercy. Feuerbach was so imbued with the consciousness that religion plays a positive part in the life of man who has not yet found his essence within himself that he asked Ruge, in one of his letters in 1842 to erase the word "atheism" from an article referring to his thought. This word, in his opinion, "is not practical" and it would be preferable to use the term "anthropotheism."[54] This phrasing attests to Feuerbach's tendency to regard religion as a human experience and, at the same time, to regard its content as the deification of man.

[47] E p. XXXVII.
[48] Ibid. p. 270.
[49] SW VII, p. 25.
[50] E 98.
[51] Ibid. pp. 92–94, 98–100, 181–183.
[52] Ibid. p. 44.
[53] Ibid. p. 57.
[54] Cf. for this issue S. Rawidowicz: *Ludwig Feuerbachs Philosophie.* Berlin 1931, pp. 119–120.

This means that Feuerbach's attitude towards religious alienation is ambivalent, to say the least. Man cannot live an authentic human life in the full sense of the word as long as he understands his own essence outside himself and attributes it to another entity; but even in a situation of externalization of the human essence and understanding of it as an essence alien to man, he is not totally abandoned to his own devices: the religious rituals lead to his unification with God, and love lulls him and helps eradicate memory of his pains and sufferings. Furthermore: alienation is essential to enable man to arrive at the view of himself as arbiter of his own fate. This aim can be achieved if he abandons the illusion which had previously characterized his life. According to Feuerbach: "The necessary turning-point of history is the open confession that the consciousness of God is nothing else than the consciousness of the species, that man can and should raise himself only above the limits of his individuality [...] that there is no other essence which can think, dream of, imagine, feel, believe in, wish for, love and adore as the absolute, than the essence of human nature itself."[55]

Feuerbach believes that religion itself contributes to this issue, and that it prepares the ground for man's self-cognition and the attainment of his freedom: "This objective, the cognition of religion as the factor spurring on human liberty, self activity, love and happines, determined the scope of my historical attitude to religion."[56] In this context the Christian religion represented in the eyes of Feuerbach the principles of criticism and freedom.[57]

All this enabled Feuerbach to argue, justifiably, that his attitude toward religion was not negative but critical.[58] Furthermore, cognition of the human essence as God created a kind of new religion. Löwith was correct when he wrote that in Feuerbach's conception "we see retention of the Christian predicates while discarding their subject."[59]

It may be stated without exaggeration that Bauer's entire network of arguments contradicts Feuerbach's system of evaluating religion, and hence the latter's criticism of it. Feuerbach also clearly saw the basic differences between his own views and Bauer's stand. Thus, for example, he wrote to Kapp in 1844: "He [Bauer] argues with me boldly, without mentioning me by name. This controversy gladdens me since

[55] E 270.
[56] *Vorlesungen über das Wesen der Religion.* SW, Vol. VIII, p. 28.
[57] E 32.
[58] Ibid. p. 270.
[59] Karl Löwith: *From Hegel to Nietzsche*, p. 336.

it exposes the great gap between us."[60] When a certain newspaper emphasized the great affinity between the author of the *Posaune* and Feuerbach, the latter regarded it as his duty to write to the editor and to state that this was an erroneous conclusion, since the anonymous author had started out from the viewpoint of Hegelian philosophy and based himself on it, while he, Feuerbach, had chosen the opposite path to Hegel and disagreed with him.[61] Feuerbach evaluated the differences in point of view between him and Bauer more correctly than did Ruge, who supported the contents of the *Posaune* and Feuerbach's theories simultaneously, and wanted to bridge the differences, writing to this end to Feuerbach: "My dear friend, have you read the *Posaune*? It is an important document and worthy of note, and constitutes a kind of detachment from the entire old Hegelian tradition."[62] But there was another fact of which Ruge was not unaware, just as many others also perceived it: Bauer attacked religion more fiercely than did Feuerbach.[63] Under the impact of the *Posaune* Ruge began to doubt the validity of Feuerbach's views and wrote to Prutz: "I am now beginning to criticize Feuerbach."[64] Bauer's radicalism was evident to all, and he was therefore denoted "Jacobite", "Robespierre of theology" and for Engels and others he was the leader of the most extreme faction of the Young Hegelians.[65]

Bauer, who was clearly aware of the basic differences between him and Feuerbach, launched a frontal attack on the latter, and particularly criticized the following ideas:

a) Religion as the love-relationship between man and God. Bauer thought that Feuerbach's views on love as "a fire consuming the uniqueness of the individual" and a framework in which "the individual is cancelled out by God" attested to a distinct, unequivocal mystical predilection. According to Feuerbach "the individual achieves rest only when he becomes a mystic, i.e. when he arrives at contemplation of God or, what is identical with this situation, when he is cancelled out in the love of God, that is to say ceases to be an individual, since his uniqueness is destroyed and he himself is completely eliminated."[66]

[60] Karl Grün: *Ludwig Feuerbach in seinem Briefwechsel und Nachlass.* Leipzig-Heidelberg 1874, p. 364.
[61] Ibid. p. 340.
[62] Ibid. p. 337.
[63] *Ruges Briefwechsel und Tagebuchblätter aus den Jahren 1825–1880*, p. 243.
[64] Ibid. p. 249.
[65] G. Mayer: *Friedrich Engels. Eine Biographie*, pp. 83, 88, 90; A. Cornu: *Karl Marx und Friedrich Engels. Leben und Werk*, pp. 299–304; MEGA I, 2, pp. 251–281.
[66] LF 83.

It is as mysticism that Bauer also sees Feuerbach's new religion, at the centre of which stands man in place of God. He was even willing to award Feuerbach the title of "the greatest mystic of all times."[67] For Bauer, love not only adds nothing to man's personality, does not enrich him and does not make him happier, but rather the contrary: it is "the culmination of the emptying of man. It is the product of weakness, reflection of the fact that man is perplexed, lacks support, and the best proof of this is the need to find something else in place of himself, the need to seek himself in others."

b) the Hegelian character of Feuerbach's views. Despite Feuerbach's harsh criticism of Hegel, Bauer believed that he had not severed his ties with the Hegelian roots. On the contrary: the fact that he had not freed his system from religion and was emphasizing the importance of the latter pointed to the joint basis of Feuerbach's thought and Hegel's system. Bauer also finds similarity between them in their view of Jesus and quotes extensively from Feuerbach's essays in order to prove that Jesus is seen by him as the embodiment of the creative logos and as a redeemer.[68]

Bauer finds a Hegelian element in Feuerbach on another point as well: in his disregard for empirical man and his representation of the divine essence as the essence of abstract man or, to be more exact, as the essence of mankind, to which the limitations of finiteness and death do not apply. This abstract man, to his mind, is another version of the Hegelian absolute spirit.

"Was Feuerbach an innovator who created change?" asks Bauer and replies: "Feuerbach and Hegel differ only on details, on marginal issues, and not on basics. [...] Both represent the same stand – the stand of substance [...] both act *arbitrarily*: both see the subject as *object* without realizing this; both start out from the *infinite* and not the *finite* and remain dependent on their starting point. What did Feuerbach do when he changed theology into anthropology? He did exactly the same as did Hegel when he elevated theology to the rank of philosophy. In anthropology, theology is sanctified, integrated and cancelled, just as it undergoes this process in Hegel's philosophy. Anthropology is religion; the species is a force which is independent of man and conducts its life outside his personality."[69]

In this context it is worth noting that, in claiming that Feuerbach

[67] Ibid. p. 91.
[68] Ibid. pp. 96–98.
[69] Ibid. p. 109.

was employing Hegelian concepts and particularly those bringing his conception close to theology, Bauer in 1845 was deviating from the atheistic interpretation of Hegel which he had previously advocated.

In general it seems that the view of the human race as a new kind of divinity is anathema to Bauer, who envisaged the active individual making his way towards understanding of the world without needing to resort to Feuerbachian religion in order to complete this task. On this point the conflict between Bauer and Feuerbach comes into the open. Bauer could not forgive Feuerbach for representing religion as worship of the essence of man, while he himself, as we know, believed that in religion the supreme essence appears as a non-human image, which imposes fear, the reflection of man's passivity and weakness. In accordance with this viewpoint, Bauer writes: "In a word, the species is a new God or the God of the new; but, as in every religion, here too man is represented as what he is not. Religion is the view of the non-human, the distorted essence, a reflection of helplessness, of complaisance, of weakness. [. . .] [On the other hand, Feuerbach's] anthropology is the decorated heaven of God, the storehous filled by the fertile imagination. When it is dazzled by the divine sun, when it is gazing at the glowing halo of God, the eye cannot grasp the essence of religion."[70]

c) Feuerbach's materialism also seemed to Bauer to reflect philosophical weakness. Bauer cites dozens of excerpts from Feuerbach's writings in order to emphasize the importance of sensibility in the Feuerbachian conception and states that the range of problems of the human self-consciousness is not accorded sufficient attention, because of the stressing of the sensual aspect of man's conceptions and of the process of cognition of the world. For Bauer, Feuerbach's view of nature as a dominant factor in human life constitutes a serious obstacle to understanding of man's spiritual life: "Nature is exalted, man is inferior. Nature is God, while man is its servant." For these two reasons: the stressing of sensibility and the view of man as part of nature, Feuerbach closed himself off from cognition of the authentic problems of human life. The postulates on man and his essence become mere phrases since Feuerbach empties man of his real contexts, and sees mainly sensibility: "He prays to sensibility, in contrast to which he himself is but nothing. He bows down to sensibility and becomes dust."[71] Referring to the Feuerbachian theory that the essence of God is but the essence of man and that this illusion of the picture of God

---

[70] Ibid. p. 110.
[71] Ibid. p. 121.

should be eradicated in order to replace the old worship by worship of man, Bauer writes: "He [Feuerbach] was, in his advanced stage, no atheist, lacking belief in God, but rather a theist in the fullest sense of the word."[72] Bauer does not regard Feuerbach as a consistent materialist, but as a split materialist, torn between two tendencies – the materialistic, which emphasized the importance of nature for human life and for the consolidation of the patterns of religion, and the humanistic, which seeks to elevate human dignity.

Bauer deduces from all this that Feuerbach had learned nothing since 1841 when the *Essence of Christianity* appeared. The pioneer of criticism had become a conciliatory moderate, lagging badly behind the intensifying radical tendencies.[73]

Bauer's radicalism as regards religion is highlighted when – again in contrast to Feuerbach – he grasps Christianity as the religion of total alienation "which takes a negative and contemptuous view of all those relations which make a man – man", "isolates man", transforms him into an egoist "sacrificing all the human objectives", suppresses the natural human needs and desires of man for the realization of his human mission.[74]

The lack of humanity is more evident in Christianity than in any other religion and reaches its height there, since Christianity is a pure religion,[75] which encompassess all of the human entity, but lends it religious interpretation, i.e. distorted and inhuman.[76]

In Judaism the lack of humanity does not go so far, since the Jew is integrally bound up with his people and lives for the sake of human interests.[77] The leaning towards the human being is even more striking in the religion of nature which is also a framework of alienation, but in which human life is combined with human interests deriving from the attachment of the folk to nature, from patriotic and artistic motifs, etc.

But just because Christianity is the religion of total alienation it prepares the ground for the negation of religion in general. Here Bauer employs a formula typical of his conception: "When the plight reaches its peak, the solution is near",[78] which means that Christianity is "a very complete religion" and as such is "the world's greatest catas-

[72] Idem.
[73] Ibid. p. 416; Cf. Rawidowicz: *Ludwig Feuerbachs Philosophie*, p. 155.
[74] ECh 126–129, 134, 157, 162.
[75] Fae 61.
[76] Idem.
[77] Idem.
[78] Fr 78.

trophe",[79] creating the conditions for the liberation of man. It is just then, under the most arduous conditions, when man is in chains and his consciousness is totally enslaved, that the bells of salvation begin to sound out. Despite the argument that after Christianity developed its principles to the end and arrived at the height of human subjugation – from the spiritual point of view and as regards the political, scientific, artistic and other aspects – Bauer does not agree with the idea that the ending of the rule of Christianity is a form of deus ex machina. He learned from Hegel that basic change occurs only after the conditions have been prepared, i.e. that the negation of the rule of religion was preceded by changes, sometimes infinitesimal, which led to the undermining of its status and thus created the suitable background for its deposition from the key position in spiritual and cultural life and in the state.

If we skip the (unsuccessful) attempt of various apostates to change the nature of Christianity and to introduce humanistic motifs into it,[80] the first manifestations of the liberation of the human spirit from the rule of Christianity are connected with the crystallization of the principles of the Reformation. As Stuke rightly says,[81] Bauer's attitude towards the Reformation is not unequivocal. On the one hand it constituted "a vital step towards completion of the religious consciousness";[82] on the other: it laid the foundations for cancellation of dogma and freeing of the spirit from its rule.[83] But this Bauerian view, which, on the face of it, contains two contradictory components, has been explained above, where we spoke of the exacerbation of contrasts and unbearable aggravation of alienation within the framework of Christianity, and of the approaching salvation. In other words: if Christianity is a pure religion or *the* religion, then the Reformation is the most abstract element of Christianity as a whole,[84] i.e. the most characteristic example of the fact that when the old principle reaches the height of its development and stands completely triumphant, forces are created which come out against it in order to cancel it and to impose the principles of the free self-consciousness. Hence also Bauer's evaluations of Protestantism as the height of development of the Christian principle in general: "This split [into various religious cur-

---

[79] ECh 95.
[80] Ibid. p. 151.
[81] H. Stuke: *Philosophie der Tat*, 156.
[82] ECh 142.
[83] *Einleitung in die Dogmengeschichte*..., p. 151.
[84] Ibid. p. 153.

rents within the framework of Christianity] is the strengthening of elements of dogma, its supreme development, its consequences, the pure depiction of the religious principle [. . .][85] and the basis for the liberation of mankind from the rule of religion and authority in general.''[86]

The struggle for emancipation of mankind is both protracted and arduous. Since Christianity is the perfect religion and attained the height of inhumanity and at the same time encompassed the entire spectrum of human life, any consistent campaign against it must be total and must expose the nature of Christianity as self-delusion. Its total character was burdened by the principles of all-embracing love and fraternity, which concealed the persecutory tendencies of the Catholic and Protestant churches, the hatred of others etc.[87]

Free thought in the sphere of philosophy and science made an important contribution to shattering the monopoly of religion, since the development and achievements of philosophy are related to opposition to dogma and its liberation from all those assumptions which it once shared with religion.[88] From this viewpoint Spinoza's thought should be regarded as a decisive stage in the development of the spirit, when "the human spirit arrived at total separation from religion and its views on the absolute."[89] But the detachment from religion could not be absolute, since the absolute is grasped in Spinoza's philosophy in in the form of substance and not as subject.[90] In addition, Spinoza still tended to identify the absolute with nature and God together and therefore Bauer denoted his system "theological materialism".[91]

This Spinozian point of view was developed more consistently in materialism, which purged philosophy of the remnants of the religious concept. The eighteenth century French materialists "deposed God and put an end to the worldwide rule of religion",[92] "liberated the human spirit in fact from religious chatter and provided a prop and legitimization for the existence of mankind without religion."[93] At the same time, materialism is incapable of comprehending man, with all his specific spiritual qualities or seeing the true place of the self-

[85] Ibid. p. 154.
[86] Ibid. pp. 154–159.
[87] Fae 61–62.
[88] *Bremisches Magazin . . .*, p. 132.
[89] *Die christliche Glaubenslehre . . .*, p. 83.
[90] Idem.
[91] LF 103.
[92] ECh 158.
[93] Ibid. p. 159.

consciousness in the world. "They [the materialists] grasped the movements of the self-consciousness as the movements of the universal essence, of matter, and were thus unable to understand that the movement of the universe materializes as the movement of the self-consciousness."[94] The main mistake of materialism derived from the view of man as an anthropological entity, i.e. a subject whose movements are determined by nature, and hence disregarding of the qualities of the human spirit and its self-definition in history, science and art.[95]

The Enlightenment deserves credit for formulating the human rights won by the French Revolution, which translated its postulates into action,[96] and because of this fact "human history, which creates human thought, and sees its task as the founding of human society, begins only with the eighteenth century."[97] But the Enlightenment was limited, as was the Revolution, as regards ideals and objectives. Deism was still hampered by the chains of religion and even the French and American Revolutions freed only the state, and not man, from subjugation to supernatural forces.[98]

Bauer does not see the course of history as an ascending line, as infinite progress. There are, in its course, "hundred day regimes" like the brief reign of Napoleon after Elba, i.e. the old and vanquished principle may regain power, particularly at a time when the Revolution has exposed itself to attack by reactionary forces.[99] Bauer sees a triumph for reaction in Robespierre's declaration during the Revolution of the new worship of a supreme entity, and in the concordat between Napoleon and the Pope, as well as the Restoration after Napoleon's defeat.[100]

But the defeat of the revolutionary forces, representing the case of the freedom-seeking human spirit, is not final: "The oppressed spirit raises its head again, in order to realize what French materialism did not succeed in doing, and to conduct the last battle against lack of spirit, against the inhuman and all the past lack of humanity."[101]

Bauer clearly divides history into two periods: the pre-historic era

[94] Ibid. p. 161.
[95] LF 109–111, 116–122; ECh 162.
[96] ECh 87–88; Jud 19; Fr 122–123.
[97] *Geschichte der Politik, Kultur und Aufklärung*, vol. I, Charlottenburg 1843, p. VI.
[98] ECh 87–88, 132.
[99] *Dr. Ammon. Die Geschichte des Leben Jesu mit steter Rücksicht auf die vorhandenen Quellen* (Rez.). An, Vol. II/1843, p. 163.
[100] ECh 88.
[101] Idem.

and the era of true human history. In the first period, from ancient times to Bauer's own day, human society was in a state of alienation, in a regime of spiritual and political oppression, represented by tyranny and religion (to exclude the French Revolution and those circles which were opposed to religion and tyranny and were the harbingers of the new era). This history, known as *Vorbereitungsgeschichte*, created the conditions for consolidation of the basic principles of the second era through gradual accumulation. The efforts of many decades were needed in order for "Enlightenment and criticism to be able to attain perfection and purity enabling them to open up a new era in human history."[102]

The start of the turning point in Hegelian philosophy, which Bauer sees as revolutionary, is directed against all the existing institutions: religion, the state, the law etc. "His [Hegel's] theory was a dangerous praxis, generalized and extremely destructive. It was revolution itself."[103] Thanks to Hegel, criticism of substance arrived at perfection, the consciousness became free and mankind was restored to itself.[104] As we have seen above, Bauer finds in Hegel's philosophy his own philosophical principles and therefore regards himself as the legitimate heir of Hegelian atheism, religious critique and the philosophy of the self-consciousness. This is how Bauer brings the world the message of salvation: "Can history fight itself? Egoism, weakness, fear, the spirit of slavery can do as they choose, they can still fight – and when the suitable means are at disposal – can even suppress; but what does this matter to mankind, which is guided by the self-consciousness and recognizes its universal power? It has arrived at a new era; for the first time it has recognized itself after realizing that all its powers are its own creation. It is now marching towards new development, which it alone will control."[105]

As far as Bauer was concerned there was no doubt that the crisis afflicting Christianity and the state enslaved by this religion, would be settled in favour of criticism, science and philosophy, whose spokesman he was. In all his essays there is a distinctly messianic and eschatological tone. When he speaks of the purpose of the struggle against the regime and religion, he emphasizes that he is fighting "for

---

[102] Fae 62.
[103] Pos 171.
[104] *Einleitung in die Dogmengeschichte...*, p. 141.
[105] Ibid. p. 156.

the happiness of mankind, for the victory of liberty over slavery, and the triumph of the truth over deception."[106]

In his critique of Gospel history, he noted that it was the task of the profound and horrific alienation to prepare and to consecrate the eternal liberty which mankind was to win.[107] In his other works he expressed his view that his philosophical activity denoted the final stage in the struggle against the alienated image of man, and all those conditions which create this alienation; "we must fight man's last enemy";[108] "We are not referring to the bestowing of philosophy on mankind instead of religion, but to the fact that mankind will be all in all."[109] "Criticism knows no dogmatism. Its slogan is: mankind or no mankind, death or life, everything or nothing."[110] In Bauer's letters to Ruge, he also spoke of the approaching last battle, and expressed his conviction that the principle of liberty would overcome hostile principles and would determine reality.[111]

The last battle to be waged for the sake of mankind and the division of history into two periods, with the liberation of mankind occurring in the second stage – both these concepts attest to the teleological nature of Bauer's conception. His entire historiosophical viewpoint revolves around one central axis: development of the Christian principle to its peak, thus making it possible to cancel it so as to carry out emancipation of mankind. When Bauer exposes the irrational nature of Christian dogmas, he asks: "Did these issues really attract the attention of mankind and cause it suffering for fifteen hundred years and more?" and replies: "Yes, it was obliged to suffer as a result of preoccupying itself with this issue, since the next giant step can be taken only after such suffering and torture. [. . .] Mankind was educated in a regime of slavery, so as to be able to prepare the ground more fundamentally for freedom."[112] Bauer gives similar expression to his views in his letter to Marx: "The future is so certain that one cannot doubt it even for a moment. [. . .] The hostile forces have come so closely that one blow will decide the issue. [. . .] The catastrophe will be terrible and of tremendous dimensions, I would almost say that it will be greater and more terrible than that which accompanied the birth of Christianity."[113]

[106] Fr 82.
[107] Syn III, 312.
[108] Fr 185.
[109] Ibid. 202.
[110] Ibid. p. 204.
[111] Cf. Bauer's letter to Ruge, 16 April 1841.
[112] Syn III, 312.
[113] MEGA I, 1, ii, pp. 241–242.

It is not surprising, therefore, that Bauer, who knew the course of history and envisaged the decisive battle, believed that "the matter [. . .] will be settled in the Prussian State."[114]

It should be noted that Bauer's basic standpoint on the universal consciousness as an objective factor led to his view of history as occurring necessarily and dialectically. From this viewpoint, it is clear that man has no control over historical processes, but things change with the approach of events which change the character of human society.

The unconscious character of history yields place to consciousness thanks to the Bauerian theory which is grounded on cognition of the universal self-consciousness or on adaptation of the free individual self-consciousness to the course of the universal consciousness, and which deciphers correctly the tendencies of world history. "The theory which has aided us so far remains our sole support, in order to liberate ourselves and to help others to become free. History, over which we have no control and which has decisive turning points which are beyond planned calculations, will cancel the illusion and elevate freedom – given us by the theory – to such power that it can give the world a new image. [. . .] Criticism is the sole force which grasps and explains the self-illusion of the existing and gives us the confidence that history will concern itself with finding a solution to the crisis."[115]

[114] ChS 37.
[115] Fr 225.

CHAPTER IX

BAUER'S POLITICAL CONCEPTION

As we have noted, Bauer saw alienation as existing not only in the sphere of religion but in other fields of life as well. The factors influencing man's destiny – for better or worse – include the state. Bauer, as a true disciple of Hegel, could not but attribute great importance to the state. As far as he was concerned, it was indisputable that the supreme freedom – that of the self-consciousness – is impossible without political liberty. It is true that at first he dealt solely with pure philosophical and theological issues; until 1840 there is almost no reference to political categories. But this was true of all the Young Hegelians: they advanced from religious problems to basic and topical political issues, as Engels was to state correctly forty years later. At the same time, Engels was wrong in thinking that the political path was then a difficult one and that this was why the Young Hegelians directed their efforts, first and foremost, against religion.[1] It is possible that the lengthy period of time which lapsed from the eighteen forty events to Engels' essay helped him forget the fact that it was not merely political difficulties but mainly the hope that the Prussian state would become more progressive and allow Hegel's disciples to play a part in its cultural policy which persuaded the latter to refrain from attacking the principles of this policy.

These hopes were reflected in Bauer's first article, which was devoted to political and religious matters.[2] The starting point of the article was the Union of Lutherans and Reformists proposed by Friedrich Wilhelm III in 1817. Bauer deduced from this fact that the essential differences between the churches had been eradicated in the face of the desire of the state that the religious organization be integrated into state institutions. This principle of integration, if it were consistently applied,

[1] *Ludwig Feuerbach und der Ausgang der klassischen deutschen Philosophie*, Karl Marx Friedrich Engels: *Werke*, Vol. 21 (Ost)Berlin 1952, p. 271.
[2] *Die evangelische Landeskirche Preussens und die Wissenschaft*. Leipzig 1840.

would, in his view, lead to eradication of the visible church. "We are treading here," he wrote, "on the soil of the state, that is to say on the soil of a form of spiritual life in which the form of the visible church is cancelled. To be more exact, it is cancelled by the unification [...] which is the product of the state, and could have been carried out thanks to it alone. The success of the project is the best proof of the cancellation of the visible church within the state."[3] Bauer regarded the state as the height of realization of the idea of morality and reason in history,[4] and as the most comprehensive being in human life.[5] Accordingly the state is not grasped from the administrative, police and legal aspect but is represented mainly as the supreme manifestation of liberty and humanity.[6] It is clear that Bauer is emulating Hegel who treated the state as actuality of the ethical idea and the substantial will[7] and absolutely rational in and for itself[8] and as actuality of concrete freedom.[9]

Bauer attributed to Prussia the qualities of the ideal state, at least in theory, and believed that the time was approaching when there would be a change in the direction of realization of the ideal: "It is necessary," he wrote, "that a change take place in the history of our country [...] we are confident of the future of history and with the same degree of confidence with which we view our prince, we expect the throne to give the sign which will lead to the change in the near future. We have confidence in his wisdom which will not disregard the course of this history [...] we may say that the great chapter of Prussian history is approaching, for what could be more noble than the attainment of the objectives of thousands of years of struggles as the culmination of the free consciousness."[10]

In formulating this conception, which sees Prussia as a state on which is imposed the universal task of realizing the principles of freedom and reason, Bauer was relying, implicitly on the later Hegel. At first Hegel was a supporter of Napoleon, in whom he saw "the soul of the world, mounted on a horse",[11] and he was distinctly unsympathetic towards Prussia. After the defeat of Napoleon he altered this attitude,

---

[3] Ibid. p. 65.
[4] Ibid. p. 95.
[5] Ibid. p. 107.
[6] Ibid. p. 97.
[7] PhRt § 257.
[8] Ibid. § 258.
[9] Ibid. § 260.
[10] LP 18.
[11] For Hegel's attitude toward Napoleon, cf. Franz Rosenzweig: *Hegel und der Staat.* München-Berlin 1920, vol. II, pp. 23–24, 27–29.

but this change of outlook should not be attributed to the fact that
he moved to Berlin or to his contacts with the Prussian authorities.
There were other reasons: the reforms of Hardenberg and Stein led
to changes in the social and economic structure of Prussia, and made
it a relatively progressive state – in comparison with other German
states. The enslavement of the peasants was abolished, the towns were
granted limited autonomy, freedom of commerce was introduced and
the king promised that a constitution would be drawn up and a parliament established. The spiritual climate was reasonably congenial for
intellectuals – the freedom of thought and of scientific research were
respected. The Minister of Culture von Altenstein, who was an ardent
Hegelian, was in no small measure responsible for creation of the freer
atmosphere.

But we should not deduce from this that Hegel took a positive view
of the Prussian situation as it stood, nor should we assume that Bauer
displayed such intentions. Hegel's political ideal corresponded to the
spirit of Stein's reforms, but in the ideas he advocated there were many
elements which were lacking in Prussia, such as a constitution, the
institution of jury in the courts, an Assembly of Estates. Hence his
ideal was shaped as the result of his speculations on a reality differing
from the Prussian, a wide European reality, and the Hegelian pattern
of the state corresponds to the essence of the modern state as evolved
in the wake of the revolutionary upheavals which occurred in Western
Europe in the eighteenth century and at the beginning of the nineteenth.[12] It is completely clear that Hegel was never the ideologist
of reactionary Prussia, as is claimed by some commentators (Haym,
Popper, Carritt).

Bauer claimed that Lutheranism enabled the state to develop the
spirit of liberty and the principles of reason which it accepted and
adopted as an integral part of itself. But the absorption of the Lutheran
principles of internal liberty, the lack of Catholic-style hierarchy, lack
of a barrier between believers and God – in contrast to the Catholic
church and its faith – made the dogma and its organization superfluous: the positive form of the decline of the Lutheran church was
reflected in the fact that it did not preserve its good principles for itself

---

[12] For this issue, see Eric Weil: *Hegel et l'État*, Paris 1950, pp. 15–16; Joachim Ritter:
Hegel und die französische Revolution. In *Metaphysik und Politik. Studien zu Aristoteles und
Hegel*. Frankfurt/M., Suhrkamp 1969, pp. 201, 203–204, 208–209. See also: T. M. Knox:
Hegel and Prussianism. In *Hegel's Political Philosophy*. New York, Atherton Press 1970,
pp. 13–29; Shlomo Avineri: *Hook's Hegel*. Ibid. pp. 71–79; Z. A. Pelczynski: *Hegel Again*.
Ibid. pp. 80–86.

but made them universal for the sake of the Enlightenment, the ethical spirit and scientific trends."[13] "No-one could possibly think that it was by coincidence that the heroes of German history belonged – by origin and education – to the Lutheran sect. Because of the cancellation of the dogma of the Lutheran church within the supreme objectives of reason, only people of limited spirit could demand the existence of a separate and independent church."[14]

There is a certain affinity here with the Hegelian idea that Catholicism is an exclusive religion which distinguishes absolutely between a hierarchy based on the authority of power and the bestowing of grace in return for obedience and discipline on the one hand, and simple rank-and-file believers on the other. Protestantism was set up in opposition to Catholicism, and it abolished the mediation of priests in relations between believers and God, and enabled people to understand that God is a spirit, that is to say eternal and universal. The Protestant community is not created as an earthly association guided by an authoritative regime, striving to dominate the secular state, but rather as a free partnership, in which man "is privileged to receive the spirit of truth [...] the absolute internality of the soul and the freedom of the church."[15]

According to Hegel, the state does not only enable its citizens to attain freedom; it is itself a kind of embodiment of freedom. It is a value and an end and not merely a means of satisfying the needs of individuals. The state does not only exist as an institution and law. Where its objective order is concerned, it is consistent with the dispositions (Gesinnungen) of those individuals who take a positive view of the realization of reason in the state and hence elevation to a universal and substantial viewpoint, identical with the interests of the state. The *Philosophy of Right* does not emphasize the mind of citizens as the basis for the stability of the state – and stress was placed on cognition of the fact that the individual takes pride of place among the universal aspirations and objectives of the state as against its particularist interests,[16] although there as well Hegel does not ignore this point. In his later essays, Hegel placed greater emphasis on the unity of the institutions and laws constituting the objective foundation of liberty and the views

[13] LP 12.

[14] Ibid. pp. 12–13.

[15] *Vorlesungen über die Geschichte der Philosophie*. Theorie-Ausgabe. Frankfurt/M., Suhrkamp 1970, p. 496. For Hegel's attitude toward catholicism and Lutheranism, cf. PhM § 552; PhH 412–438.

[16] PhRt §§ 258, 268; Eugène Fleischmann: *La philosophie politique de Hegel sous forme d'un commentaire des fondements de la philosophie du droit*. Paris 1964, pp. 257–258.

of the individuals living in the state, or unity of the political regime and religion: "For in affirming that the state is based on religion – that it has its roots in it – we virtually assert that the former has proceeded from the latter, and that this derivation is going on now and will always continue; i.e. the principles of the state must be [. . .] recognized as determinate manifestations of the Divine Nature. The form of religion [. . .] decides that of the state and its constitution."[17] Both motifs infiltrated the writings of the Young Hegelians: from the idea that the state is based on the primacy of the universal interest over the particularist and the grounding of religion on representation[18] they deduced that religion cannot serve as the basis for the existence of the state, and held that such a task can only be fulfilled by science deriving from reason.[19] Through emphasizing the Protestant spirit they arrived at the conclusion that the values of the Reformation constitute an important factor in the evolvement of the modern state. In other words: the Young Hegelians utilized these two motifs regarding the essence of Prussia and its significance in order to claim that Prussia was simultaneously a Protestant state and a rational state, based both on rational religion and on rational institutions and laws. Thus, for example, Ruge, who dealt mainly with political problems, wrote: "The light of Protestantism is the light of the world."[20] "In Protestantism the spirit of God penetrates into all spheres of life."[21] The Protestant principle was grasped by Ruge as suited to modern science, philosophy and culture and this viewpoint enabled him and other members of the Young Hegelian school to attribute Protestant character to political history, the state and its institutions. But it is clear that there is nothing in common between Protestantism of this kind and the Protestant faith and church. This appears in Bauer as well: he identifies internal liberty with freedom of the self-consciousness, absence of hierarchy with the departure or removal of a stratum of specialized interests, differing from those of the state or, as he puts it in his essay: *Die evangelische Landeskirche Preussens und die Wissenschaft*: "The

---

[17] PhH 51.

[18] For this issue, see PhRt § 270; E. Fleischmann: *La philosophie politique de Hegel...*, 282–292.

[19] In Hegel too there was a clear tendency to regard independent reason, which does not submit to external authority, as the criterion for evaluation of the essence of both the state and religion. Cf. E. Fleischmann: *La philosophie politique de Hegel...*, pp. 290–291; Eric Weil: *Säkularisierung des politischen Denkens*. Marxismusstudien. Vierte Folge. Tübingen 1962, pp. 149–150.

[20] Arnold Ruge: *Der Pietismus und die Jesuiten*. HJ 1839, p. 287.

[21] Arnold Ruge: *Preussen und die Reaktion. Zur Geschichte unserer Zeit*. Leipzig 1838, p. 91.

Church can exist only in the state, since outside it it has no legal right to existence; but since it is located in the state it ceases to be a church separate and different from the state, and an independent body operating against the state. It is nothing but the being and the depiction of the religiosity which constitutes an internal factor of the state itself."[22]

The theme of science operating so as to fashion the essence of the rational state was developed among the Young Hegelians mainly by Bauer. He believed that – since the days of Friedrich II – Prussia had been the home of free science. But the church wished to cast suspicion on science and besmirch it and was inciting the state against it. There was no escape from confrontation between the forces of reason on the one hand and the church on the other, and Bauer appealed to the state to take part in the campaign on the side of the interests of reason and scientific thought which were, in the last analysis, its own interests.[23]

According to Bauer science had exposed the secrets of apologetics and its irrational character. These revelations were completing the process of disintegration of the church, which had begun previously, when "the resentment of the people, indifference of the middle class on church matters, contempt of the upper class and general enlightenment abolished men's ties to religion."[24]

According to Bauer the state made science, thought and philosophy its own internal concern. The tension which from time to time develops between science and the state is to the advantage of the latter, since these clashes encourage the ethical principle contained in the state, further the cause of freedom and internality.[25] In other words: science need not and cannot accept the dictates of the state. But its achievements and discoveries are to the benefit of the state since science has no interest which is opposed to the rational nature of the state. The principles of science – freedom, internality, ethics, reasonability – are also the principles of the state and it can therefore never come to an end and is eternal.[26] The struggle between science and religion particularly advances the cause of liberty and reason and frees the state from "the monster of the hierarchy".[27]

It is clear that Bauerian science is nothing but speculative philoso-

[22] LP 100–101.
[23] Ibid. pp. 5–7.
[24] Ibid. p. 11.
[25] Ibid. pp. 105–106.
[26] Ibid. pp. 106, 108.
[27] Ibid. pp. 6, 105.

phy in radical guise, and there is particular identification of science with the Bauerian dialectical method. This "science" presented itself as holding the monopoly over both metaphysical and political truth and, from this point of view, Bauer formulated a principle which was acceptable to all the Young Hegelians. It is not surprising therefore that this essay was enthusiastically acclaimed by Ruge, who regarded Bauer's ideas as a shining example of historical representation of the problem and philosophical art, as well as complete intellectual control of the problems of relations between the state, philosophy and religion.[28]

Whereas in 1840 shortly after the ascension of Friedrich Wilhelm IV to the throne, Bauer had pinned hopes on the Prussian throne and expected it to give the sign for reforming the state, a year later he had abandoned all illusions as to the nature of the new monarch and his policies. It was clear to Bauer that the idea of attaining a constitutional regime through gradual reforms in the spirit of Hardenberg and Stein, deposing the church from its eminent position in spiritual life, and cooperation of the state with radical intellectual elements, was without basis. The monarch proved by his actions that he was a supporter of the reactionary ideologist Haller, and that he was striving with all his might to restore the patterns of absolute monarchy and to ground the state on tradition, Christian faith and absolute obedience.[29] Bauer's disappointment was expressed in his article on the Christian state.[30] He did not give up his basic theory that the state, even in its crudest form, is the embodiment of liberty and an act of the universal self-consciousness,[31] but he does not identify the state with a specific government, as long as the government does not recognize this essence of the state.[32] The hint is clear. Prussia is not a state as Bauer understands it: it does not implement the principles of liberty on the intellectual-spiritual and political planes. It entrusts itself to Christian apologetists such as F. J. Stahl[33] and permits the

---

[28] Arnold Ruge: *Die evangelische Landeskirche Preussens und die Wissenschaft* (Rez.) HJ/ 1841, pp. 537–558.

[29] R. Prutz: *10 Jahre. Geschichte der neuesten Zeit. 1840–1850*, vol. 1, pp. 160–163.

[30] *Der christliche Staat und unsere Zeit.* HJ 1841, No 135–140. Reprinted in *Feldzüge der reinen Kritik*, Frankfurt/M. 1968.

[31] Ibid. p. 7.

[32] Ibid. p. 32.

[33] Stahl sharply criticized rationalism and Hegelianism and demanded that the state be founded on the principles of Christian faith. Cf. F. J. Stahl: *Philosophie des Rechts nach geschichtlicher Ansicht.* Vol. I: *Die Genesis der gehenwärtigen Rechtsphilosophie.* Heidelberg 1830, pp. XIV–XV; *Der christliche Staat und sein Verhältnis zu Deismus und Judentum.* Berlin 1847, pp. 25–28, 46–48.

church to intervene in matters which are not its concern. Protestantism, which fulfilled a certain positive role – however limited –, after passing through the filter of the Young Hegelians and being integrated among their historiosophical and political principles, yielded place to Christianity, and the Protestant state – to the Christian state. When he refers to the state of this type, Bauer's full hostility towards religion comes to the surface. The Christian state is guided by the dictates of religion, it suppresses all manifestations of free and autonomous thoughts, leads to the banishing of the spirit, lulls all the predilections and aspirations of mankind, is guilty of causing crime etc.[34]

Bauer draws a straight line from the term "Christianity" to "Catholicism" and actually bases them both on a common foundation.[35] Whereas formerly Catholicism had symbolized for him external and formal religiosity, obedience and submission, narrow intellectual horizons, mysticism, conservatism, orthodoxy, dogmatism, opposition to philosophy and science, all these phenomena were now transplanted to Christianity in general, while the non-free state became its agent and the implementer of its wishes. The conflicts between Catholicism and Protestantism was replaced by a new antagonism: Christianity on the one hand and science on the other. Scientific circles in the universities and intellectual circles concentrated around progressive journals are depicted by Bauer as representing the interests of the human spirit struggling for its autonomy against the church and state hierarchy. "The opposition, accepted by the modern state and winning recognition through the granting of freedom of teaching in universities", wrote Bauer, "possesses clear advantages when compared with both – the church and the specific government – when it arrives at completion of its process of development in dialectical theory. As such it places itself at the centre of political life and the free self-consciousness. . . ."[36]

Science demonstrates the limitations of the life of religion and the empirical state and elevates the latter to higher status. It can succeed in this objective when its principles reach the people, and are adopted by them. This struggle between science and the Christian state is denoted by Bauer 'the last battle", a viewpoint which fits in with his

---

[34] ChS 9, 14, 17.
[35] Ibid. p. 17–18.
[36] Ibid. p. 35.
[37] Ibid. p. 36.

eschatological theories. History will decide this struggle and there can be no doubt as to the consequences.[37]

Bauer does not hide the fact that his views are influenced by the French Revolution, which he defines as the "bloody terrorism of reason and ethics". The principles of the Revolution undermined the rule of the church and of absolutism and the Enlightenment also operated in this direction on the ideological plane. These three factors: the Revolution, the Enlightenment and the Bauerian interpretation of Hegelian philosophy raised the issue of the state as realizing the liberty of the people. As far as Bauer was concerned, there could be no doubts that the future belonged to the people, who would support the radical philosophical principles of his thought: "The future belongs to the people; the truth is popular, for it is open, invulnerable and without fear. It will share the future with the people or, more correctly, both – the people and the truth are the same and, as such, the all-powerful ruler of the future. The style of patronage is no longer comprehensible to the people; they want the style of truth, courage and simplicity, demanding only that style which they are capable of understanding."[38]

From these remarks it is absolutely clear that Bauer was convinced that his philosophical principles faithfully reflected the dynamics of the development of history and that their general dissemination would lead to their realization. Their fulfilment is an act of rational participation in the process of constructing a new political reality, thanks to cognition of the laws of historical development, of participation of the people in the activities of historical laws. Bauerian science thus corresponds to the pattern accepted by all the Young Hegelians, defined by Stuhr as follows: "Science is active in practical fashion in the world, in order to create new forms of life and to build for them a firm foundation on the basis of its innovative principles."[39]

But Bauer's conceptions – including his political views – were influenced by the French Revolution to a larger extent than the views of other radical Hegelians, at least between 1841 43. Atheism and humanism, republicanism and revolutionism reach the furthermost limits of an intellectual movement which is not supported by the masses, under the conditions of Germany before the March 1848 revolt.

Bauer strives to liberate man from the chains of servitude, which prevent him from becoming a complete human being.[40] Bauer had

[38] *Dr. Ammon, Die Geschichte des Lebens Jesu...*, p. 185.
[39] *Lehrbuch der Universalgeschichte von H. Leo* (Rez.). An, vol. II, p. 189.
[40] Fr 39, 202.

once believed in the efficacy of gradual reforms on the part of a regime which allowed philosophers to share in shaping policies, but between 1841–43 he advocated "revolution rather than reform", the reverse of the catchword of his opponents.[41] "Is revolution forbidden to raise its head", he asked, "when the 'objective' relations are totally ruined and are in need of change of head and limbs?"[42] He believed that the Young Hegelians had learned from their mentor the principles of atheism, the revolution and the republic.[43] He was referring here to his own specific interpretation of Hegel's theories in a radical spirit. Bauerian radicalism is based on acerbic criticism of the political relations prevailing in the Prussia of his day, which saw as its objective drastic and violent change deriving from the tradition of the French Revolution, in contrast to liberalism which wanted to alter the political and cultural structure of the state through reforms alone.[44]

Bauer clearly interprets Hegel's theories in a revolutionary spirit: "His theory was an extremely dangerous, generalized and destructive praxis. It was revolution itself."[45] Hence those who take steps consistent with the essence of Hegelian philosophy, i.e. the Hegelian philosophers, are "the true revolutionaries, and the most dangerous, for they are the most consistent and uncompromising."[46] Philosophers hate the existing order and expedite the disintegration of the old institutions, the anachronistic laws. Bauer notes that "philosophy must act in the political sphere as well and attack the existing relations which contradict the self-consciousness, in order to undermine them. Servitude and patronage are intolerable to the free spirit."[47] Bauer's aim is to destroy the Christian state, to elevate freedom to the level of a force and power and thus to escape the crisis ravaging society and the state.

When Bauer uses the phrase "philosophy" he is referring to the theoretical principle that should guide intellectuals in their efforts to change reality completely, with all its contradictions, conflicts, hypocrisy. His main efforts are directed towards the concept of the

---

[41] B 81.
[42] Idem.
[43] Ibid. p. 86.
[44] For the differences between liberalism and radicalism in 19th-century Germany, cf. Gustav Mayer: *Die Anfänge des politischen Radikalismus im vormärzlichen Preussen*, pp. 24–34, 52–60, 70–96.
[45] Pos 171.
[46] Ibid. p. 170.
[47] Ibid. p. 172.

"complete man",[48] who attains "peace, tranquillity and compatability with himself."

It has been noted that Bauer speaks out against the chained man and wishes to liberate him. Political liberty is a conditio sine qua non for full liberation of man, so as to enable him to live in accordance with his essence. Bauer saw the political struggle as important and did much to advance the "good cause of liberty", but, in contrast to Stuke's theory, there is no reliance on any defined social class[49] such as the radical bourgeoisie. The reason lies in Bauer's belief in the determinist force of historical laws, operating for progress, and his extremely high opinion of science and philosophy as the factors capable of exposing the true face of the existing regime and encouraging the oppositional forces to act in accordance with the trends of history. Bauer's comments on the future as belonging to the people and the identification of the people with the truth should be viewed within this framework: truth is Bauer's truth, i.e. that of his critical philosophy. The people will recognize this philosophy as its own, but it is clear that the task of spiritual guidance is entrusted here not to the people but to the Bauerian idea. This is why the Bauerian conception is more abstract that Marx's later conception, which, by basing itself on the proletariat, lent his theories a dimension lacking in Bauer.

As noted, Bauer did not only engage in the writing of philosophical theological and historical essays. He also tried to implement his ideas and employed political journalistic writing for this purpose. On this point there was a fundamental difference between Bauer and Feuerbach, who never devoted attention to political problems. Bauer himself noted this difference between himself and the author of the *Essence of Christianity* when he asked: "How has it happened that Feuerbach has never dealt with politics?"[50]

At first Bauer was active in the *Hallische Jahrbücher*, then in the *Deutsche Jahrbücher* and in the *Rheinische Zeitung*, in which he published no less than twenty articles.[51] It was Bauer who invited Feuerbach to collaborate with the *Rheinische Zeitung*,[52] and for a time even served as its editor.[53] Under the influence of Bauer's radical ideas the paper as

[48] Fr 202, 221.
[49] H. Stuke: *Philosophie der Tat*, p. 173.
[50] See Bauer's letter to Ruge, 16 March 1842.
[51] Cf. G. Mayer: *Die Anfänge des politischen Radikalismus im vormärzlichen Preussen*, p. 61; Barnikol: *Bruno Bauer. Studien und Materialien*, p. 246.
[52] For this issue see Hans-Martin Sass: *Bruno Bauers Idee der Rheinischen Zeitung*. Zeitschrift für Religions- und Geistesgeschichte, 1967, pp. 321–322.
[53] Cornu: *Karl Marx und Friedrich Engels. Leben und Werk*, vol. I, p. 266.

a whole became a militant oppositional platform at the time when it was edited by his brother-in-law – Adolf Rutenberg,[54] who was dismissed by the authorities and thus left the position vacant for Karl Marx.

In his political journalism Bauer tried to translate into concrete language the principle that "the terrorism of the true theory must remove every obstacle from its path."[55] The word "terrorism" is not employed here by chance. In those years Bauer was studying the history of the French Revolution, as noted in his letter to Ruge of January 1842. In this letter Bauer wrote of his plan to write an essay on the French Revolution and noted: "I am studying the latter [the French Revolution] diligently, but I shall need to do more reading in order to complete my essay."[56] It was the study of revolutionary history which led Bauer to the thought that he should blow up the entire Faculty of Theology and not rest until he had carried out this project, – that only then could he leave in peace for Paris.[57] On another occasion Bauer wrote to Ruge: "Think about the Revolution; its annals cannot be studied often enough. It is the supreme law of any historical movement."[58] The content of revolution was defined by Bauer on the basis of Paul's words as a war "with ministers and rulers, ruling in the darkness of this world, with the evil forces above."[59]

In a series of articles on French subjects[60] Bauer gave expression to his views on revolution which, to his mind, is directed against all forms of tyranny. He believed that the Germans should learn from the French, if they did not want to build in a vacuum. "Courage, liberty and security are basic qualities of the revolutionary French people and no-one who lacks these qualities can carry out real tasks on earth." Hinting at the constitutional regime of Louis Philippe in France, Bauer wrote: "A people like the French, which has dedicated great efforts to establishing constitutional legislation with its noble principles [...] only appears to have tired, politically and productively speaking of the constitutional experiment [...] in actual fact its political forces

---

54 Cf. Wilhelm Klutentreter: *Die Rheinische Zeitung von 1842/43 in der politischen und geistigen Bewegung des Vormärz*. Dortmunder Beiträge zur Zeitungsforschung, 10. Band, 1. Teil, 1966, p. 90.
55 Cf. Bauer's letter to Marx, 28 March 1841. MEGA I, i, ii, p. 247.
56 See Bauer's letter to Ruge, 9 January 1842.
57 Cf. Bauer's letter to Ruge, 1 March 1842.
58 See Bauer's letter to Ruge, 9 October 1841.
59 Fr 185; cf. Bauer's letter to Feuerbach in H-M. Sass: *Bruno Bauers Idee der Rheinischen Zeitung*, p. 322.
60 Cf. *Rheinische Briefen und Akten zur Geschichte der politischen Bewegung 1830–1850*. Edited by Joseph Hansen, vol. I², Osnabrück 1967, p. 329.

have been trained and prepared to create the true product of the constitutional principle – the republic, which abolishes the contradictions of the constitutional system."[61]

Bauer is employing a transparent device here. Instead of referring to the German situation and risking the banning of his article by the censor, he presents his republican sympathies in French contexts. This is also true as regards the United States, which serves him as the ideal of the federative and democratic republican structure. This is what he has to say on this question: "The author does not mention the United States, which represents a true and exalted plane of the modern republic. The United States is the true renaissance, that is to say, an improved transplantation of the form of the Greek state, the republic of the great states, the republic of the federation, the republic which the Girondists in France founded prematurely. No-one who is thinking of the future of Europe and Germany can afford to ignore the United States.[62]

Bauer believed that Germany and France complemented one another and should therefore cooperate. This view was common to all the Young Hegelians and found striking expression in Moses Hess's book *Die europäische Triarchie*. Bauer's argument is aimed at proving that the national character of the Germans and French is different, just as they differ in geographical situation and in the principles on which their respective histories are based: practical-political for the French and spiritual-philosophical in the case of the Germans. This is the basis of their joint activity.[63]

As we have noted, Bauer's political ideal is tied up with France and the United States. This was not only because of considerations of censorship but also because of the political reality. Germany was divided politically speaking, and was backward both as regards her political regime and socially and economically in comparison with the West. Bauer's political ideal was a challenge to the radical forces in Germany but was a political actuality where Germany's western neighbour was concerned.

The principle of democratic republicanism in the style of the United States or the French Girondists was clearly directed against absolutism, but no less against constitutionalist monarchism. This sequence

[61] *Deutschlands Beruf in der Gegenwart und Zukunft von Theodor Romer* (Rez.). RhZ, Nr. 158, 7. VI. 1842, Beiblatt.
[62] Idem.
[63] *Die deutschen Sympathien für Frankreich*. RhZ, Nr. 37, 6. II. 1842, Beiblatt.

of events, which attests to Bauer's detachment for his previous constitutionalist views, as reflected in his first political essay, is the outcome of the evolution of his views. His revolutionary-democratic
stand, which calls for drastic and violent changes of the existing
German political situation was in flagrant contrast to the moderate
liberal line. It is not surprising therefore that Bauer sharply criticizes
the compromisory constitutional principle which seeks to bridge the
contradictions between two real extreme standpoints. The *juste milieu*
tries to mediate between the reactionary and revolutionary-progressive
sides and thus neutralizes the effort to change the face of things and
helps the old to preserve its advantage and power. In addition, constitutionalism is divided by its contradictions between the principle of
the rule of the people on the one hand and the rule of the despot on the
other.[64]

Bauer also sharply attacked the stranglehold of the Prussian censorship which tried to suppress any manifestation of free thought which
naturally took an oppositional form. The article *Was ist Lehrfreiheit?*,
which also appeared in the *Rheinische Zeitung*, was dedicated solely to
this issue. Bauer argued that freedom of conscience was a personal
matter which every person utilized in accordance with his needs and
considerations and that there was no point in passing a special law on
this matter. On the other hand, freedom of written expression should
be permitted so that views contradicting those of the existing regime
could reach the general public through the press and journals: "When
on the firm soil of freedom of conscience there arises the structure of
freedom of instruction or, to be more exact, this structure rises to its
highest storey through the addition of freedom of instruction, then the
contradictions will be reconciled, liberty will be ensured and the state
can be the guide of the movement."[65]

Bauer's republican ideal, which is a kind of fusion of the Greek polis
with American federal principles, is the form of man's being which has
attained full self-consciousness and created for itself suitable conditions
for free creativity. Such a socio-political organization enables him to
overcome the duality of his historical existence between essence – as a
free being – and his empirical being – in submission to earthly gods; to
arrive at the historic objective; enables man to be reconciled with himself and with the products of his social activity. The distraction, split
and alienation which characterize man's life on the political sphere – like

---

[64] *Die Parteien im jetzigen Frankreich.* RhZ, Nr. 23, 23. I. 1842, Beiblatt; see also *Die deutschen Sympathien für Frankreich.*

alienation in other spheres of life – will disappear. But it is clear that
what Bauer envisaged was not immediate political aims. Policy, political journalistic activity, the political movement were grasped by
Bauer as means of realizing universal values, relating to the wider
principles of human being. Liberty, like man, is totality. Thus, it is not
enough for man to be liberated from despotic rule and to establish a
republic. He will not cease to be a slave as long as he is in a state of
spiritual servitude, subjugated to religious patterns, to spiritual authority, not until his conscience becomes his guiding light and compass.
One can agree with Stuke[66] that for Bauer political revolution was
linked to intellectual revolution, which was supposed to precede it and
that the attempt to bring about radical political change before completing the process of changing the self-consciousness is useless and
purposeless.

A similar train of thought may be discerned in Bauer's theory of
alienation: at first man's alienation from himself must be exposed and
his essence as a free man in the sphere of the self-consciousness must be
restored. To this end it is necessary to fight prejudice and the chains
binding the human spirit.[67] Only subsequently is it possible to overcome alienation in the political situation. Without the first factor the
second is not possible: the struggle for liberation of the self-consciousness, in which the overcoming of the division of the spirit is a vital link,
constitutes a presupposition of the postulate of political freedom.
It is to this point that all of Bauer's conception of theory and praxis
is also anchored. He was imbued with awareness of the fact that the
realization of philosophy leads to victory of the spirit over alienation
in the intellectual sphere alone.[68] But the philosophical ideal of the
self-consciousness guided man in his struggles aimed at changing the
face of reality, i.e. without the light of theory, praxis is blind. In this
context Bauer's definition of the theory as "terrorism" is clear. He is
referring to uncompromising revolution in the sphere of the spirit and
ideological life as well as to the destruction of existing political frame-
works. Against this background it is clear why Bauer saw theory as a
"mighty praxis"[69] and demanded, first, the completion of theory in
order "to prepare history to march along the new path."[70] Therefore

[65] *Was ist Lehrfreiheit?* RhZ, 12.4.1842, Beiblatt.
[66] H. Stuke: *Philosophie der Tat*, p. 174.
[67] Fr 209.
[68] *Die christliche Glaubenslehre in ihrer Entwicklung...*, p. 86.
[69] Cf. Bauer's letter to Marx, 31. March 1841, MEGA I, 1, ii, p. 250.
[70] Fr 209.

"philosophy is criticism of the existing reality"[71] and also an instrument for shaping a new reality or, as Bauer puts it: "Things must arrive at utilization in the principle of praxis, practical opposition [...] the theoretical principle must become praxis and action [...] philosophy must act in politics, attack existing relations and undermine them, when they conflict with the self-consciousness."[72]

[71] Pos 172.
[72] Idem.

PART TWO

KARL MARX AND BRUNO BAUER

CHAPTER I

THE PERSONAL RELATIONS AND LITERARY COLLABORATION BETWEEN BAUER AND MARX

Marx was a student of Bauer, his senior by nine years, and attended the latter's class on Isaiah[1] during the summer semester of 1839. On the basis of a letter which Marx wrote to his father in 1837[2] we know of the strong affinity between Bauer and Marx, and it is reasonable to assume that this acquaintance led Marx to attend this particular university course.

Bauer is mentioned in the letter as recommending the publication of an essay by Marx, and is described as playing a leading role in the Hegelian school. Bauer's name also appears in another context: as an active member of the Doktorklub, of which we know very little,[3] although many commentators refer to it.

Marx was a constant visitor to the Bauer home, and his visits continued after Bauer's transfer to Bonn.[4] Bruno advised his brother Egbert to ask the third brother, Edgar to establish contact with the writer Meyen, through Marx, in order to obtain the writer's advice on ways of distributing those books in which Egbert was interested.[5] This incident attests to the fact that Marx was consulted on Bauer's family affairs. Edgar was on close terms with Marx after Bruno left Berlin, and wrote to his brother of various social encounters with Marx.[6] In the letters Bruno wrote to Marx, he referred nostalgically to the days when they had taken walks through Berlin together.[7]

Bauer's 13 letters to Marx, which were published by Ryazanov, cast considerable light on the relations between the two. It is unfortunate that Marx's letters to Bauer have not been preserved, since they would

---

[1] Cf. MEGA I, 1, ii, p. 248.
[2] Ibid. pp. 213–221; ET 1–10.
[3] For this issue see Bauer's letter to Marx, 11 December 1839 (MEGA I, 1, ii, p. 235) and Sepp Miller-Bruno Sawadzki: *Karl Marx in Berlin*, Berlin 1956, p. 68.
[4] BE 55–56.
[5] Barnikol: *Bruno Bauer. Studien und Materialien*, p. 14.
[6] BE 123–124.
[7] MEGA I, 1, ii, p. 236; see also BE 33.

undoubtedly have helped us to understand the issue more clearly.

Bauer advised Marx to take his final examinations at Berlin University as soon as possible.[8] "Put an end to hesitation", he wrote, "and to your attitude towards the examination, which is nothing but a farce." He gives Marx information on the procedures for bestowing a Ph.D. and for academic appointments. Bauer, who was much more of a radical, or was thought to be such at the time, advocated "being frank only on the cathedra"[9] and believed that lectures and research could help change reality. This was the reason why he advised Marx to make haste in writing his Ph.D., so as to be able to take part in the philosophical struggle against the oppressive system in Prussia. "Everywhere", he noted, "decisive conflicts are being created and the Chinese police system which endeavours to suppress them only leads to their strengthening. Philosophy is freeing itself from the methods of Chinese oppression and will conduct a struggle against them, while the state, in its blindness, will lose control of affairs. There have never been times in which it was necessary to do as much as now."[10]

Bauer wanted to attract Marx to Bonn University, at which he lectured, and even began to plan the subjects of the courses Marx would deliver.[11] He cautioned Marx against over-radical formulation of his philosophical views lest he harm his academic career.[12]

Bauer made plans for the publication of a journal devoted to critique of religion and theology, to which he wanted Marx and Feuerbach to contribute.[13] He hoped for the collaboration of the latter, despite reservations expressed by Marx.[14] This fact does not, of course, fit in with the theory which tries to emphasize the Feuerbachian sources of Marxian thought at the beginning of the forties, and we will return to this issue below. "Dr Marx, Dr Bauer and L. Feuerbach are joining forces for the publication of a journal of theological-philosophical affairs", Jung wrote to Ruge, "and it will then be necessary to assemble all God's angels around Him, and to exercise Heavenly mercy towards Him, since it is certain that the three of them will banish Him from Heaven and what is more He may even face trial at their hands."[15]

[8] Ibid. p. 234.
[9] Ibid. p. 239; cf. ibid. p. 252.
[10] Ibid. p. 237.
[11] Ibid. p. 240.
[12] Ibid. p. 252.
[13] Ibid. p. 246.
[14] Ibid. p. 253.
[15] Ibid. pp. 261–262.

Bauer turned to Marx after the publication of the second edition of Hegel's *Philosophy of Religion*, which he edited, and asked him to write a critique on this subject. At the same time he cautioned him against criticizing Marheineke so as to avoid bringing trouble on him, Bauer. This comment makes it abundantly clear that the friendship between Bauer and Marx was a well-known fact, since otherwise it would be hard to understand why Marheineke, when criticized by Marx, should turn against Bauer of all people?

All these plans – a university post for Marx, publication of a journal, etc. – never reached fruition, because of the increased opposition of the regime to radical elements and because of Bauer's dismissal from his position at Bonn.

Marx left Berlin, moved to Trier and from there went with M. Hess to Bonn, in order to visit Bauer and attend his lectures. In Bonn Marx was regarded – to employ Bauer's colorful term – as the last emissary of justice.[16]

Another matter worthy of consideration is the literary collaboration between Bauer and Marx. At the time, Jung claimed that Marx and Bauer had written the *Posaune* together,[17] but this statement was based on an incorrect guess and not on any actual information. From his knowledge of the close personal relationship between the two, Jung deduced that they had written the work together, but after the author's anonymity was lifted, there was no longer any doubt that Bauer was the sole author.

In contrast, the question of the authorship of *Hegels Lehre von der Religion und Kunst* was more complicated. This essay was originally planned as the second part of the *Posaune*, but after the prohibition of the latter its name was altered. Marx was supposed to write the second half of this book, which dealt with art, particularly Christian, in Hegel's thought, while Bauer was to write those chapters dealing with Hegel's attitude towards religion and theology. Marx prepared his contribution, though somewhat late because of his own illness and that of his father-in-law, who died shortly afterwards, but – because of the stringency of Saxonian censorship and his disappointment at the parodistic tone of the book – he did not hand it in.[18] On the basis of examination of the time schedule and Marx's arguments on these issues, most commen-

---

[16] Ibid. pp. 259–260.
[17] Cf. ibid. 262 Jung's letter to Ruge, 29 November 1841.
[18] See ibid. pp. 264–269, 270–278.

tators have concluded that Marx cannot be regarded as the author of the work.[19]

Counter-arguments were put forward by Gustav Mayer, who cited, for example, the comment in the introduction to this essay that two are better than one, and referred to the gap in the timetable as proof that Marx did in fact submit his contribution.[20] But, apart from examination of the various dates and of Marx's considerations, there is a much more important reason for rejecting Mayer's theory and that is comparison of the text with texts by Bauer on the one hand, and Marx on the other. It is surprising that Mayer formulated this theory without examining the matter more fundamentally. It is his view that it is impossible to determine by textual analysis to whom to attribute the second half of the essay. This is a hasty conclusion which is not sufficiently founded. The text was written by Bauer alone, and there are several reasons for arriving at this conclusion:

1) The section which should have been written by Marx, was entitled: "Hegel's hatred of sacred history and of the divine art of writing sacred history". As regards the problems it raises it encompasses a much wider area than Marx's essay on Christian art.[21] The 115 pages of this section deal with the critique of religion and theology in characteristically Bauerian fashion, while only 20 pages are devoted to the Marxian subject.[22]

2) In this section of the essay the tendency to combine Hegelian ideas with the concepts of the French atheists is clearly evident, a tendency already expressed in the *Posaune*. There is no such trend in the works of Marx and the reason is simple: Marx never believed that Hegel represented an atheistic outlook. Furthermore: Bauer uses the same expressions in both essays when he writes of Hegel's admiration for the French and his great esteem for their ideological achievements.

3) In referring in the *Posaune* to Hegel's views, Bauer several times employs the term "hatred" – hatred of Jews, hatred of God.[23] In *Hegel's Lehre* he reiterates this expression and other similar terms,

---

[19] For this issue cf. A. Cornu: *Karl Marx und Friedrich Engels. Leben und Werk*, vol. I, pp. 251–252; Walter Sens: *Die irreligiöse Entwicklung von Karl Marx. Christentum und Sozialismus. Quellen und Darstellungen*. Edited by Ernst Barnikol, Halle 1935. *Beilage: Wer ist der Verfasser des zweiten Teils der Schrift: Die Posaune des jüngsten Gericht über Hegel den Atheisten und Antichristen*, pp. 139–145.
[20] *Marx und der zweite Teil der Posaune*. Archiv für die Geschichte des Sozialismus und der Arbeiterbewegung. Edited by Carl Grünberg. No 7/1916. Heft 3, pp. 332–363.
[21] Cf. MEGA I, 1, ii, p. 268.
[22] HL 138–157.
[23] Pos 165, 169, 186, 192.

when speaking of Hegel's views on the church, religion, Judaism etc.

4) The fusion of Hegelian motifs with the ideals of French philo-sophers creates an illusory picture of Hegel's hostile attitude to-wards the Jews – again in both essays. We may search in vain in Marx's writings for such an approach – he never attributed antisemit-ism to Hegel, nor did he cite French antisemitic literature in support of his conception of Judaism.

5) In the last section of the text, Bauer returns to his polemic against Strauss and again cites arguments against Strauss's views, which had appeared frequently in his previous critical articles – such as the historical nucleus of the Scriptures, contempt for the self-consciousness etc.[24]

All this attests clearly to the fact that the essay, in its entirety, was written by Bauer. He wrote the first half in ten days and was undoubtedly capable – after Marx failed to meet the planned deadline – of writing the second section in a similar period of time.

But there is another aspect to the question of the literary collabora-tion between Bauer and Marx. Bauer would never have established a friendship with Marx, and allowed him to share in his research and literary plans, had there not been intellectual affinity between them and similarities between their conceptions. Only a misguided view could ignore this affinity and argue that Marx, in his dissertation, had already criticized Bauer (as Cornu, for example, claimed)[25] or attribute to Marx increasingly anti-Bauerian sentiments from 1837 onwards.[26]

The truth is that Marx never accepted Bauer's theories in their entirety, even at the time when Bauer clearly influenced the shaping of his views. There can, however, be no doubt as to Marx's dependence on Bauer for a number of years.

The differences of opinion between Marx and Bauer surfaced towards the end of 1842 against the background of the savage attacks of the *Die Freien* group in Berlin, whose patron Bauer was, on the church and religion. Marx, who edited the *Rheinische Zeitung*, refused to publish articles by Meyen, Buhl, Köppen, Rutenberg, Stirner and other mem-bers of the group, since he believed that religion was not a subject in its own right, and that the critique of religion – without reference to the political reality – had no constructive contribution to offer and was not consistent with the tasks of the journal.[27] Marx asked Bauer to cease

[24] HL 187–191.
[25] Cornu: *Karl Marx und Friedrich Engels. Leben und Werk*, vol. I. p. 164.
[26] Sepp Miller-Bruno Sawadzki: *Karl Marx in Berlin*, p. 76.
[27] Cf. Marx's letter to Ruge, 30 November 1842 (MEGA I, 1, ii, p. 285).

supporting the group which was engaged in provocation against the authorities and could cause the closing-down of his paper. But Bauer, in his letter of 13.12.1842, supported *Die Freien*[28] and this led to deterioration of the friendship and increasing controversy between the two. The outcome is well-known: Marx published his polemical essays against Bauer and the latter responded, though his reply was more restrained and moderate than the violent and often unrestrained attacks launched by Marx. Thus the two arrived at a complete breach.

Years later, however, Bauer reestablished contact with Marx. When he was in London in 1855–56, Bauer demonstrated that he harboured no resentment towards Marx and often visited the latter's home, as Marx reported in his letters to Engels.[29] In their conversations, Marx and Bauer discussed a whole range of problems: the development of German philosophy, the class struggle, political economy, the role of Germany and England in Europe etc. For Marx, who had long since ceased to deal with Hegelian philosophy, this was an opportunity to delve into these subjects once more. It is even possible that these discussions had their impact on Marx's renewed interest in Hegel, which was to find striking expression in the *Grundrisse*, written shortly afterwards, in 1857–58.

[28] Ibid. pp. 291–292.
[29] Cf. Marx's letters to Engels, 14 December 1855 and 12 February 1856 (MEGA III, 2).

CHAPTER II

BAUERIAN MOTIFS IN MARX'S CONCEPTION OF RELIGION

From the very beginning of his philosophical career, Marx displayed great interest in the problems of religion. This predilection was shared by all the Young Hegelians, and Marx was no exception. Like other personalities who played a part in this movement, and first and foremost Bruno Bauer, Marx started out by recognizing the central role which religion had played for so long in the life of man and society. Man and society were in a state of submission to supernatural forces, since their self-consciousness had not arrived at maturity enabling it to be a supreme value and a decisive factor in shaping the image of the human cosmos.

Marx's critical attitudes towards religion found expression in his *Preliminary Notes on Greek Literature*, which he began to write in 1839, and in which he compiled material for a dissertation, which was accepted in 1841. It was from this literature that he drew his knowledge of the views of Epicurus and Democritus. In his notes and in the introduction to the dissertation, Marx devotes considerable space to the relations between philosophy and religion and the relations between man and the supreme powers. Marx's remarks were mostly written as comments on Plutarch's polemic with Epicurus, in which Marx found confrontation between the theological viewpoint represented by Plutarch and the pure philosophical conception of Epicurus.[1] Marx naturally supports the latter, and strongly criticizes the approach of Plutarch, who sees the main source of religion in man's sense of dependence on Heaven and emphasizes awe in the face of the divine world as a factor deterring men from doing evil deeds.

According to Marx, the fear of God is, in fact, the main evil, since it cancels human freedom and turns man into a non-sovereign creature. In obvious affinity with Bauer, who was apparently influenced on this

---

[1] MEGA I, 1, i, p. 10. See also ET 12–13.

point by Hegel, Marx claims that fear causes man to deteriorate to the animal level, and animals have no need of restraint by the norms of religious ethics. "In fear man is determined as an animal [. . .], and for the animal there is no importance to the question of how he is restrained."[2]

For the young Marx all the evil in the world derives from the view of the human world in the divine cosmic sphere and from negation of the independence of human beings, who, through religion, forfeit the most precious thing – human nature, since man was meant to be sovereign and free and not to be an instrument of the external forces, and it is beneath his dignity to regard these forces with awe and to see them as a source of terror. Plutarch who, according to Marx, represents the opposite view, can note to his credit the following statement by Marx: "If the philosopher sees nothing contemptible in the view of man as an animal, then he is incapable of understanding anything at all discursively."[3]

In contrast to Plutarch, Epicurus is depicted positively. He is the fighter for humanity and for its authentic life. His main objective, as Marx understands it, is spiritual consolidation of man's sovereignty, the ensuring of his freedom and happiness. "As long as a single drop of blood pulses in her world-conquering and totally free heart, philosophy will continually shout at her opponents the cry of Epicurus: the atheist is not the one who destroys the gods of the multitude but the one who foists the multitude's doctrines onto the gods. Philosophy makes no secret of it. The proclamation of Prometheus: In a word I detest all the gods, is her own slogan against all the gods of heaven and earth."[4]

It is worth noting that the admired image of Prometheus, to whom the above slogan is attributed, was Bauer's ideal,[5] and it is certain that during the four years of friendship Prometheus must often have been the subject of exchanges of views between Bauer and Marx. For Marx, as we know, Prometheus was the ideal of a champion of humanity in its struggle against all servitude, and he held this view all his life.

In total contrast to Feuerbach, who held that religion insists on the projection of human qualities to the illusory divine world, Marx claimed that the process of alienation is based mainly on the transplantation of non-human qualities to the religious sphere. For Marx religion is not objectivization of the essence of man but of negative phenomena such as the sense of dependence, fear, the splitting of man's personality etc.

[2] Ibid. pp. 55, 114.
[3] Ibid. p. 114.
[4] Ibid. p. 10; ET13.
[5] Cf. BE 36–37; Barnikol: *Bruno Bauer. Studien und Materialien*, p. 39.

According to Marx, who follows Bauer, the divine idea is a list of omissions, flaws and defects in human beings. The essence of religion, in this respect, corresponds to the essence of animals. Marx wrote extensively in this spirit, and his statements are dispersed through numerous essays; it is surprising to note that the commentators tend to disregard these statements. Thus, for example, Marx wrote in his article *Debates on the Freedom of the Press:* "As regards *animal party names* in particular, let us remark that religion itself reveres the *animal* as the symbol of the spiritual."[6] And elsewhere: "In the countries of naive feudalism, in the countries in which the caste system operates [...] they have torn, slashed, forcibly pulled off the free limbs of the great saint, of the holy Humanus, and we therefore find there the *worship of animals*, the animal religion in its original form, because for man what constitutes his true essence is regarded as the supreme essence."[7] This was why Marx declared totemism to be a religion true to itself, since in animal worship the non-human qualities of man find objectivization. In one of his letters to Ruge, Marx wrote in this context: "It is strikingly evident that the belief in man's transformation into animal took on the character of the faith of government and a ruling principle. But this does not conflict with religiosity, since the animal religion is the most consistent form of religion, and it may very soon be necessary instead of speaking of religious anthropology, to use the term religious zoology."[8]

There is a direct reference here to Feuerbach's conception and, at the same time, it is invalidated, and preference is accorded to the Bauerian terminology which is relevant to essential presentation of the principles of religion by Marx.

In 1842 Marx already saw religion as fetishism, as human worship of the product of imagination.[9] Fetishism empties human life of human content and kills it in its lifetime, since all human activity is offered up on the altar of the belief in a fetish and, on this point, the true character of religion and its denial of humanism find very frank reflection: "[...] animal worship is *a higher* religious form than fetishism. But doesn't animal worship degrade man below the animal and make the animal man's God?"[10]

Marx's essay, in which he formulated his attitude to fetishistic

---

[6] MEGA I, 1, i, p. 191.
[7] Ibid. p. 272.
[8] Ibid. I, 1, ii, pp. 270–271.
[9] Ibid. I, 1, i, p. 236; Ph 115.
[10] Idem.

religion, *The Leading Article of the Kölnische Zeitung*, is filled with Bauerian ideas. Among these may be classified the theory that the Christian state does not realize the principles of freedom, but rather engages in dissemination of dogma and its implementation; that it is not an association of free people but rather a multitude of people, who are seen as lacking in initiative and, as such, in need of patronage; that no differentiation should be made between religion as belief and the religious establishment, that the latter collaborates closely with the secular authorities, that religion teaches that all authorities were determined by Heaven, that censorship and the police protect the religious-church regime etc.[11]

In continuation of these theses, Marx tried to prove that philosophy had always been hostile towards religion, of whatever school. The conflict between philosophy and religion, according to Marx, is fundamental and applies to all the spheres in which both operate. Philosophy appeals to man's reason, while religious faith appeals to the emotions. Philosophy promises nothing but the truth, does not demand belief in its conclusions, but merely examination. On the other hand, religion promises salvation, eternal life in the next world, imposes the burden of faith on the believer, creates a regime of fear and obedience. Unlike philosophy, which strives for general recognition, the objective of religion is to emphasize its uniqueness, its specific immanent content, which distinguishes it from other religions, and to represent itself as the absolute truth.[12]

In his critique of religion, Marx highlights the political dimension of the activity of various religious organizations, but does not content himself with this. He advocates, with relative clarity, an idea which is astonishingly similar to Bauer's ideas on the individual self-consciousness and its adaptation to the universal self-consciousness, when he points to the fact that the truth is contained in the human self-consciousness which is consistent with objective metaphysical principles: "It is out of the *world's own principles* that we develop for it new principles. We do not say to her: 'Stop your battles, they are stupid stuff.' [...] We merely show it what it is actually fighting about, and this realization is a thing that it must make its own even though it may not wish to. The reform of consciousness consists solely in letting the world perceive its own consciousness by awaking it from dreaming about itself in explaining to it its own actions [...] So our election cry must be: reform

---

11 Ibid. pp. 234, 238, 239, 241–243, 248; Ph 117–118, 124–127; ET 39–41.
12 Ibid. pp. 243–250; Ph 122–130.

of consciousness not through dogmas, but the *analysis of mystical consciousness that is not clear to itself*, whether it appears in a religious or political form. It will then be clear that the world has long possessed the dream of a thing of which it only needs to possess the consciousness in order to really possess it."[13]

Marx does not employ the problematic concept of universal self-consciousness, but it is clear that it is the metaphysical principles which are the basis of the world or, as Marx puts it: "the world's own principles" lead to awakening of the self-consciousness, which adopts these principles. We should recall that for Bauer these principles find expression in reason realizing itself in history and in liberty as its product, and we will then understand that there is an additional important aspect to the relations between philosophy and religion. Philosophy exposes the hidden principles and acquaints human beings with their essence. It alone is capable of arriving at the hidden knowledge of the era. Philosophy does not criticize the existing situation alone, but also the consciousness which lags itself, first and foremost the religious consciousness and those forms of political consciousness related to it. Both find expression in what Marx calls "the mystic consciousness". He is referring to the theological way of thinking in religion and to a reactionary political theory which is expressed in conservative Prussia and its oppressive regime.

Similarly to Bauer, Marx was convinced that fusion of the two forms of mystic consciousness – the religious and the political – inevitably causes the struggle for political liberation to be tied up with criticism of religion, since critique of religion is not an objective in itself, but should be related to critique of the state or, as Marx wrote in his article *On the Jewish Question*, written in 1843: "But since the existence of religion implies a defect, the source of this defect must be sought in the *nature* of the state itself [. . .] The question of the relation *of political emancipation to religion* becomes for us a question of the relation of *political emancipation* to *human emancipation*. We criticize the religious weakness of the political state by criticizing the political state in its *secular* constitution *apart from* the religious defects. In human terms we resolve the contradiction between the state and a *particular religion* such as *Judaism* into the contradiction between the state and *particular secular elements*, the contradiction between the state and *religion generally* into the contradiction between the state and its presuppositions."[14]

---

[13] Ibid. pp. 574–575; ET 82.
[14] Ibid. pp. 581–582; Ph 222–223.

Towards the end of 1842 Marx was undoubtedly still totally enslaved to Bauer and this is attested to by the following sentence from his letter to Ruge: "[...] religion has no content of its own and does not live from heaven but from earth and falls automatically with the dissolution of the inverted reality of which it is the theory."[15] All of Marx's ideas as expressed in this excerpt are of characteristically Bauerian origin. Whereas the idea of the origins of religion as anchored on earth can be attributed to all the Young Hegelians, the conception of inverted reality as the root of religion is a word-for-word repetition of Bauer's favourite formulation, which takes up extensive space in his writings and this is also true of the expression "religion is theory of such reality".

Marx repeats these ideas, in more detailed fashion, in the well-known excerpt from *Towards the Critique of Hegel's Philosophy of Right. Introduction*.[16] Various commentators have seen in this excerpt characteristic expression of the revival of Feuerbachian motifs in Marx's philosophy,[17] but this interpretation is baseless. Marx's statement that man creates religion and not vice versa, is valid for all the Young Hegelians from Strauss to Moses Hess and is not the fruit of Feuerbach's thought alone. More thorough perusal of religious issues as presented by Marx shows that everything – from the ideas themselves to their formulation – is repetition, sometimes verbatim, of Bauer's well-known ideas. This is best reflected in the following points:

1) Marx, like Bauer, sees religion as the self-consciousness and self-feeling of man, who has not yet comprehended his true relation to the world around him and his own authentic nature as the creator of the social actuality within which he lives. Therefore man, who "has not yet found himself" or has "already lost himself" is explicitly identified with the individual with flawed self-consciousness who has not attained understanding of the fact that his authentic interest is in conflict with religion. Under these circumstances the content of man's self-consciousness is grasped as existing outside man or, as Bauer defines it, is grasped as "absolute and as history".[18]

2) Marx clung to Bauer's view of the world as "inverted" and claimed, in his wake, that religion is inverted self-consciousness, i.e.

15 Ibid. I, 1, ii, p. 286; ET 53.
16 Ibid. I, 1, i, pp. 607–608; Ph 249–251.
17 For example, see Jean-Yves Calvez: *La pensée de Karl Marx*, Paris 1956, pp. 85–88; H. Gollwitzer: *Die marxistische Religionskritik und der christliche Glaube*. Marxismusstudien 4/1962, p. 56; D. McLellan: *Marx before Marxism*, London, MacMillan 1970, p. 143; Werner Post: *Kritik der Religion bei Marx*, München 1969, pp. 162–163.
18 Cf. part one, ch. VI, n. 46, 47, ch. VII, n. 47, 49.

basically distorted like the distortion characterizing reality. The Bauerian conception, which grasps religion as ideology, was transplanted in entirety to the framework of Marx's ideas on the essence of this issue. We will discuss Marx's debt to Bauer in the chapter on Marx's conception of ideology.

3) When Marx refers to religion as the general theory of the inverted world, as its moral sanction etc., he is repeating, with only slight modifications, Bauer's statement in his essay *Die gute Sache der Freiheit*, which Marx knew well:[19] "It [religion] is the expression, isolated manifestation and sanction of the omission and disease of existing relations. It is the general essence of all relations and tendencies."[20]

4) Marx, like Bauer sees in religion "an expression of real suffering and a protest against it." The word "suffering" replaces Bauer's definitions "deprivation, plight, poverty" etc., but the essence of the phenomenon, as grasped by Bauer, remains: no man can live an authentic life as long as there endures a reality permeated with religious principles, which creates suffering again and again.

5) Marx often employs the term "critique" which is characteristically Bauerian, and characterized Bauer's oppositional attitude, towards reality, primarily because of its religious and anti-rational nature. Shortly afterwards, in *The Holy Family*, Marx gave his polemical essay the satirical subtitle: *Critique of Critical Critique*, arguing that Bauer's critique was not mere criticism but criticism without limitation.

6) Marx is saying nothing new when he claims that religion should be cancelled as the "illusory happiness of the people", since this thesis was not only presented by Bauer, but was also, to a large extent, the central principle of fulfilment of the free and creative self-consciousness. The word "illusory" is of clearly Bauerian origin – Bauer often compared religion to both universal- and self-illusion.[21] Logically speaking the postulate of abolition of the illusion fits into the Marxian concept which negates the principle of illusory happiness, so as to enable man to "think, act and shape his reality like a disillusioned man who has come to his senses." This postulate is Bauerian from the point of view of principle and content, and as regards its formulation. This is also true of the expression "flowers on the chain", a vivid expression which Bauer often uses,[22] which he employs in referring to the natural religions, in which alienation was not so strongly felt because of their ties

[19] See MEGA I, i, iii, p. 250.
[20] Cf. part one, ch. VIII, n. 32.
[21] See part one, ch. VIII, n. 22.
[22] See part one, ch. VIII, n. 10.

to folk, nation, family and nature. Marx detached the expression from its original context and it therefore forfeited its original significance and appeared to be more a metaphor than a clear formulation.

7) Marx remained loyal to himself and to Bauer at the same time, when he claimed that man found in Heaven non-human being, in accordance with the conception mentioned above, that alienation is based on the projection of non-human qualities to the religious sphere.

8) The famous phrase "religion is the opium of the people" is but a repetition of Bauer's theory that religion lulls the consciousness of believers, reconciles them to miserable reality through drawing an illusory picture of happiness awaiting them in the next world. Bruno Bauer was not the first to compare religion to opium. A similar view was voiced, for example, before him by Holbach, who grasped religion as the art of intoxicating human beings,[23] or Maréchal, who said that "until now mankind has been ruled by religious means of intoxication" and specifically referred to opium.[24] In Feuerbach there is almost no reference to this problem, at least not in the *Essence of Christianity*, and this fact may be cited against Schaper's[25] attempts to represent Feuerbach as the inventor of this phrase. The term appears only once, in *Pierre Bayle*, but is underplayed there and lacks the significance which was attributed to it in Bauer's and Marx's writings.[26] In the *Philosophy of Religion* Hegel compares the Indian religion to a man suffering in body and spirit, in an intolerable situation, who therefore strives, though opium, to create a dream world and the joy of madness. Benz called attention to the possible influence of this idea on the Young Hegelians.[27]

Bauer, who was greatly interested in the philosophy of the French Enlightenment, attended, edited and prepared for publication Hegel's lectures on the philosophy of religion, and drew inspiration from both sources: Holbach's ideas on religion as opium and Hegel's view of the Indian religion as founded on means of intoxication and tranquilliza-tion. He absorbed both and hence his utilization of a widerange of terms consistent with the view of religion as a dream, illusion, delirium

---

[23] Holbach: Le Christianisme devoilé. Edition 1761, p. 226.
[24] *Dictionnaire des athées anciens et modernes* par Sylvain M[aréchal]. Paris. An. VIII (1800), p. XLIX.
[25] Ewald Schaper: *Religion ist Opium fürs Volk*. Zeitschrift für Kirchengeschichte, 1940, pp. 425–429.
[26] Ludwig Feuerbach: *Pierre Bayle*, Ansbach 1838, p. 249.
[27] E. Benz: *Hegels Religionsphilosophie und die Linkshegelianer. Zur Kritik des Religions-begriffes von Karl Marx*. Zeitschrift für Religions- und Geistesgeschichte, 7/1955, pp. 247–270.

on the one hand, and opium on the other.[28] As Seeger rightly noted, Bauer was the mentor of Marx and Hess on this question.[29] But Seeger was acquainted with only a few of Bauer's articles and therefore his argument is not sufficiently well-grounded. The problem is not restricted to use of the term opium alone, but should be regarded as a narrow section of a whole range of problems. Only from this angle is it possible to understand that Marx, who followed in Bauer's footsteps on all the points noted above, also took over from him the concept of opium, just as he adopted the terms inverted world, inverted self-consciousness, illusion, flowers on the chains, and a whole series of other Bauerian terms. It is also clear from this that the use of the term opium, for example, by Heine[30] (about a year before Bauer wrote *Der Christliche Staat und unsere Zeit*, in which he twice compared religion to this intoxicant) could not have influenced Marx, since Heine was not integrated in and connected to all those contexts which characterize Bauer's (and Marx's) conception of religion.

Thus, in the wake of Bauer, the view of religion as the "opium of the people" is the summary of Marx's conception of religion. Religion is the product of a situation in which man is deprived of the possibility of realizing his essence. As long as the suitable conditions for radical change are lacking, man cannot develop his authentic human qualities and is in need of consolation, of an imaginary picture of the world, of mystification. In the absence of true happiness, man clings to the illusion of happiness.

But it would be an exaggeration to claim that Marx mechanically transplants Bauer's ideas and does nothing more. It has already been said that Marx does not follow Bauer in everything, and did not accept his ideas in their entirety. This trend is also evident in the excerpt we are examining. The thought that man is the world of men, state, society, is directed against Feuerbach and not against Bauer, who tended to emphasize the importance of the political factor in history and blamed human alienation, to no small degree, on a political situation, but in Marx emphasis was placed on abandonment of "a condition which requires illusions", and this condition was seen as essentially social; on the proletariat was imposed the historical task of redeeming all mankind. In *Towards the Critique of Hegel's Philosophy of Right*,

[28] Cf. part one, ch. VIII, n. 21–24, 31, 37.

[29] Reinhart Seeger: *Herkunft und Bedeutung des Schlagwortes: Die Religion ist Opium für das Volk*. Theologische Arbeiten zur Bibel-, Kirchen- und Geistesgeschichte, Halle 1935, pp. 40–42.

[30] Heinrich Heine: *Sämtliche Werke*. Vol. VIII, p. 478.

Introduction, Marx first formulated his communist theories,[31] and in this context religion, the critique of which is represented as a premise for all criticism, – and here Marx is completely in accord with Bauer – ceases to play a decisive part, in clear contrast to Bauer's views. Hence Marx's statement that state and society produce religion, whereas in Bauer in certain cases there is a two-way relationship between society and religion, and in others religion creates the image of society. This belief in the sometimes decisive significance of religion is non-existent in Marx's thought, which started out from the splitting of society into classes, identified the bourgeoisie with egoism and the proletariat with the principle of universality and held that the emancipation of mankind would occur when the proletariat put an end to the corrupt wordly order of private property, political and social inequality. Marx's conception of religion is tied up with the universal conception and as a result of this fact the struggle against distorted reality is identical with the struggle against the religion which gives this reality legitimization, whereas the struggle against religion is seen as an indirect struggle against the social order which creates religion.

This theory can also be presented in the opposite fashion: the criticism of the state and of society which is central to the critic's argumentation does not exempt him from the obligation to take a critical attitude towards religion. Criticism knows that religion is not the main cause of all the catastrophes visited upon the world – and in this Marx differs from Bauer – but religion also contributes to the maintenance of non-human social arrangements. The contribution of religion is reflected in a positive attitude towards a regime which is in conflict with the essence of man, in apologetics where the state is concerned, in the moral sanction which religion gives the society of social gaps and of property. The existence of religion and its development may be accredited to the miserable cultural, political and social conditions which lead man to need a supernatural and irrational explanation for his situation within the world and for the nature of this world. Marx sees in the "real suffering" the root of evil and directs his attack against it. This struggle has consequences for the relations between man and the heavenly forces as well: religion as something related to the wordly order and as part of it is doomed to disappear, when existing society is replaced by another society, enabling man to be free and to realize his essence. The realization of man's essence in reality creates a new

---

[31] MEGA I, 1, i, pp. 619–621; Ph 262–264.

situation in which man no longer has need of the illusion of fulfilment of his aspirations and qualities in the next world.

Hence Marx's conception is specifically atheistic, and not only because of its rejection of the existence of a supernatural world but also, perhaps mainly because it sees religion as imaginary realization of man's essence. Religion serves, according to this Marxian-Bauerian conception, as an expression of man's weakness, his passivity, his inability to find himself, and is a kind of dehumanization.

It is not surprising therefore that for Marx atheism enjoys eminent status and is declared to constitute the theoretical basis of communism, while the abolition of private property is its practical basis or, as Marx says in *Economic and Philosophic Manuscripts*: "[...] atheism which transcends God is the emergence of theoretical humanism, and communism which transcends private property is the vindication of actual human life as man's property, the emergence of practical humanism. Or atheism is humanism mediated through itself by the transcendence of religion, and communism is humanism mediated through itself by the transcendence of practical humanism."[32]

Why did Marx base communism on atheism from the theoretical point of view instead of grounding it on philosophy or on political economy? It is clear to us that Marxian atheism is inextricably bound up with his philosophical conception, but this is not the crux of the problem. The fact that he pointed to the transcendence of religion and linked it to the transcendence of private property as the main issue of real communist activity is worthy of examination. The influence of his friend Bauer is evident in this conception which could not free itself, despite the view that socio-economic factors are decisive in human life as regards sociological analysis and the historiosophical aspect, from the evaluation that religion is the truest barometer of the human plight, suffering and the suppression of man's personality.

In the light of the above, the standpoint of Reding, who claims that Marxian theory is not basically atheistic and can definitely be reconciled with a religious outlook[33] is based on complete misunderstanding.

Marx, who grasped religion as a means of intoxication, as an illusion and as reconciliation with a social reality based on exploitation and oppression, naturally regarded it as a conservative element, reactionary and hindering progress. From this point of view religion is represented

---

[32] Ibid. I, 1, iii, p. 166; Ph 331.
[33] Marcel Reding: *Der politische Atheismus*. Wien-Graz-Köln 1971, pp. 174–176; *Universitätstage 1961. Marxismus-Leninismus. Geschichte und Gestalt*, pp. 160, 167.

as bestowing sanction on appalling social conditions and a social gap
and as an obstacle to human liberation on the one hand and to universal
emancipation of the proletariat on the other. This evaluation finds
expression in Marx's attitude towards the social principles of Christianity: "The social principles of Christianity justified the slavery of an-
tiquity, glorified the serfdom of the Middle Ages and equally know,
when necessary, how to defend the oppression of the proletariat, although they make a pitiful face over it. The social principles of Christianity preach the necessity of a ruling and an oppressing class, and all
they have for the latter is the pious wish the former will be charitable.
The social principles of Christianity transfer the adjustment of all in-
famies to heaven and thus justify the further existence of those in-
famies on earth [. . .] The social principles of Christianity preach cow-
ardice, self-contempt, abasement, submission, dejection, in a word all
the qualities of the *canaille* . . ."[34]

According to Marx's outlook, religious principles, – in this concrete
instance in their Christian manifestation, – have, throughout history,
faithfully served the ruling class and opposed any attempt by the
people to cast off the yoke of class oppression.

Marx persisted in his belief in the anti-human character of religion
throughout his life. This viewpoint found various extreme expressions,
which recall Bauer's theories of *Das entdeckte Christentum*. One example
is his enthusiastic attitude towards Daumer's book, *The Secrets of
Ancient Christianity*, which preached hatred of religion in general and
Christianity in particular, and is a perfect example of the vulgar atheistic approach. In an address delivered in a Communist circle devoted
to popular education, in London in 1847, Marx said, inter alia: "Of
everything which German philosophy has done the most important
thing is *criticism of religion* [. . .] but what has not so far been investigated is Christianity's practical ritual. *Daumer* has proved, in his
recently-published book, that the Christians really did slaughter people,
eat their flesh and drink their blood [. . .] the offering of human
sacrifices was sacred to them and was really carried out. Protestantism
transplanted it to the sphere of spiritual man, and thus slightly miti-
gated it. This is also the reason why among Protestants more are inflicted with madness than in other religious sects. Daumer's book,
which depicts this affair, deals Christianity a death-blow. To the question of the significance of all this for us, we may reply: this affair makes

[34] R 84.

us confident that the old society is coming to an end and that the structure of deception and prejudice is collapsing."[35] This excerpt clearly shows that Marx accepted the anti-Christian libel, and, what is more, was convinced that this dramatic revelation could hasten the collapse of a corrupt society founded on the principles of the Christian religion. The atheistic education which Marx received from proximity with Bauer, had borne fruit: Marx was willing to attribute to religion inhuman and horrifying characteristics in order to condemn it, and to this end he sanctioned Daumer's theories, which are the development of motifs which are to be found in Bauer. It is hard to understand the viewpoint of certain Marxologists on this issue. Lobkowicz, for example, said that "he [Marx] was always somewhat surprised, indeed annoyed by the persistent attacks on religion of such militant atheists as Feuerbach or the Bauer brothers."[36]

Lobkowicz's statement is groundless, since Marx, following in the footsteps of Bauer, conducted an uncompromising campaign against religion. There is obvious confusion here between two kinds of atheism: that which sharply attacks religion but does not call for administrative measures against it, and that which seeks to depose it through political and police pressure. It is known that Marx criticized the Gotha programme, and opposed the use of police methods against religion,[37] but this fact does not detract from the harshness of his ideological onslaught on religion. It should be stressed that this rule also applies to the views of Bruno Bauer, who, for all his attacks on dogma and ritual, was not in favour of administrative repression. Those who claim, like Lobkowicz, that for Marx religion does not take pride of place, but is of secondary importance, since its roots lie in economic and social conditions of society and that he does not see it as the main enemy, in contrast to views of Feuerbach and Bauer, who see in it the main cause of the world's plight – are ignoring the fact that this problem is irrelevant to the problems of militant atheism.

The essence of this question lies in correct evaluation of the nature of the struggle against religion: is the issue ideological struggle or are administrative measures and police repression recommended? It is a well-known fact that many proclaimed Marxists deviated from Marx's

---

[35] *Geheimnisse des christlichen Altertums*, von G. F. Daumer. *Mit einer einleitenden Rede von Karl Marx.* Wissenschaftliche Bibliothek des proletarischen Freidenkertums. Vol. IX, Dresden 1924, p. V.

[36] Nicolas Lobkowicz: *Marx' Attitude Toward Religion.* The Review of Politics, vol. 26/1964, p. 319.

[37] R 144.

theories and employed violence against religion and believers. Lenin changed Marx's statement on religion as the opium of the people, which derives from *objective* creation of religious predilections and tendencies because of the existence of suitable social conditions, to the formula of religion as "opium of the people and for the people", and this addition lent the problem the dimension of a struggle against those for whom religion serves as an instrument maintaining the workers in a regime of submission. Accordingly religion was imposed from above and is based mainly on deception. In other words: according to Marx religion is created and develops as the result of social and political processes originating in production relations and in the class structure of society, that is to say outside the human consciousness, while for Lenin, religion, to a large extent, should be regarded as the fruit of the conscious efforts of circles interested in its maintenance and prosperity, and in restraint of the masses.[38]

At the same time it is worth stressing the nature of Marx's criticism of religion. Scholars have justifiably wondered at it: this Marx, who often recommended the dialectical method (and admired the dialectical idealist, Hegel, inestimably more than the materialist, Feuerbach) and utilized it for complex socio-economic and historical analyses – how could he regard all religions at all times as ideology hampering progress, and under all historical circumstances playing a reactionary part?[39] How did it occur that in Marx's writing there is no mention of the fact which is so well-known to scholars, that in various periods religion served as a factory integrating various strata and entire nations, and was even the symbol of various revolutionary movements (Anabaptists, Socinians, Tabborites etc.)?

A typical example of the essence of his approach is his evaluation of Christianity, since its social principles are grasped as serving the interests of the ruling class and he sees this rule as valid for all historical periods from ancient times to his own day.

The view of religion as "the opium of the people" is no less schematic, and is an inseparable part of the critique aimed at exposing the reactionary nature of religion. Since Marx does not take into consideration those situations in which religion played a progressive role and ignores all the positive aspects – (the statement that religion is the expression

---

[38] Iring Fetscher: *Marx and Marxism*, New York, Herder & Herder 1971, pp. 270–271.
[39] Klaus Bockmühl: *Leiblichkeit und Gesellschaft. Studien zur Religionskritik und Anthropologie im Frühwerk von Ludwig Feuerbach und Karl Marx*, Göttingen 1961, pp. 213–215; Reding: *Der politische Atheismus*, pp. 43–45.

of real suffering and, at the same time, the protest against real suffering, does not change this general picture) – the evaluation of religion as opium and as antihuman is a kind of dogma binding in all situations and circumstances.

The tendency to represent religion as reactionary in all situations and towards its total rejection derives from Bauerian influence. Both Bauer and Marx saw in religion, above all, man's alienation from his own essence and saw it as spiritual illusion and as the expression of the dehumanization of mankind. Both criticized it harshly and angrily, with evident destructive intentions. Both aspired to total abolition of religion, in order to restore to man his alienated essence (but differed, as noted, in their ways of attaining this objective). Even in style and phraseology Marx resembles Bauer whenever he speaks of the cancellation of religion. As noted, many of the expressions Marx uses originate in Bauer's essays.

We should not deduce from this that Marx's atheism is not rooted in his own thought and is an alien element, artificially adopted under the influence of Bauer. On the contrary, as noted, Marx's atheism is an inseparable part of his theories and well-anchored in his outlook. Bauer's influence is evident in the extremity of his attitude to religion and to everything it entails, in his sweeping evaluations, in dogmatism and onesidedness.

CHAPTER III

BAUER'S INFLUENCE ON MARX'S DISSERTATION

Almost all the Marxologists agree that Bauer influenced Marx's choice of a subject for his thesis as well as the ideas he presented in this work.[1] But they believe that this influence was exerted in non-essential and marginal issues. Bockmühl, for example, says that at the end of the eighteen thirties and beginning of the forties Marx was a typical Feuerbachian and that his utilization of Bauerian categories was solely in the sphere of terminology, whereas their content derived from the writings of Feuerbach, or, as he puts it, the Feuerbachian method appears in Marx in Bauerian guise.[2] Bockmühl's argument is unfounded: Feuerbach's *Essence of Christianity* was published in November 1841, many months after Marx submitted his dissertation; in contrast to the accepted view, this essay had very little influence on Marx. There are almost no Feuerbachian motifs in Marx's conception of religion. The opposite is the case: as we have seen, Marx advocates the Bauerian approach; he sees the essence of religious alienation as the projection of non-human qualities to the sphere of religion, and regards it as a reactionary phenomenon etc. It is not surprising, therefore, that Marx protested when Bauer wanted to recruit Feuerbach as a contributor to the atheistic journal the two were planning to produce.[3] Those who studied Marx disregarded this point for many years, since it did not fit in with the picture of Marx's development drawn by Engels. But there has been a recent change of attitude. Thus, for example, McLellan expresses doubt as to Feuerbach's influence over Marx at the time the latter's dissertation was being written, and dates the Feuerbachian

---

[1] See for example, Günther Hillmann: *Marx und Hegel. Von der Spekulation zur Dialektik*, Frankfurt/M. 1966, pp. 208, 225, 227–228; Manfred Friedrich: *Philosophie und Ökonomie beim jungen Marx*, Berlin 1960, pp. 31, 41; Armin Wildermuth: *Marx und die Verwirklichung der Philosophie*. Vol. I, Haag 1970, pp. 60, 63, 67, 118; Klaus Bockmühl: *Leiblichkeit und Gesellschaft*, pp. 113–114, 125–130; McLellan: *Marx before Marxism*, pp. 59, 64; Cornu: *Karl Marx und Friedrich Engels. Leben und Werk*, vol. I, pp. 145, 161–162.

[2] Bockmühl: *Leiblichkeit und Gesellschaft*, p. 125.

[3] Cf. part two, ch. I, n. 14, ch. VI, n. 12.

influence later in Marx's life – in 1843–1845. As will be shown further on, Feuerbach's influence was strictly limited even then.

In the outline of the new introduction to his dissertation, (towards the end of 1841), Marx wrote: "This work, which I am now making public, is an old work which should have found its place in a general description of Epicurean, Stoic and Sceptic philosophy, but my professional, political and philosophical preoccupations, which are of more topical significance, prevent me meanwhile from completing this project. Since I do not know when the opportunity of dealing with the subject will arise again, I am contenting myself [with the present form of the work]. The time has only just arrived for understanding of the methods of the Epicureans, Stoics and Sceptics. They are philosophers of the self-consciousness."[4] This statement reveals the links of the philosophers of self-consciousness with Marx's own era.

Marx did not attempt representation of the three post-Aristotelian schools of thought and concentrated on Epicurus and a comparison between him and Democritus as regards the conception of nature, but the reasons why he thought the subject topical remained valid: Aristotle, like Hegel, has tackled most of the decisive problems of his day, while those who followed him were obliged to act in the shadow of his philosophical conceptions, this fact arousing frustration and epigonal emotions. The Young Hegelians saw the Greek philosophers who were active after Aristotle as the archetype of their own philosophical activity and hence their sympathy towards them. In addition, and this may be the most important reason, they advocated a historical-philosophical approach which saw these schools as a vitally important stage of development of European thought, characterized by the struggle of the self-consciousness for liberation. There can be no doubt that Bruno Bauer exerted decisive influence on the formulation of this viewpoint.

In accordance with Bauer's view, Greek and Roman philosophy is seen as a vital preparatory stage in the creation of the European Christian world. "It's [Christianity's] emergence [...] was dependent, as regards content and force, on the achievements of the classical spirit", Bauer noted. To his mind, the debt of Christianity to Greek thought found expression in the conception of the divinity as a spirit while its links to the Roman spirit were revealed in the general form of the objective and the vital significance which Roman philosophy attributed to the self-consciousness, which was grasped as a "substantial

[4] MEGA I, 1, ii, p. 327.

foundation."⁵ Bauer also gave expression to his belief that only in the European-Christian world concrete expression was given to the trend of Roman philosophy to regard relations between man and God as the unity of the absolute self-consciousness.⁶ Furthermore: the individualist principle of Hellenistic philosophy, which grew up against the background of the disintegration of the Greek polis, detached man from his objective social ties and prepared the way for the triumph of Christianity. But it also claimed its victim, since in this religion man is conceived as the object of God who, in actual fact, is but his product. For this reason Bauer – as noted above – expressed uncompromising criticism of the principles of Christianity, as a religion which was a representative sample of total alienation. It is worth adding, in this context, that Greek philosophy, because of its development of intellectual motifs which led to advancement of the self-consciousness, won Bauer's high esteem, particularly the post-Aristotelian currents, in which he saw typical representatives of the principle of self-consciousness and fighters for atheistic ideas, who were the forerunners of the atheists and critics of religion of the eighteenth century French Enlightenment. The distinction between post-Aristotelian Greek philosophical thought and modern European rationalism serves as the key to understanding of Bauer's theory that the Hegelian element emerges triumphant from the struggle with Christianity, or as he said: "The pagan, the Greek triumphs: the church, the Christian falls and collapses and becomes the hated."⁷

These motifs were developed by Marx. Thus, for example, Epicurus becomes "the representative of the Enlightenment."⁸ When Marx compares the methods of the Epicureans, the Stoics and the Sceptics with those of the Greek philosophers who preceded them, he comments: "It seems to me that if the preceding systems are more significant and more interesting because of their content, the post-Aristotelian [...] are important because of the subjective form, the character of Greek philosophy. It is precisely the subjective form, the spiritual carrier of philosophical system which we have until now almost entirely ignored in considering only their metaphysical pronouncements."⁹

In total accord with Bauer's conception, Marx argues that the schools

⁵ RAT, pp. LXXVII–LXXVIII.
⁶ Ibid. p. LXXVIII.
⁷ Pos 192.
⁸ See Norman D. Livergood's translation of Marx's dissertation in *Activity in Marx's Philosophy*. The Hague, Martinus Nijhoff 1967, p. 109 (MEGA I, 1, i, p. 51).
⁹ MEGA I, 1, i, p. 15; Dif 64.

of self-consciousness evolved in Greece were transferred to Rome and hence to the modern world: "Finally, if we take a glance at history, are Epicureanism, Stoicism and Scepticism special phenomena? Are they not rather prototypes of the Roman mind, the form in which Greece emigrated to Rome? Are they not such intense and eternal beings, so full of character, that even the modern world has to allow to them their full spiritual citizenship?"[10]

Bauer's views on this issue were evidently influenced to a large extent by Hegel, who in his *History of Philosophy*, emphasized that post-Aristotelian philosophy was the philosophy of the self-consciousness,[11] but there are modifications and serious differences between Hegel's and Bauer's evaluations of this philosophy, and in particular its essence and significance. Whereas Bauer sees it as a relatively high level of development of the universal self-consciousness, and regards it as a spiritual factor which enabled man to preserve his internal freedom at the time of political and ideological oppression reminiscent of his own times, Hegel saw it as a characteristic manifestation of dogmatism, desire for seclusion of the self-consciousness within itself and detachment of man from the world around him. Hegel therefore evaluated this philosophy as an obstacle to man's endeavours to fashion his world. "The pure relation of self-consciousness to itself" he wrote "is thus the principle in all these philosophies. [...] The principle of this philosophy is not objective but dogmatic and rests on the impulse of self-consciousness towards self satisfaction. [...] The subject seeks on its own account a principle for its freedom, namely, immovability in itself: it must be conformable to the criterion, i.e. to this quite universal principle in order to be able to raise itself into this abstract independence. Self-consciousness lives in the solitude of its thought, and finds therein its satisfaction."[12]

Marx emulates Bauer in his evaluation of Epicureanism and other conceptions belonging to that period. This is expressed in his statement that "these systems are the key to the true history of Greek philosophy,"[13] a sentence which could never have been formulated by Hegel, who greatly preferred the systems of Plato and Aristotle to those of the various Epigoni. Marx goes further and openly criticizes Hegel on this question. After praising Hegel lavishly and, inter alia, stating that the

[10] Ibid. p. 14, Dif 64. For this issue cf. H. P. Adams: *Karl Marx in his Earlier Writings*. New York, Russel & Russel 1965², p. 30.
[11] HPh II, p. 233.
[12] Ibid. pp. 233–234.
[13] MEGA I, 1, i, p. 9; Dif 62; ET 12.

true historical depiction of philosophy commenced with the publication of Hegel's *History of Philosophy*, he says that because of his giant system, Hegel was unable to "enter into details" (i.e. of conceptions which he regarded as of secondary importance) and, what is more important: the conception of those philosophical currents which appeared to him speculative par excellence, hindered him from evaluating Greek philosophy after Aristotle in the way it deserved, as regards its place in the history of Greek philosophy and for the Greek mind in general.[14]

Marx openly criticized Hegel on another point, and here too he is in accord with Bauer, namely the proofs of the existence of God, which Hegel supported. Marx disregards the fact that Hegel's God has nothing in common with the transcendent God of Christianity, that he is immanent in the world, that reason serves as the criterion for all religious problems etc. According to his view, these proofs are pure tautologies; for example, in the case of the ontological proof the significance is that man's image of God is true, i.e. impells him to act in accordance with this image (according to Marx: "What I really imagine is for me a real imagination") or proof of the existence of the human self-consciousness. Marx writes in this context: "[. . .] the proofs for the existence of God are nothing but proofs for the existence of an essentially human self-consciousness and logical elaborations of it. For example, the ontological proof. What being exists as soon as it is thought? Self-consciousness."[15]

There is a certain degree of paradox in the fact that Marx represents Hegel's theories as conflicting with those of Bauer, since Bauer attributed to Hegel's conception an atheistic character and therefore also ignored the presentation of proofs of God's existence by Hegel, while Marx brings about confrontation between the views of both and, according to his conception of religion, prefers Bauer's views to the Hegelian theories, when he claims that the theory should be reversed and that the exact opposite should be deduced from all the proofs, i.e. that they attest to the absence of God in the world. "All the proofs for the existence of God are proofs of his non-existence, refutations of all conceptions of God. The true proofs should be reversed and read: 'since nature is badly constructed, God exists! Because the world is irrational, God exists! Because there is no thought, God exists!' But

---

[14] Idem.; Dif 61.
[15] Ibid. p. 81; ET 18.

this merely means that God exists for anyone who finds the world rational and thus is irrational himself. In other words, irrationality is the essence of God."[16]

Marx employs Bauer's slogan on the struggle of the free self-consciousness which fights "against all the gods of heaven and earth who do not recognize man's self-consciousness as the highest divinity,"[17] i.e. transforms human self-consciousness into the supreme value and the norm for human behaviour.

His reliance on Bauer is so obvious here that no-one has ever expressed doubt as to his philosophical dependence on Bauer on this issue. But the amazing fact is that several years later, in *The Holy Family*, Marx was to criticize Bauer for advocating the self-consciousness as a hypostasis, and to mock him for detaching self-consciousness from man, the standard-bearer of this consciousness. Marx forgot the fact that he himself was the faithful disciple of Bauer on this point.

It is clear that Marx, who based himself on the human self-consciousness as a supreme value and as a metaphysical and historiosophical criterion, should have evaluated the philosophical problems dealt with in his dissertation from the viewpoint of the self-consciousness. And this is what happened. Thus, for example, Epicurus is seen as representing the principle of the individual abstract self-consciousness, which could maintain its liberty only by turning its back on the world and preserving its internal specificity.[18] All the differences between Democritus and Epicurus are evaluated in accordance with this criterion and this rule applies to the entire development of philosophy.[19] But it would be an exaggeration to claim that here too Marx relies on Bauer, since Hegel had already regarded the sphere of self-consciousness as "the native land of truth" and asked to examine its developments through its attitude to the objective world.[20]

As regards the universal principle which is the foundation of the Marxian conception of the significance of the free and creative self-consciousness it is possible to ascertain characteristic Bauerian motifs, which include even almost identical formulations by Bauer and Marx, but as regards identification of stages in the development of the self-consciousness with the abstract, the concrete, the individual and the universal, Marx relied on Hegel, to at least the same degree that he was

[16] Idem.
[17] Ibid. p. 10; ET 13.
[18] Ibid. pp. 50–51; Dif 108.
[19] Ibid. pp. 52, 117–120.
[20] Phen 219–220, 241–267; PhM §§ 424, 425, 427–439.

influenced by Bauer. But one factor should be excluded from this picture: when Marx refers to an apocalyptic situation, preceding the war of the titans and constituting its basic premise, he unreservedly supports the Bauerian conception. In order to understand this issue more clearly, let us examine the Bauerian-Marxian idea more extensively.

In most of the letters which Bauer wrote to Marx, he argued that the present was bad, almost intolerable, because of the regime of spiritual-cultural and political repression, which forced the philosophical opposition to betray the objectives of the free self-consciousness. But this would pale in comparison with the heavy pressures and repressive measures soon to be employed which would force the critics of the existing situation to initiate a counter-attack. The clash between the two sides would be in the nature of a cosmic catastrophe, but its outcome was certain: the forces of progress would deal a decisive blow to the political and theological-apologetic reaction and would radically change the situation. "Here, as elsewhere, we will be in an oppositional position for a certain time to come, and there will shortly be a worsening of the situation. But people [. . .] have no idea of the increasing conflict between the state and science [. . .] between the state and philosophy [. . .] the catastrophe will be terrible and of tremendous dimensions, I would almost dare to say that it will be greater and more terrible than that which accompanied the birth of Christianity [. . .] but the fate of the future is too certain for us to be uncertain – even for a moment – of the outcome. If the opposition could finally prevail in France after a regime of such extreme reaction, then victory in a sphere in which we are dealing with apologetics, is more certain and will be more rapid. The hostile forces have come so close that one decisive blow will determine the issue. Those people who were concerned only for themselves when they exploited the state for their own needs, deserve our thanks, since by their deeds they prepared the ground for their final deposal."[21]

Similar ideas are to be found in abundance in other letters as well: "The rascals will be beaten in any case, even if governments defend them for ever [. . .] when you come to Bonn, it is possible that the place will become the focus of general interest: we can cause a crisis here with all its important implications. The struggle against the local Faculty of Theology will be expanded and will become more and more

---

[21] Bauer to Marx, 5 April 1840 (MEGA, I, i, ii, pp. 240–242).

serious. [. . .] I shall first of all prepare a long essay in which I will attack
government policy. The dogs can do nothing to us, they are afraid but
they are stubborn."[22] "Here and everywhere else the struggle is raging.
Act, so that you will be able to come and the new fight can be launched."[23]

These Bauerian ideas derive, of course, from his historiosophical conception; reaction, which limits the opportunities of the creative self-
consciousness can hold the reins of power only until the latter arrives
at the necessary level of maturity and no longer has need of the
patronage of the conservative state and its ally – the church. The
deposing of these forces by the philosophy of the general self-consciousness is preceded by a mighty struggle in which the latter prevails.

But Bauer does not only envisage this principle in its actual dimensions, and this is clearly demonstrated by the phrase on the upheavals
which accompanied the birth of Christianity in the Roman Empire.
The rule established by Bauer relates to all the turning points in the
development of the human self-consciousness which find outward expression in sharp clashes with old forms of consciousness.

In accordance with these principles, Marx claims that post-Aristotelian philosophy which existed in the shadow of totality, was torn
between total enslavement to a system (because of the analogy with
Hegel, Marx attributes to Aristotle the establishment of a system) and
the trend towards preservation of the principle of freedom in the sphere
of the individual self-consciousness, as noted above. Employing Bauerian language, Marx notes that at first what occurs is catastrophe, cosmic
confrontation which undermines the structure of the state, society and
culture, and immediately afterwards a new era commences, a time of
joy or grief according to the path chosen. And this is what he has to say
on this question: "Nor should we forget that the period that follows
such catastrophes is an iron one, happy if it is marked by titanic
struggles, lamentable if it is like the centuries that limp behind the good
periods of art and busy themselves with imitating in wax, plaster and
copper what sprang from Carrera marble. [. . .] Titan-like, however,
are the times that follow an implicitly total philosophy and its subjective forms of development. [. . .] Thus, Rome came after the Stoic,
Sceptic and Epicurean philosophies."[24]

Marx sees two possible ways of development after the crisis which

[22] Bauer to Marx, 31 March 1841 (Ibid. pp. 248–249).
[23] Bauer to Marx, 12 April 1841 (Ibid. p. 253).
[24] Ibid. I, 1, i, pp. 132–133; Ph 53.

exacerbate the conflicts in the sphere of thought until they find their solution. One is epigonal in nature, lowering the level of development of philosophy, the second is related to the struggle against the old; it symbolizes joy since, by essence, it expresses the new, life, real spiritual activity.[25] Post-Aristotelian philosophy took the path of the search for individual happiness and this was a relatively good choice in the given circumstances. Rome entered the philosophical arena after the three schools began to decline.

This statement with regard to Rome is very close in significance to Bauer's belief that "the worldwide rule of Rome and philosophy are movements of universal power, which tried to rise above the limitations of nature and the people – mankind and its consciousness,"[26] but at the same time there are differences in approach here between Bauer and Marx, since the former explains in this context that religion was then a total factor and therefore liberation of the self-consciousness could not occur outside it; mankind was obliged to go through the stage of unlimited alienation in order to arrive at full emancipation, while Marx points to Rome as an additional stage in the development of the self-consciousness, but does not tend to see in Christianity a positive factor in this context. With the exception of this case, all the identifying signs of Bauer's conception are to be found in Marx; the apocalyptic struggle, the happiness arising from the war against the old for the sake of the victory of free self-consciousness, the stages in the development of this consciousness with Rome serving as the turning point.

This similarity takes more real form when we take into consideration that Marx explicitly identifies Aristotle with Hegel, and the Young Hegelians with the self-consciousness schools of philosophy in Greece, and because of this comparison Roman history is repeated in modern times.[27] Against this background it is not hard to comprehend that all of Bauer's ideas on clashes between the philosophy of self-consciousness and the forces of the past, this entire apocalyptic picture is inferred in Marx as well, and this has been noted by commentators.[28] Furthermore, it should be emphasized that Marx, like Bauer, advocated a radical and uncompromising approach. It is reflected in Marx's theory that the compromisory and divided philosophers, who lived in the shadow of Aristotelian philosophy, tended to combine the elements of

[25] For this issue, cf. Hillmann: *Marx und Hegel. Von der Spekulation zur Dialektik*, p. 198.
[26] Cf. part one, ch. VIII, n. 15.
[27] For this issue, see Heinrich Popitz: *Der entfremdete Mensch*, Frankfurt/M. 1967, p. 60.
[28] See for example A. Cornu: *Karl Marx und Friedrich Engels. Leben und Werk*, vol. I, p. 168.

the old system with new ideas. As against this trend to conciliation and compromise Marx points to Themistocles, who demanded of the citizens of Athene, when the city was in danger of destruction, that they abandon it and found a new Athens in the sea, i.e. on completely new foundations.[29]

It is unthinkable to discuss the philosophical relationship between Marx and Bauer without touching on the problem of theory and praxis, as discussed in the dissertation. Marxological literature displays astounding lack of information on this issue, which results from the large degree of disregard for Bauer and his theories. With the exception of the phrase that "theory is the most tremendous praxis", which appears in one of Bauer's letters to Marx, nothing more concrete is known on this question. The situation deteriorates into absurdity when Hillmann, for example, analyses at length Cieszkowski's ideas on this issue, despite the total lack of certainty as to whether Marx was acquainted with his historiosophical essay at all, particularly before he wrote his dissertation. While it is well-known – on the evidence of Marx's many comments as well – that in those years Bauer and Marx enjoyed a very close personal and intellectual relationship, the former's ideas have not won the attention they deserve.

Let us first turn to the Marxian text. We read there the following statements: "It is a psychological law that the theoretical mind, having become free in itself, turns into practical energy. Emerging as *will* [. . .] it turns against wordly actuality which exists outside it. (It is important, however, from the philosophical point of view, to specify these aspects more clearly, because deductions about a philosophy's immanent determination and world-historical character can be made from the particular manner of this turn. [. . .]) The *praxis* of philosophy, however, is itself *theoretical*. It is *criticism* which measures individual existence against essence, particular actuality against the Idea. [. . .] The former inner light becomes a consuming flame, turning outward. The consequence, hence, is that the world's becoming philosophical is at the same time philosophy's becoming wordly. [. . .] This is the one side when we look at the matter *purely objectively*, as immediate realization of philosophy. But there is also a *subjective* side – actually only a different form of the other side. This is the *relation* of the *philosophical system* which is actualized to its intellectual supporters and to the individual self-consciousness in which its progress becomes manifest."[30]

[29] MEGA I, 1, i, p. 132.
[30] Ibid. 64–65; Ph 61–62.

A comparison of these ideas with Bauer's theories reveals surprising similarity,[31] and it is no exaggeration to state that the deciphering of Bauer's ideas is the key to the understanding of Marxian thought. For Bauer, the problem of the actualization of philosophy was related to the idea that spiritual overcoming of alienation is in the sphere of thought alone. The theory in itself is extremely important, since it enables man to consolidate, within the consciousness, an ideal of a better society, in which man is assured of "peace, tranquillity and self-balance."[32] But as long as philosophy contents itself with this, it is but "contemplation."[33] Therefore it strives to actualize its principles, not for its own sake but for the sake of mankind.[34] The first, immediate and possibly principal meaning of this fulfilment is criticism, negation of the existing from a radical viewpoint, and hence Bauer's well-known phrase regarding "the terrorism of true criticism". Criticism prepares the soil for the actualization of philosophy through introduction of the conditions which make it possible to translate the postulates of philosophy into the language of action. With criticism philosophy abandons – on the one hand – the intellectual battlefield, placing itself in confrontation with the irrational existing situation, and – on the other hand – is transformed into the theory of the future society. The self-consciousness contains the true forms of actuality at first ideally within itself[35] and subsequently causes their transplantation outwards. This phenomenon is related to practical activity, and without it there is no chance of implementing ideals. Against this background it is easy to understand Bauer's statement: "We think so far that our theory is praxis,"[36] since it includes "deposing the existing".

This trend of thought is to be found in Marx as well, when he points to philosophy's urge for actualization,[37] to the fact that "it enters into tension with everything else" (i.e. reality), or that "philosophy lies, in her realization, in opposition to the world."[38] Criticism plays a vital part in the realization of philosophical principles. It is no accident that Marx highlights its importance both through underlining in the manuscript and through linking it to the idea according to which existing reality is evaluated. That is to say that criticism is an instrument for changing

---

[31] For this issue, see also part one, ch. VIII, n. 103, 104, 106.
[32] Fr 39.
[33] Pos 81.
[34] Cf. part one, ch. VIII, n. 109, 110, 112.
[35] B 81.
[36] Ibid. p. 89.
[37] MEGA I, 1, i, p. 64; Ph 61–62.
[38] Ibid. p. 65; Ph 62.

the existing situation, which suffers from irrationality, whereas the philosophy which Marx advocates is permeated with the spirit of rationality. Like Bauer, Marx sees the self-consciousness as placing itself in opposition to existing reality, which Marx defines as "non-philosophical", namely lacking those qualities which characterized his own approach. It is clear that Marx, who advocates a criticial conception, is not merely regarding the confrontation, but trying to take an active part in it. His philosophical analysis is not analysis for its own sake; it is aimed at playing an important part in shaping another reality, differing from that now prevailing, which is grasped, to use Hegel's term, as bad, incidental, not corresponding to its own essence. Philosophy is the product of the self-consciousness, which activates its intellectual powers in order to lend new significance to actuality. In other words: the self-consciousness realizes the principles of philosophy and is therefore the force furthering the interests of the world – true evidence of Marx's philosophical dependence on Bauer.

Like Bauer, Marx claims that criticism is theoretical praxis or that praxis is essentially theoretical. Marx is referring to the unity of theory and praxis, since theory can only criticize but is unable to change reality in radical fashion. And it is clear – in the light of the notes – that Marx wanted to cancel religion which, in his day, played an important role in society and in intellectual life. He was not as extreme as Bauer, who saw in criticism "an infernal machine which can blow up the Christian state,"[39] but he shared the opinions voiced by Bauer in his 1841 essay, i.e. at the time when Marx was engaged in writing his dissertation, to the point where the *Posaune* was believed by many to have been written by the two in collaboration. Hence there can be no doubt that at that time Marx already favoured political changes, a trend which was to find expression several months later in articles he wrote in the *Rheinische Zeitung*. This also makes it clear why Marx claimed that the self-consciousness was directed against both reality and philosophy.[40] It was opposed to reality because of its flaws and omissions, which derive from its irrational and nonphilosophical organization. When Marx makes this claim against philosophy he may seem to be contradicting himself, since he has always praised philosophy and demanded its realization. But herein lies the key to the understanding of his criticism of philosophy; he is referring to that philosophy which believes that through theoretical criticism and the raising

---

[39] Pos 128.
[40] MEGA I, 1, i, p. 65; Ph 62.

of rational principles alone it is possible to arrive at a rational, better organized world. If he was referring to Hegelian philosophy (as is generally thought) then motifs are evident here which were to find fuller and more formulated expression in *Towards the Critique of Hegel's Philosophy of Right*, but this critique disregards those Hegelian ideas which contradict Marx's conception, such as that which sees philosophy as a "revolutionary principle" (Introduction to: *Lectures on the History of Philosophy*, 1829–30). But Marx, who was strongly influenced by Bauer, apparently failed to identify the conception of philosophy as pure theory with Hegel's approach. The author of the *Phenomenology* was represented by Bauer, as we know, as a republican and revolutionary and such an evaluation could not but have influenced Marx at the time. On the other hand, it is reasonable to assume that Marx attributed these qualities to positive philosophy, since in this context he notes that the self-consciousness is revealed to be twofold; on the one hand it is represented by the Liberal Party and on the other by positive philosophy. Various scholars have wondered at Marx's intentions on this issue and do not understand the issue. But it is not difficult to interpret Marx's theories if we start out from Bauer's remarks in the *Posaune*, where such philosophers as Fichte Junior, Fischer, Weisse and others are described as "positive philosophers,"[41] who know the truths of Christianity and impose on philosophy the task of substantiating the personal nature of God, the divine revelation, immortality etc. Bauer explicitly says that this philosophical system "should serve the kingdom of God, the church and the state."[42] The Liberal Party obviously symbolizes the Young Hegelians, of whom Marx was part, and therefore Marx identifies himself completely with it. He stresses that this party voices criticism, that it is the outward drive of philosophy, i.e. against existing reality, while the positivists advocate internalization of philosophy in the sphere of the self-consciousness and evade the use of praxis which is aimed at changing reality.

On the other hand there can be no doubt that the unity of theory and praxis is still seen by Marx within the framework of a conception similar to that of Bauer; theory serves as a torch illuminating the dark and complex paths of reality. Without it there is no possibility of practical constructive activity. On the other hand, theory remains barren and cannot achieve reasonable results if it does not serve as the basis for active behaviour in criticism of religion and the existing state.

---

[41] Pos 129–140.
[42] Ibid. p. 135.

Two facts should be emphasized in this context: *a*) theory comes before praxis, but it must appear practical and therefore the statements regarding the primacy of theory or praxis are not compatible with the Marxian approach at that time. What may be stated with a reasonable degree of certainty is that first it is necessary to complete the process of changing self-consciousness and only then should its objectives be fulfilled, i.e. intellectual change should be brought about before the radical changing of actuality. *b*) Marx is still remote from the communist conception of the praxis as social-revolutionary action, and does not pin his hopes for change on the proletariat; these hopes found expression only in the last section of *Towards the Critique of Hegel's Philosophy of Right. Introduction*. Like Bauer he favours the view that intellectuals, who grasp the needs of the self-consciousness and propose solutions for its enrichment, also act to further its objectives in the world, both through proposing political and antireligious ideas and through taking part in political publicistic activity. Bauer's slogan: "Philosophy should operate in politics and attack existing relations, when they conflict with the self-consciousness, and undermine them" is, according to all the signs, a theory which Marx accepts.

CHAPTER IV

BAUERIAN MOTIFS IN MARX'S CONCEPTION
OF ALIENATION

The problem of alienation in Marx's theory has, as a certain philosopher once put it, proven to be a gold-mine for many scholars. An examination of the number of scholarly studies which deal with the question of alienation in the works of Marx, particularly the early writings, proves this remark to be correct. Since the *Economic and Philosophic Manuscripts* and the *German Ideology* were first published, many articles have appeared which examine the various aspects of the problem of alienation: the political, the religious, the ideological, the social and the economic. The concept of alienation has, to a certain extent under the influence of these studies, invaded literature, sociology and psychology – which proves the wide, almost universal range of states of alienation and their human and social significance.

At the same time it should be emphasized that the large number of publications dealing with alienation and the great interest which scholars have displayed in this question, should not obscure the fact that the study of alienation within the framework of Marx's thought is still in its infancy, and that many problems have not yet been sufficiently elucidated. The question of the sources of Marx's concept of alienation is one of the most important, and perhaps the central, of these problems.

This may sound paradoxical. Did not Marx himself point to Hegel as his source of inspiration on this subject? Do the *Economic and Philosophic Manuscripts* leave any room for doubt regarding Marx's attempt to come to terms with Hegel's conception of alienation, as expressed in the *Phenomenology of Mind,* and particularly in those chapters on the lord and the bondsman and on the self-alienation of spirit? Is it not obvious that, in his struggle against the Hegelian system, Marx based himself on Feuerbach's transformation method, and in particular on those sections in which he exposed the speculative and idealistic character of Hegel's thought? And if all this is true, then we should deduce that Hegel and Feuerbach are the sole source and basis of Marx's analyses regarding the problem of alienation. Marcuse,[1] Löwith,[2] Bloch[3] and, subsequently, others arrived at this conclusion.[4]

But this problem is not as simple as it may appear at first glance. On the one hand, there is no room for doubt regarding Marx's dependence on the above-mentioned sources, on condition that we remember that Marx's philosophy was, almost from the first, original in character, and that the adaptation of certain Hegelian and other elements was carried out in accordance with Marx's system and that they were thus isolated from their original context becoming an integral part of a new conception, so that at times they constituted an essential contradiction to their former meaning (for example: the conception of the civil society in Hegelian and Marxian thought; the universality which Hegel attributes to the state and Marx to the proletariat; the character of labour and its meaning within the framework of these two theories etc.). On the other hand, it is not sufficient to single out Hegelian and Feuerbachian sources in order to solve the basic problems entailed in the question of alienation. The reason is that we cannot limit ourselves to a study of visible surface facts. We must strive to uncover the deep and hidden roots of the Marxian conception, and only then can we answer several questions raised in this context, which have not yet found their solution.

How can we explain, for example, that alienation, which Marx generally regards in his early work as an anthropological category, is nevertheless described as becoming more and more acute under the conditions of the civil society of the nineteenth century, as a phenomenon which came into being long before, but which reached its peak within the framework of the society in which Marx actually lived? There is another question, the essence of alienation, which is grasped by Marx as negative under all conditions and circumstances, to which there is no satisfactory answer within the limits of an explanation which sees Hegel and Feuerbach as the sources of Marxian theory.

---

[1] *Neue Quellen zur Grundlegung des historischen Materialismus.* Die Gesellschaft, vol. VII/ 1932. Recently published in *Ideen zu einer kritischen Theorie der Gesellschaft*, Frankfurt/M. 1969, pp. 22–30, 42–54; Marcuse: *Reason and Revolution*, pp. 22–30, 42–54, 235–285.

[2] *From Hegel to Nietzsche*, pp. 295–304; *Man's Self-alienation in Early Writings of Marx*, Social Research 21/1954.

[3] *Das Prinzip Hoffnung*, vol. I, pp. 289–318; *Subjekt-Objekt. Erläuterungen zu Hegel*, pp. 408–411.

[4] Gajo Petrović: *Marx in the Midtwentieth Century*. New York, Anchor Books, Doubleday & Co. 1967, pp. 136–137; Jean Hyppolite: *Studies on Marx and Hegel*. London, Heinemann 1969, pp. 113, 130, 133; Henry J. Koren: *Marx and the Authentic Man*, Pittsburg, Duquesne University Press 1967, pp. 75–78.

In order to understand better why Hegel represents a standpoint remote from that of Marx on this question, it is necessary to survey his views on the issue, however briefly.

Hegel attributes alienation to the self-alienated spirit which he identifies – apparently under the influence of Rousseau – with education, formative development and culture (he uses the term *Bildung* which has various meanings, in accordance with the context or intention). This spirit appears on two planes, with dialectical reciprocal influence between them; on the individual plane as consciousness, self-consciousness and reason, and on the plane of objective actuality, as the objective spirit operating in the state, society and world history. The process of cognition of the world and its *Bildung*, depicted in the *Phenomenology*, on which Marx relies, is both an individual process – like the individual conciousness – and a universal one, in accordance with Hegel's views on the activity of the spirit in the three spheres – subjective, objective and absolute. The consciousness is the starting point for Hegel's analyses, externalizing itself in objects, imagining that the world of substance is totally independent; furthermore, that it is a totally different world from itself, or as Hegel puts it, "otherness" (*Anderssein*). But because of its acquisition of knowledge of the nature of objects and their essence, the consciousness absorbs these objects into itself and returns to itself as an enriched consciousness, which has taken over all those objects with which it has established contact during the process of revelation in otherness, in the world of objects. In other words: the subject experiences various states of externalization and alienation, overcomes its illusory and incorrect opinions on the world and eventually arrives at absolute knowledge of itself and its place in the world. But, as noted, the spirit is also revealed in the universal-objective sphere in which it is grasped as an objective spirit, and it is externalized in culture, society etc. Thus it becomes a world alien and even hostile to itself. Thanks to its energetic and protracted efforts the spirit emerges successfully from its bitter and tragic experiences (such as despotic-feudalist rule, the domination of the Catholic church, the horrors of the French Revolution etc.), until it achieves identification with universal actuality. Since, for Hegel, liberty is the substance of the spirit, it is easy for us to understand why philosophy as absolute knowledge became a demonstration of intellectual freedom, history became progress towards consciousness of freedom, and the state – as actualization of the rational idea of universality – became the full freedom of the individual.[5]

[5] Cf. Phen 457–461, 509–518, 561–610.

Hence, in Hegel the human spirit overcomes alienation, both through the knowledge of the absolute (the spirit, the eternal truth, God) in the sphere of art, religion and in more perfect fashion – in philosophy, and in the historic process of the development of culture and the state. As against this conception, Marx grasps alienation as the essence of the existing society and the problem of its cancellation is linked to processes which will occur in the *future* so as to put an end to its existence. It transpires from this that there were additional sources of inspiration apart from the Hegelian ones. This conclusion is borne out by the fact, which various scholars have already noted, that for Hegel the process of alienation is vital and essential for the shaping of reality and its cognition and is of positive significance.[6] Without it the spirit cannot constitute a creative force, and the subject cannot bridge the gap between it and the objective world. We may concur therefore with the opinion of Garaudy that "alienation corresponds to culture in the widest sense of the world, it is identical with all of man's activity from technical skill to poetry, from economics to religion, from politics to philosophy, in short with all action. Through it the individual is elevated – through negation of his self – to the universal. Thanks to it the subject endows itself with substantial reality."[7]

In the light of the above it is easy to understand that alienation exists in order to arrive at its own negation, or, in Hegel's words: "the alienation will be found to alienate itself, and the whole will take all its contents back into the notion."[8] We should not deduce from this that Hegel sees alienation as always playing a positive part. He was aware of the negative manifestations accompanying the process of externalization and alienation, such as the view of the human element and the products of human activity as something alien to man and even hostile to him. This trend is reflected in the early writings in his attitude to the positive religion, which he sees as coercive, authoritative, conflicting with the nature of man and with reason,[9] and in the writings of the Jena period, in which he discussed, inter alia, problems of political economy and society, and stated that man had become the slave of his work: "The more he conquers it [nature] the more powerless he himself

---

[6] Marcuse: *Reason and Revolution*, pp. 73–90; Jean Hyppolite: *Studies on Marx and Hegel*, pp. 89–90.

[7] Roger Garaudy: *Dieu est mort*, Paris 1962, p. 262.

[8] Phen 517.

[9] ThJ 139, 143, 145, 165. See also: Walter Kaufmann, *Hegel. A Reinterpretation*, pp. 36–37; H. S. Harris: *Hegel's Development Toward the Sunlight 1770–1801*, Oxford, At the Clarendon Press 1972, pp. 237–243, 297–298, 317–319, 403–406.

becomes. [...] The more mechanized labour becomes, the less value it has, and the more the individual must toil."[10] "A great many people are condemned to stupifying, unhealthy and precarious labour in factories, manufactures, mines etc."[11] It may be determined safely in accordance with this approach that individuals are under the control of economic forces which are but the products of their own activity.[12]

The negative aspects of the alienation process were described in the *Phenomenology* as well: when Hegel analyses the unhappy consciousness – which, historically speaking, appears as Judaism and as pre-Protestant Christianity – he exposes its torn and divided character and its nothingness in the face of God, to whom it attributes its activity, thereby depriving itself of confidence in its own destiny. In this context Hegel claimed that "instead of returning out of its activity into itself and instead of having confirmed itself as a fact for itself, consciousness reflects back this process of action into the other extreme which is thereby represented as purely universal, as an absolute might from which the movement in every direction started."[13]

The negative motif in the self-alienation of the spirit appears in Hegel in his view of self-consciousness as opposed to the world, which it sees as alien and as standing apart, without the self-consciousness having access to it or a part in it. According to Hegel: "That spirit finds its content over again in the form of reality that is just as impenetrable as itself, and the world here gets the characteristic of being something external, negative to self-consciousness."[14]

Marx could not have been acquainted with the content of Hegel's early writings, which were published only at the beginning of the 20th century, but it is evident that he disregarded the negative aspects of the process of alienation in the Hegelian conception. And what is more, he criticizes Hegel's view of alienation as an essentially positive process.[15]

As noted above, Feuerbach's attitude to alienation is also critical rather than negative.[16] The question of alienation is related to his view

[10] Jen I, 237.
[11] Ibid., vol. II, p. 232.
[12] For this issue, see Marcuse: *Reason and Revolution*, 77–81; M. Friedrich: *Philosophie und Ökonomie beim jungen Marx*, pp. 124–133; Shlomo Avineri: *Hegel's Theory of the Modern State*, Cambridge University Press 1972, pp. 91–98; Raymond Plant: *Hegel*, London, Allen & Unwin 1973, pp. 113–114.
[13] Phen 166.
[14] Ibid. p. 509.
[15] MEGA I, 1, iii, pp. 155, 158; Ph 320, 323.
[16] See part one, ch. VIII, n. 54, 58.

of religion, and it is clear that religion plays a positive role in human life, as long as man has not found his essence within himself. To a large extent Feuerbach's conception of alienation is close to that of Hegel, when he claims that alienation is necessary in order for man to arrive at the view of himself as the arbiter of his own fate. Elsewhere we have cited sufficient evidence to illustrate this theory, but it is worth adding Feuerbach's theory in his own words. In the appendix to *The Essence of Christianity* he writes: "Why does man grasp his essence outside himself, and why does he cause its reification? I ask: why does man compose poems? Why does he humanize his own feelings? Why does he submit theories and grasp them in their activity? [...] Why does he embody thoughts and principles in signs and picture – he is creating them in his head, so why should he transplant them outwards?"[17]

The very phrasing of these question is symptomatic. Feuerbach believed that alienation is the most important means of realizing man's creative powers. From this point of view religion resembles other forms of human creativity: poetry, world outlooks etc, without which it is impossible to contemplate human activity. In order to complete the picture, let us quote Feuerbach, in *The Essence of Christianity*: "In religion man seeks contentment: religion is his highest good. But how could he find consolation and peace in God if God were an essentially different thing? How can I share the peace of a being if I am not of the same nature with him? If his nature is different from mine, his peace is essentially different, it is no peace for me. [...] Thus, if man feels peace in God, he feels it only because in God he first attains his true nature, because here, for the first time, he is with himself. [...] The grand characteristic of religion and of the Christian religion especially is that it is thoroughly anthropotheistic; the exclusive love of man for himself; the exclusive self-affirmation of the human nature."[18] It is abundantly clear that it was not from this source that Marx could have drawn inspiration when he attributed to alienation solely negative and non-human qualities. We are left with Bruno Bauer, and he is indeed an unfailing source of ideas which undoubtedly bear affinity to Marx's theory of alienation.

It is, of course, possible to evaluate Bauer's influence on Marx's view of alienation from another aspect. We have seen that Bauer exerted significant influence over the consolidation of Marx's opinion on religion, and criticism of religious alienation is the archetype of criticism of

[17] SW I, 367.
[18] E 45–46.

all forms of alienation in human life. Marx himself gave expression to this conception when he noted that "criticism of religion is the premise of all criticism."[19] This statement gives him away; it attests to his dependence on Bauer even in formulation of the idea of the primacy of criticism of religion over all other forms of criticism. There is no contradiction between this idea and Marx's belief that religion should be criticized more within a critique of the political situation than the political situation within a critique of religion,[20] for, in his intellectual way of thinking, Marx commenced with criticism of religion, moved on to critique of philosophy and at a later stage to critique of politics; from this viewpoint the early criticism served as the basis and premise for the later critique. On the other hand, Marx, when editor of the *Rheinische Zeitung*, accepted the primacy of political criticism – because of both censorship conditions and fundamental motifs – but, at the same time, did not neglect criticism of religion. On the contrary: in all his attempts to abolish social and economic alienation, he noted that the starting point for his critical analyses was critique of religious alienation. In order to illustrate this theory, it is worth citing some of the many statements in the *Economic and Philosophic Manuscripts*, in which Marx emphasized that the mechanism of realizing alienation in the sphere of labour corresponded completely to what occurred in the process of religious alienation. Inter alia, he writes: "The more the worker exerts himself, the more powerful becomes the alien objective world which he shapes against himself, the poorer he and his inner world become, the less is it that belongs to him. It is the same in religion. The more man attributes to God the less he retains in himself."[21] Elsewhere he writes: "Every self-alienation of man, from himself and from nature, appears in the relationship which he postulates between other man and himself and nature. Thus religious self-alienation manifests itself necessarily in the relation of laity to priest, or also to a mediator, since we are here now concerned with the spiritual world. In the practical real world, self-alienation can manifest itself only in the practical real relationships to other men."[22] In order to complete the picture, let us add an additional quotation from Marx in *Towards the Critique of Hegel's Philosophy of Right*: "Just as it is not religion that created man but man who creates religion, so it is not the constitution that creates the people but the people which creates the

---

[19] MEGA I, 1, i, p. 607; Ph 249.
[20] Ibid. I, 1, ii, p. 286; ET 53.
[21] Ibid. I, 1, iii, p. 83; Ph 289–290.
[22] Ibid. p. 91; Ph 297.

constitution. In a certain respect democracy is to all other forms of the state what Christianity is to all other religions."[23] Therefore political alienation is grasped as operating in accordance with the mechanism of action of religious alienation: alienation is raised to the level of totality and creates the conditions for its total cancellation, a phenomenon defined by Marx as follows: "Monarchy is the fullest expression of this alienation. The republic is the negation of this alienation within its own sphere."[24]

Marx, as we know, eventually gave up using the term *Entfremdung* (but returned to it in *Grundrisse*) and in *The German Ideology* placed it within quotation marks. Nevertheless Marx was to persist in his theory on the common traits of the process of fetishism (which, for him, took the place of alienation) in the sphere of religion and socio-economic life. There is conclusive evidence that Marx upheld this belief all his life. This trend finds expression in the *Capital*, from which the following statement is taken: "As is the case with man in the sphere of religion, where he dominated by the product of his own thought, so in capitalistic production he is controlled by the product of his own efforts."[25]

It is clear from this that religious alienation serves as the archetype of other forms of alienation and that through it Marx arrived at understanding their structure.[26]

If this is true, then he should have been concerned with the negative qualities when trying to clarify the essence of alienation in work and in social life. And this is in fact what happened. The social forces ruling man's life, which are the fruit of his own activities, are represented by Marx as hostile, non-human, damaging his humanity, and alienation in work is expressed in similar fashion: in negation of the human character of work, as the worker becomes crude, barbaric, deprived of value and the slave of nature.[27] According to this conception work creates crippled and flawed creatures: this is exactly the idea which Marx took over from Bauer, who regarded the properties of religion as a series of flaws, weaknesses and infirmities in mankind. It is not feasible to assume that Feuerbachian influences underly this conception – taking into consideration the fact that the product of alienation is monstrous

---

[23] Ibid. I, 1, i, p. 434; Cr 30.
[24] Ibid. p. 436; Cr 32.
[25] K I, 653.
[26] For this issue, see Calvez: *La pensée de Karl Marx*, p. 92; Robert Tucker: *Philosophy and Myth in Karl Marx*, Cambridge University Press 1971, pp. 137–140.
[27] MEGA I, 1, iii, pp. 84–86; Ph 293–297.

and the exact opposite of authentic human qualities, or, to be more exact, what we have here is total dehumanization of man.

Bauer influenced Marx on yet another issue. Hegel's conception of alienation is grasped in accordance with the exegetic tendencies of Bauer, who attributed to Hegel subjectivism and negation of substance. The difference between Bauer and Marx is reflected in the evaluation of this fact – Bauer believed that he was deciphering the authentic content of Hegel's theory and made this principle the foundation of his theory, namely he saw himself as the continuer of Hegel, whereas Marx attacked Hegel precisely because of his erroneous conception, in other words, took a negative view of the Bauerian subjectivism attributed to Hegel.

The process of alienation described by Hegel in the *Phenomenology* is seen by Marx as "the history of the production of abstract, logical, speculative thought". Marx notes in this context: "The alienation thus forming the real interest and transcendence of this externalization is the opposition of *in itself* and *for itself*, of consciousness and self-consciousness, of *object and subject* – that is, the opposition within thought itself between abstract thinking and sensuous actuality [...]."[28]

Marx criticizes Hegel since he alleges that for the latter real forms of human alienation, such as property, religion, political rule etc. are grasped as pure forms of thought and consequently alienation is attributed to abstract-philosophical thought and not to actual man, who lives his life on earth.[29] Thus, according to Marx, Hegel transformed the alienation of real-empirical man into the alienation of the self-consciousness. This mystification finds expression subjectively speaking in the total identification of man with the self-consciousness, and objectively – in the identification of alienation with thinghood (*die Dingheit*). In this Marx remained consistent to the end. He believed that "*human nature, man,* is equivalent to *self-consciousness.* All alienation of human nature is thus *nothing* but the *alienation* of *self-consciousness.* [...] The *externalization of self-consciousness* establishes *thinghood.* Since man equals self-consciousness, his externalized objective nature or *thinghood* is equivalent to externalized self-consciousness [...] thinghood can only be externalized self-consciousness."[30] Hence Marx's confidence that Hegelian alienation is "only appearance of the alienation of actual human nature", and thinghood is not real but "a

28 Ibid. pp. 154–155; Ph 319–320.
29 Ibid. pp. 155–156; Ph 320–321.
30 Ibid. p. 159; Ph 323–324.

mere artifice established by self-consciousness." It is not surprising in this context that Marx employs Bauer's remarks from the *Posaune* on substance (which for Marx became thinghood): "It is clear that thinghood thus completely lacks *independence, essentiality*. [...] And what is established, is only a confirmation of the act of establishing which for a moment, but only a moment, fixes its energy as product and *apparently* gives it the role of an independent, actual nature."[31] To Marx's mind there exists the same attitude towards the problem of subject-object relationship in Hegel, which was characteristic of Bauer's understanding of Hegel: the substance disappears and only the self-consciousness remains and it creates the world with all its differences. Marx's criticism of Hegel on this point suffers from the same flaws as Bauerian interpretation. The reconciliation of thought with the objective world is the objective of philosophy, according to Hegel, but this reconciliation is not grasped as the movement of pure thought alone, as Marx claimed, but also as the movement of objects. Hegel displays no tendency to cancel objectivity within subjectivity and to grasp the world of things as nullity, as Marx says. Rather the contrary: as we have seen in our chapter on Bauer as a commentator on Hegel, the object is grasped as subject and vice versa – the subject as object, and this is how Hegel displays his interest in the empirical world of objects, on the one hand and bows to reason and its cognition on the other. Hence the objective world does not disappear in order to yield place to the self-consciousness and the relations between subject and object should not be reduced to the theory that objects are established by the subject, since the subject is also shaped by the objective world. It is true that the subject wins the objects through absolute knowledge, but he wins them as things, and thinghood is not totally cancelled by this process.

Bauerian ideas are intensively evident in Marx's first polemic essay against Bauer, *On the Jewish Question*, not only in the characterization of Judaism – but also in the conception of current political alienation and in the relations between religion and the state. This is an interesting fact if we take into consideration that Marx heaped abuse on Bauer and differed with him on all the question under discussion.

According to Marx, the banishing of religion from the state to the private sphere (i.e. separation of the state and religion) cannot solve the basic problems of civil society (i.e. the bourgeoisie), such as selfish-

[31] Idem; Ph 324–325.

ness, the accumulation of capital at the expense of others, social and economic oppression, etc. Marx's objections refer to two points: *a*) the absence of separation between religion and the state is only one of the components of the democratic political revolution which put an end to the feudal structure (or the vestiges of feudalism) and to absolutism. The democratic changes include many far-reaching alterations: the eradication of corporations, guilds and feudal privileges and of the superior status of a certain religion as the state religion, the expansion of voting rights, recognition of the rights of the man and citizen. *b*) At the same time all these changes cannot solve the problems of political and social alienation, anchored in the selfishness of man, in self-advantage, in oppression and exploitation. Marx's conclusion on this problem is expressed in the following words: "Feudal society was dissolved into its foundation, into *man*. But into man as he actually was the foundation of that society, into *egoistical* man. This *man*, the member of civil society, is now the basis and presupposition of the *political* state. He is recognized as such by the state in the rights of man. But the freedom of egoistic man and the recognition of this freedom are rather the recognition of the *unbridled* movement of the spiritual and material elements forming the content of his life. Thus man was not freed from religion; he received religious freedom. He was not freed from property. He received freedom of property. He was not freed from the egoism of trade, but received freedom to trade."[32]

Only human emancipation can put an end to the dismemberment and splitting of man who lives a double life within the framework of bourgeois society: as a citizen of the state and as a member of civil society. It can do this through the elimination of private property and of the rule of selfishness and self-advantage.

The polemical aspects of *On the Jewish Question* are obvious. But there is an additional trend in this essay, which has as yet remained unremarked: Marx had need of the Bauerian ideas of alienation so as to develop his theory regarding the existence of alienation and its exacerbation within the framework of bourgeois society.

Bauer identified the Christian state with the feudal-absolutist state. The latter is based on the negation of freedom of expression and conscience. It enjoys longevity, thanks to the granting of legitimation to the status of Christianity as the ruling religion, it cooperates with it, oppresses man and does not permit him to be free and to live a human life. Christian alienation — as had already been noted — was much

32 Ibid. I, 1, i, p. 598; Ph 240.

stronger than any kind of alienation which preceded it in history, because it penetrated into all spheres of life and totally dominated man. Marx takes over the Bauerian argumentation, but – wonder of wonders! – that which in the Bauerian conception was one of the distinguishing features of Christianity and the clerical-monarchical regime, is attributed by Marx to the democratic-bourgeois state, which has proclaimed the representational-parliamentary regime, civil equality and other democratic freedoms and separation of religion and state.

Marx does not regard the Christian state as an earthly state, human in its reality, but as a chimerical state in which state is negated by religion, which stands above it and wishes to rule in its stead. At the very best cooperation emerges between the two for the perpetuation of Christianity and the rule of the Christian monarch, emphasis being placed not on the monarch but on the Christian aspect or, as Marx puts it: "The so-called Christian state is a Christian denial of the state, not in any way the political actualization of Christianity. The state that still professes Christianity in the form of religion does not profess it in political form because is still behaves religiously towards religion – that is, it is not the actual expression of the human basis of religion since it still deals with the unreality and imaginary form of this human core. The so-called Christian state is an imperfect one, which treats Christianity as the supplement and sanctification of its imperfection."[33]

Regarding the state which recognizes the Christian religion as the state religion and grants it special rights, Marx employs the term "the so-called Christian state" (*der sogenannte christliche Staat*) but the term "Christian state" is attributed to a state of a totally different type. We can safely say that this term – which is of such great importance in Bauer's conception – undergoes a process of transplantation in Marx, which is quite astounding. Marx explains to the astonished reader that, of all states, it is that which proclaims freedom of religion and conscience and separates itself from religious institutions, which is the complete Christian state: "Indeed, the perfected Christian state is not the so-called Christian state acknowledging Christianity as its foundation in the state religion and excluding all others. It is rather the atheistic state, the democratic state, the state that relegates religion to the level of other elements of civil society."[34] In accordance with this view, the so-called Christian state, i.e. the imperfect state, treats religion politically and politics religiously. In contrast, the democratic state can

[33] Ibid. p. 587; Ph 228.
[34] Idem.

ignore considerations emanating from the interests of Christianity as a
church organization and an establishment, but it has need of religion as
an ideological seal, even if this be religion in its private and non-state
form. But what is more important: the Bauerian conception of the
alienation of Christianity thus undergoes an additional transformation
and takes on the form of the bourgeois society with all its contradictions
and tensions. After Marx identifies true Christianity with the democratic state, he identifies this state, to a great extent, with the relations
prevailing in the civil society of his times. In this matter he relies both
on the Bauerian thesis that Judaism and Christianity are religions of
dismemberment and egoism and on Hegel's interpretations of the
structure of civil society in *The Philosophy of Right*. In this context
Marx writes: "The members of the political state are religious by
virtue of the dualism between individual life and species life, between
the life of civil society and political life. They are religious inasmuch
as man regards as his true life the political life remote from his actual
individuality, inasmuch as religion is here the spirit of civil society
expressing the separation and withdrawal of man from man. Political
democracy is Christian in that it regards man – not merely one but
every man – as *sovereign* and supreme. But this means man in his
uncivilized and unsocial aspect, in his fortuitous existence and just as
he is, corrupted by the entire organization of our society, lost and
alienated from himself oppressed by inhuman relations and elements."[35]

Man, in his uncivilized and unsocial aspect as an egoist, who regards
himself as the sovereign and others as the source of his income and his
life (a motif developed in *Economic and Philosophic Manuscripts*) is
the true Christian man. So as to explain his views on this subject,
Marx first attributes to the Jew and to Judaism certain qualities which
fit in with Bauer's conception of Judaism. There can be no doubt
that Marx, who was Bauer's close friend at that time, read Bauer's
essay against Hengstenberg, and utilized the Bauerian system for
his own purposes. The accepted story that Feuerbach was the first
to lay the foundations of the conception of Judaism as the religion
of practice and the worship of Mammon and that he thus influenced
Marx decisively has nothing to support it, if we take into consideration
the fact that Feuerbach's book *The Essence of Christianity* was published in 1841, two years after the publication of Bauer's essay. Only lack
of acquaintance with Bauer's work can explain the view that Feuerbach was the source of Marx's views on the subject.

[35] Ibid. p. 590; Ph 231.

Marx also follows Bauer in his view of the other qualities of Judaism: hostility towards theory, art, science and progress in the history of society. It is interesting to note that the *Jewish Question*, the book against which Marx is arguing in his essay, is wholly devoted to a pseudo-historiosophical analysis of the situation of the Jews in the world, in the light of their opposition to the progress of science, the arts and human society.

Marx transplants the qualities of Judaism to the sphere of Christianity so as to prove that it is Christianity which is suited to serve as the religion of a bourgeois society based on commercialization, egotism and self-advantage. To his mind, Judaism was not capable of building a new world since its principles were too abstract, and it was obliged to wait for the creation of a society which would enable it to realize its essence. When this society was created there was no longer any need for Judaism, and its place was taken by Christianity, which accepts the views of Judaism but differs from it from the point of view of its universality and cosmopolitism and its formal attitude towards God. There exists an inter-relation between Christianity, which is but a continuation of Judaism, and the civil (bourgeois) society, the common denominator being the disintegration of the society into individual atoms, i.e. individuals on the one hand and the conception of them as egoistical creatures by their very nature, on the other.

The artificial construction of both Judaism and Christianity enables Marx to describe alienation as a basic quality of bourgeois society. At first he argues, repeating Bauer's phrase verbatim, that what is valid in the so-called Christian state is not man but alienation; and he then notes that alienation reaches perfection in the Christian world, that is, the capitalist world.[36] These are already typical echoes of the motif of the *Economic and Philosophic Manuscripts*, as Marx writes that Christianity (read: capitalism) "had completed the aliention of man from himself and from nature."[37] And, furthermore, Marx also notes that "money is the alienated essence of man's labour and life, and this alien essence dominates him and he worships it."[38] These conclusions are clearly a springboard to the view of bourgeois society as the height of alienation of man from himself and from nature, and the need to conduct an analysis of alienated labour.

A most important role is allotted in Marx's early writings to the

---

[36] Ibid. pp. 590, 597–599; Ph 231, 238–240.
[37] Ibid. p. 605; Ph 247.
[38] Ibid. p. 603; Ph 246.

Bauerian idea of alienation and its cancellation as the criterion for periodization of human history. At this point it is worth repeating some of Bauer's views on this issue and dwelling on them, because of the importance of this subject for the understanding of Marx's thought.

According to Bauer, alienation, in its Christian form, causes total dehumanization of man, who is entirely under the sway of external forces, over which he has no control whatsoever. What is more: alienation becomes total, penetrates all the areas of human behaviour and mainly his thought and consciousness. This totality of the consciousness is the basic premise for the universal cancellation of all forms of alienation. Bauer emphasizes that when man finds the daring to tackle alienation as a whole and to bring freedom to all spheres of life, the struggle for freedom will end in such a way that there will never again be need to engage in such a struggle.

In accordance with this view history is split into two periods: past and future. The past was under the sign of man's self-alienation and alienation. This state of affairs has continued into the present, but there is now a firm basis for the changing of values and for far-reaching changes, which will create a situation in which alienation will yield place to humanity of a new kind, which is not enslaved to external forces outside man and above him. This change cannot come about without upheavals. There is need of a serious crisis and of a spiritual and political revolution, in order to bring about the longed-for change. There is a distinct eschatological tone in Bauer's statement and this is not surprising since he was convinced that his intellectual activity symbolized the last stage of the fight against alienation for removal of all restraints from man's free activity.

Bauer's conception of alienation as the basis of human periodization, the division of history into the era of alienation and the era of lack of alienation and of freedom, the view of philosophy as aimed at bringing redemption to mankind – all these ideas made a profound impression on Marx's intellectual development. The background for this was the intellectual climate of Germany in the early forties, the tightening of censorship and the introduction of terror by the authorities,[39] which led people to believe that the extremism of the authorities would bring about extremist response on the part of the opposition and that there would be a frontal clash between the forces of progress and of reaction.

[39] Cf. Reinhart Seeger: *Friedrich Engels*, Halle 1935, pp. 103–106.

In such an atmosphere Marx could not rely on Hegel, who, as he saw it, had transformed the constitutional monarchy, i.e. an empirical fact at that time, into a "metaphysical axiom"[40] and presented the estates as the embodiment of political consciousness and particularist strata consciousness, as the synthesis between the state as universality and civil society as particularity. For Marx on the other hand "the estate [...] separates man from his universal nature, it makes him an animal."[41] Thus Hegel, who accepted the principle of monarchy (though in moderate constitutional form) as an axiom and took a positive view of alienation, could not serve as Marx's source for inspiration, and this is certainly also true of Feuerbach, who never engaged in politics and represented an ambivalent stand on alienation.

There were apparently certain elements of Bauer's thought which – at least temporarily – attracted the attention of Marx and evidently influenced him, such as the eschatological desire to ensure the happiness of man and of the entire human race through the realization of philosophy and cancellation of alienation, and the view of all of human history as the preparatory stage for the implementation of this task. In *Towards the Critique of Hegel's Philosophy of Right. Introduction* there is evidence that Marx wanted the postulate of human happiness to be realized through the cancellation of religion – in the spirit of Bauer. Marx points there to the need to put an end to religion as illusory happiness in order to supply true happiness. According to Marx, the immediate task of philosophy is to remove the threat of alienation hanging over the heads of mankind and he includes in the concept of alienation both religions and secular manifestations. The abolition of alienation is the beginning of a new era, in which men will be free, arbiters of their fate and masters of themselves.[42]

Marx reiterates these motifs in the *Manuscripts*, with certain serious modifications, his main ideas appearing in the form of economic categories, such as private property and its abolition, production etc. But here too, as Tucker correctly noted, the economic analysis is still secondary while the view of alienation as the foundation of human history and the need for radical change of reality, meaning the abolition of alienation and commencement of a new era – take pride of place. Marx does not hide the teleological trend of the historical conception: alienated man can comprehend the meaning of events only in the light

[40] MEGA I, 1, i, p. 428. Cr 25.
[41] Ibid. p. 499; Cr 82.
[42] Ibid. p. 607–608, 614–615; Ph 249–251, 256–258.

of the realization of his true essence in the future, i.e. through taking his fate into his own hands he will be capable of understanding that his entire past did not, in fact, belong to him. According to this, all of history, – according to Bauer's view – is seen as the history of preparation, and it should not therefore surprise us to learn that Marx employs the term *Vorbereitungsgeschichte*, which Bauer used to denote the same objective which appears in Marx: preparation of freedom and the eradication of mankind's alienation.[43]

History takes on significance because of its final objective. Marx sees in the existing forms of life a characteristic expression of the dehumanization of mankind and he demands the humanization of life through the cancellation of alienation. The idea of cancellation from alienation is the central idea of the *Economic and Philosophic Manuscripts*, and one can agree with Popitz, who writes: "Eschatological philosophy stands in first place and the empirical tendency has not yet paved its way. [. . .] The historiosophical interest [which Marx reveals] is generally lost as long as the problem is not directly related to the idea of emancipation."[44] The reason is clear: Marx is still under the spell of the Bauerian construction and therefore the cancellation of private property and the communist idea to a large extent serve an *a priori* aim, which basically does not lack eschatological elements, while the empirical analysis – typical of Marx's later writings – is aimed at proving the justness of the objective.

Bauer's conception of the alienation afflicting man since the beginning of his historical existence, took root in an additional issue in Marx's philosophy. This was the question of the relations between alienated work and private property. Marx, who adopted Bauer's idea of the primacy of alienation over social factors and advocates the Bauerian theory that alienation takes first place both as regards its universal significance and historically speaking, explicitly identifies alienated life with alienated work,[45] and claims that alienated work precedes private property. "Alienated labor is the direct cause of private property. The downfall of one is necessarily the downfall of the other."[46] And elsewhere he writes: "*Private property* is thus product, result and necessary consequence of *externalized labor*. [. . .] *Private property* thus is derived, through analysis, from the concept of *ex-*

---

[43] Ibid. I, 1, iii, pp. 114, 123; Ph 304–305, 311–312.
[44] *Der entfremdete Mensch*, p. 141.
[45] MEGA I, 1, iii, p. 91; Ph 297.
[46] Ibid. p. 92; Ph 299.

ternalized labor, that is, *externalized man,* alienated labor, alienated life and *alienated* man."[47]

Among scholars dealing with the question of alienation in Marx's thought there is an almost general tendency to evaluate Marx's views with the aid of his socio-economic system of a later period, and this has caused considerable misunderstandings. Thus, for example, it has been claimed that alienated labour leads to the creation of capital and accumulation of property alone and that Marx was not referring to the institution of private property,[48] while others have suggested that Marx was referring only to capitalist property[49] and in this case it is clear that alienated labour had existed previously: in pre-capitalist economic regimes.

---

[47] Ibid. p. 91; Ph 297–298.
[48] Richard Schacht: *Alienation,* New York, Doubleday 1970, p. 108.
[49] Bertell Ollman: *Alienation. Marx's Concept of Man in Capitalist Society.* Cambridge University Press 1971, p. 159.

CHAPTER V

THE IMPACT OF BAUERIAN IDEAS ON MARX'S CONCEPTION OF IDEOLOGY

Scholars studying ideology in general and Marx's conception of ideology in particular, tend – in accordance with the accepted approach to the early writings – to highlight those sources originating with Hegel or Feuerbach, and to ignore all other ideological factors. It is evident that Hegel exerted considerable influence over the formulation of Marx's ideas, both in the positive aspect – the continuation of Hegelian motifs in Marx, and in the critical sense – through negation of Hegelian ideas by Marx. This does not apply when we try to attribute to Feuerbach influence over Marx's concept of ideology. Thus, for example, Barth claimed that the reduction of theology to anthropology, the critique of religion, demand for the cancellation of alienation, the postulate of the realization of human essence, as formulated by Feuerbach were accepted by Marx with "unlimited admiration" and had a decisive influence on him.[1] Others are of the same opinion.[2] We have proved above that the critique of religion and the view of man as the creator of religious principles were common to all the Young Hegelians, that Bauer was immeasurably more radical than Feuerbach in his conception of religion, that he voiced harsh criticism of the existing state and formulated radical political principles while Feuerbach devoted no attention to politics, a fact which Marx protested vehemently. But what is much more important: Feuerbach's principles of religious criticism are completely irrelevant to the problem of ideology as phrased by Marx, and it is surprising that the scholars have not noticed this. In order to illustrate this problem, it is not even necessary to arrive at Marx's *Theses on Feuerbach*, which contain strong criticism of Feuerbachian ideas. If we disregard the theory which finds sharper and

---

[1] Hans Barth: *Wahrheit und Ideologie*, Zürich 1945, pp. 98–107.
[2] George Lichtheim: *The Concept of Ideology and other Essays*, New York, Random House 1967, p. 16; Jacob Barion: *Ideologie, Wissenschaft, Philosophie*, Bonn 1966, pp. 115–116; Paul Kägi: *Genesis des historischen Materialismus*, Wien 1965, p. 355.

more emphatic expression in Bauer than in the work of the author of the *Essence of Christianity*, namely that it is necessary to ascend from earth to heaven and not vice versa in order to comprehend man's place in the world – we do not find in Feuerbach's thought any explicit reference to issues which were central links in Marx's network of claims on ideological matters, such as the distorted world, the distorted consciousness, the objective conditions inevitably causing the evolvement of the false consciousness, the transition from self-illusion to deliberate falsehood etc.

From this point of view, Bauer's ideas supply material for ideological research and it is not hard to comprehend that they served as the focus for formulation of numerous Marxian ideas relating to this problem. It is no chance that Marx's ideas on ideology found their first systematic expression in *Towards the Critique of Hegel's Philosophy of Right*, or to be more specific, in the opening section, in which Marx speaks of the significance of religion as ideology, since it was here that religion was criticized from the Bauerian viewpoint; who, more than Bauer, dedicated efforts to exposing the essence of religion as ideology?

Although Bauer did not use the term "ideology" in his writings – neither did Hegel – his version of ideology, the principles of which were formulated as part of the levelling of criticism against religion and theology, is a clear paradigm of a modern approach to this issue, and if we borrow Mannheim's phraseology, we find here a combination of the idea of particular ideology with total ideology. On the one hand, religion is represented as ideology, ruling human beings, causing them to be deluded on the question of existing reality, confusing their minds. It is seen as self-illusion and as the spreading of general illusions, and in certain situations – as conscious falsehood.[3] On the other hand, the essence of ideological consciousness is grasped as lack of understanding of a historical situation, which leads to this fundamental illusion, i.e. as function of objective factors emanating from the regime of alienation and its various manifestations, over which men have no control. Mannheim claimed that in the past an adversary who represented a hostile position would be accused of distorting the facts either consciously or unconsciously, whereas with time the attack had become more fierce, until the adversary was seen as incapable of formulating correct facts, and the structure of his consciousness was invalidated in its entirety.[4]

---

[3] Cf. part one, ch. VIII, n. 20–24.

[4] Karl Mannheim: *Ideology and Utopia*, London, Routledge and Kegan Paul 1954, pp. 68–69.

Mannheim's theory applies to Bauer more than to any other of Marx's predecessors. This conclusion is almost self-evident from perusal of these Bauerian statements: "Theological freedom is lack of freedom, freedom as illusion and hypocrisy, but hypocrisy not in the sense that the theologians understand the rules of the game and use the word freedom premeditatedly in order to organize a regime of slavery and to make it universal, but in the sense of hypocrisy of *objective relations and the state of the world*, which was not created as the result of the deliberate calculations of individuals."[5] And elsewhere he writes: "Illusion does not penetrate the consciousness of the people living within it."[6] Views of this type are abundant in most of Bauer's writings, and two additional quotations will suffice: "It [religious patronage] was explained in distorted fashion: it was accused of crude and malicious cheating, but the true source of religion, illusion, self-deception of the dependents, remains, and even the rationalists, who are free of one illusion, though not completely from this one, are totally subjugated to it."[7] Referring to ways of elucidating the sources of religion, Bauer wrote: "[...] first and foremost it should be noted that the true explanation does not start out from religious illusion as the falsehood of the priestly caste, but from its comprehension as the universal illusion of mankind in general."[8] From these Bauerian ideas we may draw several conclusions of great importance even for the understanding of Marx's philosophical method as regards ideology.

1) At the basis of the ideological consciousness lie objective processes, which necessarily cause the creation of the universal illusion as regards the nature of the world and the place of man within it.

2) Ideology, and the various motifs it contains, characterizes all ways of thinking, including those of the rationalists (Bauer toyed extensively with the idea that theological rationalism is the most perfect form of religion).[9] Bauer himself, of course, should be regarded as an exception to this rule, since science and philosophy, according to his specific understanding, help him to comprehend the laws of historical development.[10]

3) In contrast to Bauer's dialectical-scientific approach, the ideological consciousness, which is in a state of alienation and division, does not

---

[5] Fr 16.
[6] Ibid. p. 17.
[7] Fae 62.
[8] Ibid. p. 69.
[9] *Einleitung in die Dogmengeschichte von Theodor Kliefoth*, pp. 153–157; *Dr. Ammon: Die Geschichte des Leben Jesu...*, pp. 167–169.
[10] See part one, ch. VII, n. 74 and ch. VIII, n. 115.

comprehend the laws of its own development. It claims that it exercises control over the processes of human activity, which it examines in accordance with theological criteria, but in actual fact it does not grasp the relations prevailing in the world, since it is incapable of penetrating into their internality and cannot understand the dialectical character of the processes behind these relations;[11] in other words, it restricts itself to a standpoint of visible motifs and does not expose the essence of things. Bauer means that the ideological consciousness is incapable of rising to a level of understanding of the fact that man is the creator of earthly reality, and attributes the role of architect of the human cosmos to supernatural forces. At the same time, the principles of the world do not depend on individuals, and as such are objective, according to the status which Bauer lent to the category of the universal self-consciousness and to the sphere of universality in his historiosophical conception.[12]

4) The Bauerian theory of the almost universal character of the ideological consciousness is more than understandable in the light of his view of the world as inflicted by general, steadily worsening alienation. Ideology is alienation in the sphere of the human consciousness. The universality of alienation in all spheres of life finds its necessary expression in the monopoly of ideology as regards patterns of consciousness.

The category of religion, which is grasped entirely through ideological concepts, serves as the archetype of alienation. Religion transplants human contents to the celestial, unearthly sphere and despite this, cannot free itself from earthly and human motifs, which are the foundation of its existence. "It [religion] is but transplantation into the air, to the sphere of the imagination and simultaneously it is still an imaginary reflection of reality, which it regards as far inferior to itself."[13] It transpires, therefore, that religion is the distorted consciousness of the worldly order, which is seen by Bauer as distorted and inverted.[14] As noted elsewhere, distortion characterizes both the world and the ideological consciousness.[15] This conclusion derives from Bauer's claims that the ideological consciousness is torn, divided and self-alienated,[16] and as such is grasped as "inverted reason" (*verkehrte*

---

[11] Fae 67.
[12] Cf. part one, ch. VII, n. 65–69, 79.
[13] Fae 67.
[14] Cf. part one, ch. VIII, n. 25–32.
[15] See part one, ch. VIII, n. 33.
[16] ThB 156–170.

Vernunft)[17] since it loses its authentic qualities in the world in which it is persecuted and in which man's weaknesses and passivity win esteem,[18] a phenomenon faithfully reflected in the tendency of ideology to take a favourable view of reality and to lend it legitimation.

The link between ideology and reality is a two-way one: the distorted consciousness or the inverted reason gives its tendencies dominion in the world, and thus contributes to the consolidation of the flawed order, characterized by the irrationality of the forces and factors operating in the world and by the gaps and contradictions between the world of phenomena and the essence of things, but it itself is under the increasing influence of the "inverted world", a phenomenon which in Bauer's eyes gained dimensions to the point where it could not be disregarded.[19] This view caused him to grasp religion, which from his point of view symbolized the ideological consciousness, as a reflection of the inverted world.

These comments contain only partial reference of this problem, and it will be necessary further on to complement them by additional Bauerian evaluations, but at this stage they constitute a sufficient basis for opening a discussion of Marx's ideas on ideological problems.

Marx, like Bauer, sees ideological activity as taking place mainly in the sphere of religion, but expands its scope and adds to philosophy and ethics. Marx's tendency to see in religion, historically speaking, the first form of ideology is attested to by the sentence which appears, in his handwriting, in the margin of the text of *German Ideology*, which notes that "the first form of ideologists, priests (Marx uses the derogatory word, *Pfaffen*) is concurrent"[20] while elsewhere he leaves no doubt that, in his view, religion – until the beginning of modern times – exclusively fulfilled all those tasks which ideology in general now plays: it serves as illusion, clouds the true situation, lends justification, moral sanction, ceremonial legitimation etc. to the social and political order.[21]

Like Bauer, Marx claims that in the past human beings did not arrive at understanding of themselves and thought that their superficial views on their motives were correct, when, in fact that "made up for themselves false conceptions about themselves, about what they are and what they ought to be." What Bauer claimed on history in

---

[17] Fr 182.
[18] ECh 94–96, 100–101.
[19] Fr 16–17.
[20] GI 43.
[21] MEGA I, 1, i, p. 160; cf. ibid. pp. 607–608.

general and Gospel history in particular, namely that it was grasped in distorted fashion and based on abstract principles – God, the spirit of the world etc. – is reiterated in Marx in the form of the accusation he hurls at ideology that it constitutes "a distorted interpretation of history or a complete abstraction from it"[22] and that "the speculative idea, the abstract conception is made the driving force of history."[23]

Following on Bauer and under the impact of his views, Marx sees in ideology – imagination, mystification, spectre, illusion, the illusion of an epoch etc.,[24] which as such cannot arrive at cognition of reality. This phenomenon is clear and almost self-evident: imagination and mystification have nothing in common with science and truth. They are outside the domain of critical thought or, to use another term, they constitute characteristic signs of distortion, characterizing the approach of the opponents to progress, truth and "real and positive science" founded by Marx.[25] It seems that the entire course of Marxian thought in exposing the illusion which lies at the foundation of the ideology which sees itself as truth, is influenced by Bauers argumentation. According to Bauer the differentiation between the truth and falsehood does not apply to the religious-ideological consciousness, which necessarily advocates false motifs, but to the critical-scientific theory alone. He grasps the problem as follows: "The freedoms [of theology and religion] are hostile to freedom, its researches hostile to research, its truths to truth, its sciences to science. Its freedoms are freedoms based on privilege, its research – on excessive rights, i e the total opposite of true freedom and true research. They are feudalistic and barbaric truths and freedoms." And elsewhere: "Our praxis is necessity, which cancels all the illusions which religion creates as regards itself. Theory has released us from this illusion."[26] Bauer's critical theory draws its yardsticks from science, that is to say from the Hegelian dialectical philosophy as grasped by Bauer, and from praxis as well (hence the highlighting of the importance of praxis in the above quotation, which notes its significance for the abolitions of the clerical-reactionary regime).

Illusion is, at first, the product of ideological consciousness, which is not guided by evil intention and reflects a state of self-illusion, and only in times of crisis, when the situation reaches frontal clash between

[22] GI 28.
[23] Ibid. p. 134.
[24] Ibid. pp. 37, 43, 50, 63, 135.
[25] Ibid. p. 38.
[26] Fr 21, 208.

free science, criticism and the conservative und theological elements, does the structure of illusion and self-illusion collapse, since the hidden fabric of existing relations becomes visible, and for this reason the covering up of the flaws and faults of reality is done out of awareness of the falsehood which is the basis of the ideological argument.[27]

Marx also believes that ideology was created and operated at first as an universal illusion that ideologists share. In a marginal comment, which he jotted down in the *German Ideology*, he said that "in the beginning this illusion is true,"[28] i.e. did not derive from a malicious falsehood and deliberate deception. Marx adopted the Bauerian theory on the crisis as the cause of the basic change of ideology, which is transformed from illusion to crude lie and from self-deception to malicious deception, from a phenomenon of objective character to subjective distortion and to apologetics based on a deliberate lie. All this may be ascertained from Marx's idea that the monarchic-clerical regime in Germany was, at first, based on a general error, but in time – with the degeneration of this regime and the consolidation of opposi- tional forces, exerting more and more pressure on the political and social situation in order to bring about its collapse – the objective error yielded place to subjective deception and hypocrisy. "The history of the *Ancien Régime* was *tragic* so long as it was the established power in the world, while freedom, on the other hand, was a personal notion – in short, as long as it believed and had to believe in its own validity. As long as the *Ancien Régime* as an existing world order struggled against a world that was just coming into being, there was on its side a historical but not a personal error. [. . .] On the other hand, the present German regime – an anachronism, a flagrant contradiction of generally accepted axioms; the nullity of the *Ancien Régime* exhibited to the whole world – only imagines that it believes in itself and demands that the world imagine the same thing. If it is believed in its own *nature*, would it try to hide that nature under the *semblance* of an alien nature and seek its salvation in hypocrisy and sophism?"[29]

A similar idea was put forward by Marx in the *German Ideology*, but in accordance with principles which found their first systematic formu- lation in this essay: on the decisive significance of relations of pro- duction and the division of society into a ruling class, concentrating in its hands material power and consequently ideological power, and

[27] Cf. part one, ch. VI, n. 32.
[28] GI 62.
[29] MEGA I, 1, i, p. 610; Ph 253–254.

oppressed and exploited classes – Marx drew a line between the material forces of production and the ruling conditions of the dominant class and the changes occurring within them, in short between the *crisis of capitalist society* on the one hand and the transformation of the character of ideology on the other. "The more the normal form of intercourse of society and with it, the conditions of the ruling class, develop their contradiction to the advanced productive forces, and the greater the consequent split within the ruling class itself as well as the split between it and the class ruled by it, the more untrue, of course, becomes the consciousness which originally corresponds to this form of intercourse (i.e. it ceases to be the consciousness corresponding to this form of intercourse) and the more do the earlier traditional ideas of this intercourse in which actual private interests etc., are expressed as universal interests descend to the level of mere idealizing phrases, conscious illusion, deliberate hypocrisy."[30]

The same thought, which sharply distinguishes between objective falsehood, deriving from the estrangement of the conscious structure from its human substance, and the malicious falsehood of apologetics, is to be found even in *Das Kapital*, where Marx notes that since the taking over of political power by the bourgeoisie in England and France, the class struggle has taken on threatening forms which endanger the regime. As the result of this fact the bourgeois political economy has betrayed its scientific purpose, turned its back on the truth and begun to concern itself consciously with safeguarding the interests of capital and property. "In place of disinterested scientific research comes the bad conscience and the evil intent of apologetics."[31] In another essay, all economists are referred to as "scientific representatives of the bourgeois class."[32]

This thought helps us to understand an additional Marxian idea, which would also appear to have been influenced by Bauer: in the past there was objectivity in scientific disciplines related to subjects of public interest and sensitivity, and they lacked – to a lesser or greater degree but not absolutely – ideological motifs. But at the time of Marx's activity, from 1830 onwards, the situation changed, and there is not a single conception in this sphere – (we are not taking into account the natural sciences, because of the lack of clearity as regards Marx's standpoint) – to which the rules of ideology do not apply. This is true,

[30] GI 316–317.
[31] K I, 21.
[32] *The Poverty of Philosophy*, Ph 494.
[33] GI 516–517.

of course, of moral, political and other doctrines, which Marx called "theoretical products of consciousness", and even as regards political and social conceptions formulated from a socialist standpoint (excluding, of course, Marx's theories). The last part of *The German Ideology*, which dealt with "true socialism" serves as an excellent illustration of this theory. Thus socialism is accused of all the possible ideological sins: its phraseology weakens the consciousness of the conflict between the proletariat and the bourgeoisie and thus strengthens the capitalist regime,[33] it constructs a dream-like kingdom of light,[34] advocates philosophical mystification, its conclusions lack logic,[35] it transforms the self-consciousness into the sovereign factor, it is detached from history and nature[36] – this last argument, as we know, served Marx for the invalidation of ideology.[37] The terms: mystic, illogical, trivial, pure fantasy, are scattered through the text and attached in turn to Hess, Grün, Kuhlmann and other thinkers. For the same purpose Marx does not hesitate to employ various derogatory terms, such as cheat, charlatan etc. It would not be hard to prove that Marx's attitude to Proudhon, Louis Blanc, Weitling is not fundamentally different. It is clear that this general conception, which started out by rejecting, because of its ideological character, all the philosophical thought of his day, which differed from his own ideas, was based on the principles of his own philosophy. The author of *The Holy Family*, who thought that in the proletariat's revolutionary activity thought is reconciled with the true needs of the social praxis, saw himself, consequently, outside the trends of ideology, since he was the author of this new revolutionary principle.

The rejection of all non-Marxian thought – because it was ideological – is explicitly spelled out in *The Manifesto of the Communist Party*. Even systematic perusal of the chapter on communist and socialist literature reveals that all forms of socialism – the feudal, the petit-bourgeois, the "true", the conservative, the utopian – are regarded by Marx (and Engels) as either reactionary or utopian. Whereas Marx was willing to admit that the methods of the past still contained revolutionary elements, "their disciples have, in every case, formed mere reactionary sects."[38] Marx was referring to the Fourierists, the Saint-Simonists and

---

[34] Ibid. pp. 517–518.
[35] Ibid. p. 520.
[36] Ibid. p. 521; For all of this, cf. Isaiah Berlin: *Karl Marx. His Life and Environment.* Oxford University Press 1963, third edition, pp. 145–149.
[37] Ibid. pp. 29–39.
[38] Pol 39.

the Owenists. But it is well-known that those same arguments which he
employed in writing the *Manifesto* also served him for denunciation of
his opponents within the framework of the First International. Thus,
for example, Marx represented Bakunin as the ideologist of the bourgeoisie, who, inter alia, wanted to transplant into his proposed anar-
chistic system a control apparatus separate from society, which characterized the old society and the bourgeois state.[39] Marx's attitude
towards the leaders of the Paris Commune – various Proudhonists and
Blanquists – was also very critical, and there is a clear tendency to a
favourable attitude towards the revolutionary struggle of the masses
and to denunciation of their leaders who did not advocate Marx's
ideas.[40] Hence also Marx's negative attitude towards the Paris uprising
– even before it took place – for fear it would be led astray by Blanquist
dreams, which were doomed to failure.

Wherein lie the similarities to Bauer's ideas? It would seem that
in the general course of his thought, Marx remains dependent, to a
large extent, on the philosophy of his former friend, whom he criticizes
harshly in *The German Ideology*, since – in accordance with Bauer's
own viewpoint – his views are completely free of ideological motifs,
which characterize every ideological network which is not directly
connected to his theories. The reason for this is clear: according to
Bauer, he had deciphered correctly the course of human history, unlike
others who were still enslaved to reactionary theological-clerical con-
structions. The example, of Feuerbach and Bauer's attitude towards
him make it possible to understand, that it was particularly those who
were close to Bauer as regards rejection of theism and the rule of
clerical-reactionary elements whom he grasped as mystics, hidden
theologians etc. This approach helps us to understand why those who
advocated a different set of ideas – even if these do not differ greatly
from those of Bauer – are represented as remote from the correct
standpoint, which holds the monopoly over scientific truth, according
to the conception guided by the slogan of "all or nothing".[41] This
viewpoint is almost self-evident, since Bauer was convinced that he
was conducting a campaign against all the conceptions outside the
ideological current which he represented, or, as he himself put it: "The
whole world is a battle arena, and the issue of all of human values [. . .]
in one word: we are speaking of the principle of all future history."[42]

[39] For this issue cf. Shlomo Avineri: *The Social and Political Thought of Karl Marx*, p. 238.
[40] Ibid. pp. 239–249.
[41] Fr 203.
[42] Ibid. p. 220.

Bauer saw himself as a fighter against the non-truth, the illusion and the lie[43] and it was from this viewpoint that he objected to the views of scholars and thinkers who represented other views. His evaluation of world history and of human philosophy is carried out in this light: even the progressive philosophers and the revolutionary movements which combated religion, ideological, cultural and political subjugation are accorded partial and restricted admiration – let us recall, for example, Spinoza and the French atheists, the American and French Revolutions[44] – since their theories or, in the case of the radical movements, the teachings on which they are based, were still insufficiently mature, or else were compromisory or irreconcilable with the principle of the creative self-consciousness and the free spirit.

But Marx's attachment to Bauerian ideas cannot conceal the fact that in Bauer the eschatological element is more dominant than in Marx, and that Bauer deduces from it his own rightness, the inevitable triumph of his ideas and the establishment of a state and society of a new type. There are signs of an eschatological approach in Marx as noted above: the proletariat plays the role of a messianic force, communism is the message of redemption etc. At the same time it is clear enough that for Marx the need to bring about change in the structure of society, the economy, culture and other fields does not emanate mainly from a religious approach or from a belief that lacks supernatural principles but basically fulfils roles similar to those characterizing religion, as is often claimed in literature – but derives first and foremost from analysis of the economy, society and history. It is for this reason that there are indeed many similarities between the ideological approaches of Bauer and Marx, but from the point of view of the pertinent argument, Marx far surpasses his former friend. It is enough to compare *The German Ideology* with *Das entdeckte Christentum* in order to ascertain Marx's superiority: behind his ideas lies a wide spectrum of arguments taken from the spheres of history, social, economic and political life, the attempt to delve to the depths of phenomena, wider intellectual horizons. He is the only one of the Young Hegelians who, from these points of view, could successfully have tackled the ideas of Hegel himself.

An additional point on which Bauer influenced Marx is the conception of the products of the ideological consciousness as spectres of insanity. This idea which was formulated by Marx very early, in the

[43] ThB 154.
[44] See part one, ch. VIII, n. 89–98.

appendix to his dissertation, appears in a most interesting context: in attacking positive philosophy, which aspires to preserve the existing political and religious situation, Marx explicitly attributes to it ideological qualities: "In this party [. . .] the conversion is revealed, that is to say insanity as such."[45] This idea appears for the second time, attributed this time to religious ideologists, as follows: "For him who sees a *mere idea* in the *perceptible world*, *mere idea*, on the other hand, becomes a *perceptible being*. The figments of his brain assume corporeal form. A world of perceptible sensible ghosts is begotten within his mind. That is the mystery of all pious visions, and at the same time it is the general form of insanity."[46] This statement, unlike the previous quotation, aroused the attention of scholars, who justifiably see it as a general characterization of ideology,[47] but they do not know that Bauer served as the source for these Marxian evaluations, and are incapable of comprehending the exact significance of this Marxian text. We encounter here the same phenomenon which we have noted elsewhere: Marx strongly disagrees with Bauer and makes mock of his beliefs, but this does not prevent him from using them and exploiting them for his own purpose.

Bauer attributes to the religious-ideological consciousness qualities of insanity, from 1841 onwards and is consistent in this belief throughout the radical stage of his activity. He believes that religion encourages tendencies to deny humanity and its obligations, ethics, freedom and reason, and to sacrifice family, state, art, science and all the products of the free spirit on the altar of faith. Those who behave themselves – who are guided by reason, seek answers to life's problems in philosophy, are inspired by radical-revolutionary principales – are seen as madmen, since, from the point of view of him who is inflicted with insanity, the whole world is mad.[48] Those who are ruled by ideology behave like madmen; they are in a frenzy, they curse, cry out and try, by this method to force those who advocate a scientific approach to accept their will, since they do not take into consideration criteria of truth.[49] Bauer describes in detail the emotional apparatus which underlies the phenomena of insanity: hysterical fear of exposure of the truth,[50] a

[45] MEGA I, 1, i, p. 65.
[46] HF 245.
[47] Cf. Hans Barth: *Wahrheit und Ideologie*, p. 150; Jacob Barion: *Ideologie, Wissenschaft, Philosophie*, p. 105.
[48] ThS 44.
[49] Ibid. pp. 47–48.
[50] ThB 155–161.

split within the consciousness and self-alienation,[51] self-delusion,[52] intoxication and partial loss of consciousness, a sense of spiritual impoverishment, spiritual suffering and dissatisfaction.[53] The pathological
symptoms of mental disease are: the cancellation of unity of personality, a split within the soul, the view that the entire world is suffering
from a split, the view that all the products of one's activity were created
by others,[54] the view of oneself as an object, in short symptoms
characteristic of schizophrenia.[55] Furthermore, Bauer cites Leo, who
represented conservative-clerical tendencies and was among the outstanding opponents of the Young Hegelians in order to illustrate the
theory that ideology is insanity on the basis of his personality. "Herr
Leo screams, barks, grits his teeth and behaves as if in a frenzy."[56]

According to Bauer, the world of insanity is based on alternate
dulling of the senses and their sharpening. Inter alia, he noted that
from the viewpoint of the madman, the perceptive world is blurred, all
colours disappear. "He does not behave like a spirit conscious of its
object, but the alcohol ignited in his internality leads him [...] to
transform all things into ghosts and abstract schemes and deprives
them of the colours of their lives."[57] Bauer's ideas and his conclusions
are clear: he who is in an ideological state (for Bauer the notion of
ideology, in all its possible contexts, has a pejorative significance, as it
has for Marx) does not grasp the world as it is, since he is not interested
in its existential form but imposes on it his abstract ideas regarding
God, sovereign of the world etc. As a result the forms of the world
become phantoms and illusions. In this way the ideological consciousness was invalidated once more: it is incapable of confronting the
problems which are the focus of the human world and therefore it sets
up an imaginary world, which is dependent on superhuman and supernatural entities. Marx, who follows in the wake of Bauer, explicitly
stresses that the idea he has formulated can help explain the secret of
the *religious* vision, and thus he revealed that ideological insanity in the
religious sphere serves as a representative model of ideological insanity in general.

[51] Ibid. pp. 156–157.
[52] Ibid. pp. 161–162.
[53] Ibid. pp. 162–163.
[54] Ibid. pp. 156, 158, 160–161, 164–167.
[55] The truth of Bauer's abstract conception has been demonstrated in our times. This
may be ascertained, for example, in Gabel's monograph, which sums up numerous studies by
psychiatrists, psychologists and sociologists. Cf. Joseph Gabel: *La fausse conscience – essay
sur la réification*, Paris 1962.
[56] ThS 54.
[57] ThB 162–163.

It is not superfluous to note here that there is a reasonable possibility that, in regarding insanity as a characteristic of religious consciousness, Bauer was relying on an old Hegelian idea. In the *Philosophy of Religion* Hegel noted that the Indian religion should not be understood through the prism of the miracle, since the entire world of this religion is basically insane: "It is impossible to speak of miracles here, for all is miracle; everything is insane (verrückt) and nothing determined by means of a rational connection of the categories of thought."[58]

An additional Bauerian idea, absorbed by Marx is the idea of the inverted world. This idea is also to be found in Hegel,[59] although it may be traced to other thinkers and writers, including some who preceded Hegel, like Rousseau.[60]

Marx could, of course, have based himself directly on the Hegelian idea and we cannot exclude the possibility of direct influence on this issue, and particularly in a later period. An example of this is the Marxian idea, contained in *Das Kapital*, that the ideological consciousness contents itself with describing the appearance of reality, while philosophical-scientific thought sees its main task as grasping the essence of things or, in Marx's own words: "It pertains to the activity of science to conduct a reduction of visible movement which is mere appearance, into true and internal movement."[61] It is not hard to see that this theory is based on the Hegelian idea that the "essential world is the positing ground of the appearing world,"[62] or "the problem or aim of philosophy is often represented as the ascertainment of the essence of things: a phrase which only means that things, instead of being left in their immediacy must be shown to be mediated by, or based upon something else."[63]

The idea that the existing world is inverted was integrated in Marx's thought through Bruno Bauer, for Bauerian identifying traits are to be found in various contexts in which the above phrase appears in Marx. Let us first examine Marx's letter to Ruge of May 1843, which could have been written by Bauer, so numerous are the Bauerian motifs which appear in it.[64] In this letter Marx employs Bauerian ideas on religious alienation and, in the wake of Bauer, extends their scope to

[58] PhR II, 34.
[59] Phen 203–206; Log. II, 139–141. For this issue cf. Eugène Fleischmann: *La science universelle ou la logique de Hegel*, Paris 1968, pp. 182–183.
[60] Kägi: *Genesis des historischen Materialismus*, pp. 196–197.
[61] K I, 297.
[62] Log II, 159.
[63] LH § 112, Zusatz.
[64] MEGA I, 1, i, pp. 561–566; ET 74–79.

the sphere of politics and ethics. He explicitly identifies human beings with free men and with free republicans and the non-human with the animal and the slave. In clear affinity to Bauer, who characterized the religious element as animal and saw political conservatism as inextricably bound up with the repellent qualities of religion and theology, Marx wrote: "Human beings are beings with mind. The narrow-minded bourgeois want neither of these. What is left for them to be and wish? Their desires to exist and procreate [. . .] are the same as those of animals [. . .]"[65]

According to Marx, the fact that there are human beings who do not feel themselves to be such and behave like "a breed of slaves or horses" is the consequence of "barbaric centuries" which "begot and reared this world and now it stands as a consistent system whose principle is the de-humanized world"[66] (Marx here employs the well-known Bauerian phrase *entmenschte Welt*). The contemptible man, who is not grasped as a man and does not see himself as such is "the monarchical principle" within the framework of which "the inverted world is the real one." Marx believed that it was necessary to work for "the change to the human world of democracy."[67] There is an evident tendency here to emphasize the human character of progressive people who fought for democracy as against the non-human character (Marx, like Bauer, uses the term *entmenschter Mensch*), i.e. lacking all authentic human qualities, of those elements who defended the conservative and despotic regime prevailing in Germany. This is in total accord with the Bauerian conception which rejects in this way religion and conservatism and identifies humanity with those endowed with free self-consciousness and holding atheistic and radical views. Furthermore: like Bauer, Marx extends this evaluation to whole historical epochs and political regimes – the period of lack of humanity, the prehistoric eras as against the epoch of democracy and the view that the principle of humanity is the foundation of the republican-democratic regime on the one hand and the principle of dehumanity and animalism of the autocratic monarchy on the other.

It is worth noting here that for the two years prior to the writing of Marx's above-quoted letter, Bauer did more than any other individual to cast doubt on the legitimacy of the monarchic regime with its autocratic tendencies and advocated the introduction of a republican-

[65] Ibid. p. 561; ET 75.
[66] Ibid. pp. 561–562; ET 75.
[67] Ibid. p. 564; ET 77.

democratic regime in Germany. From his viewpoint it was clear that the conservative political regime which was collaborating with ortho-dox-clerical elements, was based on ideology, i.e. on distortions in the sphere of the consciousness, while democracy and the republic became for him the rule of reason and the free self-consciousness.[68] Marx's statement that "the King of Prussia will be the hero of his times as long as the inverted world is the real one" is based on the idea that man is by essence free but in reality oppressed and despised, that democracy is the sole political regime suited to the human essence but in reality the forces of reaction and conservatism prevail, that in the free human regime man can live his authentic life while in actuality it is the enemies of humanity and progress, the animal elements anxious to create a "world without humanity" who prevail.

The world is inverted because it is in conflict with the essence of man, it is organized in a manner which contradicts the human right to freedom and self-definition and to establish institutions consistent with their aspirations and abilities.

When we compare this viewpoint with Bauer's theory of the inverted world, we see that the emphasis has been shifted. The latter placed greater stress on the religious aspect of this problem, but, at the same time, levelled harsh and uncompromising criticism at these institutions and authorities in the political sphere which do not permit man to develop in accordance with this mission, bind his hands and transform him into an inferior and contemptible creature.[69] Marx is not as in-terested as Bauer in presenting the religious aspect, although he transplants Bauer's arguments to his critique of the existing state and concentrates mainly on exposing the reactionary principles of the world around him and on bringing them into confrontation with the principles of democracy. There is, however, no essential difference between this outlook and Bauer's viewpoint, since the Bauerian evalu-ation of the inverted world regarded political alienation as negative to the same degree as religious alienation and supplied Marx with the weapons for criticism of existing reality on both the ideological and political plane. Hence Marx's use of all the basic terminology of the Bauerian conception of the animal world lacking in humanity, man without humanity, the distorted structure of the world which trans-

---

[68] For all of this cf. B 86; Fr 220, *Deutschlands Beruf in der Gegenwart und Zukunft; Die Parteien im jetzigen Frankreich.*
[69] Cf. part one, ch. VIII, n. 31.

forms its creators into instruments in the hands of celestial and earthly forces which are but the products of man's efforts etc.

At the same time, Marx also devoted attention to the inverted world from the point of view of the religious aspect of this evaluation. In order to comprehend this problem it is worth reexamining *Towards the Critique of Hegel's Philosophy of Right*. Marx claims there explicitly – like Bauer – that "religion is the generalized theory of this world [i.e. the inverted world – this term appears in the previous sentence], its encyclopaedic compendium, its logic in popular form, its spiritualistic point d'honneur, its enthusiasm, its moral sanction." In accordance with what was claimed in the letter to Ruge, this text also claims that state and society are an inverted world and there is nothing new in this. But religion is also described as an inverted world or, to be more exact, in accordance with Bauer's view of religion, as "inverted consciousness." It has been stated elsewhere that the religious-ideological consciousness is grasped by Bauer as torn, split, self-alienated,[70] and transplanting its tendencies to the earthly world. On the other hand Bauer advocated a reciprocal relationship between the earthly actuality and the illusory world of the religious consciousness and therefore also regarded religion as "the imaginary reflection of reality."[71]

Does Marx represent a different trend to Bauer's ideological conception? Did he regard religion solely as the mirror of reality? On the face of it, the answer appears to be positive, the theory being confirmed by Marx's statement that "this state and this society produce religion which is an inverted consciousness of the world because they are an inverted world," i.e. the distorted and alienated social order inevitably engenders a distorted and flawed consciousness, which takes on the form of religion. We will return to this theory and see that the "mirror" theory finds no substantiation in the case before us. At the same time, it is clear that for Marx, the economic-material factor takes pride of place among the various factors existing in human life and in society. He believes that it is necessary to emerge from the developmental dynamics of economic life in general and production in particular, in order to explain the character of consciousness and not vice versa. This conception, which Marx regarded as his main contribution to comprehension of the relations prevailing between the social consciousness and social existence, was formulated by Marx as follows: "The mode

---

[70] See part one, ch. V, n. 35, 36 and ch. VIII, n. 25.
[71] See part two, ch. V, n. 13.

of production of material life conditions the general process of social, political and intellectual life. It is not the consciousness of men that determines their existence, but their social existence that determines their consciousness."[72] In proximity to this sentence, there appears his no less known statement on "the totality of those relations of production constitutes the economic structure of society, the real foundation on which arises a legal and political superstructure and to which corresponded definite forms of social consciousness." Against the background of these statements and as a conclusion from his statement that "the phantoms born in the human brain are also necessarily sublimates of their material life process. [. . .] Morality, religion, metaphysics, all the rest of ideology and their corresponding forms of consciousness, thus no longer retain the semblance of independence. They have no history, no development, but men developing their material production and their material intercourse alter along with this their real existence, their thinking and the products of their thinking. Life is not determined by consciousness, but consciousness by life"[73] – against this background the theory was evolved, – which became popular among Marxists and critics of Marxism, – that regarded ideology as a "reflection" of material social activity, or of the material life process. As we know, Engels tried to correct what he regarded as the false impression among admirers of Marx regarding the direct influence of the economic basis on the super-structure and on the human consciousness in general; he claimed that he and Marx had never held the view that ideology does not affect socio-economic factors, and that the economic factor is always the decisive one; he said that they had only claimed that this factor is the last instance in the process of shaping the image of society.[74] But the problem is not how Engels grasped Marxian theory, since it is known that there was never total accord between them on vital questions, but rather relates to the authentic Marxian interpretation. It is customary, on this issue, to cite Marx's view of Greek art as proof that he regarded conceptions of this art and creation as the external example of artistic creation in general, i.e. as proof that Marx

---

[72] *A Contribution to the Critique of Political Economy.* London, Lawrence & Wishart 1971, pp. 20–21.
[73] GI 37–38.
[74] Cf. Engels' letters to Schmidt (5 August 1890 and 27 October 1890), Bloch (21–22 September 1890) and Starkenburg (25 January 1894). Marx-Engels *Selected Correspondence 1846–1895, with Commentary and Notes,* London, Lawrence & Wishart pp. 475 ff, 477 ff, 516 ff.

did not always hold that the consciousness depended on the material basis, but that it won relative independence.[75]

Those who study Bauer's ideological conception cannot disregard the affinity between Bauer and Marx – which exists despite the pronounced differences – and must ask themselves: is it possible that Marx, who utilized so many Bauerian principles in his critique of religion, in politics and ideology, could have totally ignored the two-directional link which existed in the Bauerian philosophical world between the ideological consciousness and the practical activity of human beings? Marx's response, which should, of course, be sought in the early writings, in which he takes issue with Bauer on the one hand and uses his theories on the other, is made up of two components: in the first he rejects the theory of the primacy of consciousness and demands admission of the precedence of the economic-material factor, while in the second he expresses reservations as to the theory and restricts it to such a degree that in actual fact he reaffirms the idea of the reciprocal ties between the consciousness and practical life. In one of his article in the *Rheinische Zeitung*, Marx wrote: "Since every genuine philosophy is the spiritual quintessence of its time, the time must come when philosophy comes into contact with *mutual reaction* with the actual world . . ."[76] What clearly emerges from Marx's remarks is that existing philosophy is too abstract and speculative, and therefore does not influence the existing social order but conducts its life solely on the spiritual plane; the philosophy of praxis, however, which Marx advocated (and, at that time, Bauer as well)[77] would change things and influence reality no less than it is influenced by it. Hence also Marx's well-known statement on philosophy as the head (brain) of emancipation and the proletariat as the heart of emancipation.[78] From the same standpoint of the existence of a reciprocal relationship between the theoretical consciousness and the existing reality, Marx concluded that at times historical events occur, within the framework of which practical life is mindless just as mental life is impractical.[79] And if this does not suffice, Marx notes in *The German Ideology* that the historical conception should commence from the viewpoint of production processes

[75] Cf. Vojin Milić: *Das Verhältnis von Gesellschaft und Erkenntnis in Marx' Werk.* In *Ideologie*, edited by Kurt Lenk, Neuwied, Luchterhand 1971⁵, pp. 185–187; Julius L. Löwenstein: *Vision und Wirklichkeit. Marx contra Marxismus*, Basel, Kyklos, Tübingen, Mohr 1970, pp. 71–72.

[76] *The Leading Article of the Kölnische Zeitung*, MEGA I, 1, i, p. 243; Ph 122.

[77] For this issue, see Stuke: *Philosophie der Tat*, 159–178.

[78] MEGA I, 1, i, p. 621; Ph 263–264.

[79] Ibid. p. 619; Ph 262.

but, in the last analysis, historical processes constitute a totality, and within the framework of this totality there is a mutual relationship between its various aspects: material production on the one hand, the state and the theoretical consciousness with its various manifestations on the other.[80]

If this is so, it is clear that the theory on the ideological consciousness or the consciousness in general (since Marx did not see his own conceptions as ideology) as a reflection or mirror of reality has no basis. The consciousness is grasped as an active factor, which has the power and possibility to shape reality, in many cases. It therefore transpires that Marx generally recognized the priority of the economic-material factor in society, but that this did not prevent him from supporting the theory that it is necessary to examine the relations between the various components of social reality through the prism of reciprocal activity. His famous statement: "The weapon of criticism obviously cannot replace the criticism of weapons. Material force must be overthrown by material force. But theory also becomes a material force once it has gripped the masses,"[81] gives concrete expression to this postulate. By elevating the theoretical consciousness to the level of "material force" Marx endows it with a status no less – if not more – important than that he attributed to production factors. Because of these facts we should attribute the same significance which Bauer gave the statement that "religion is the imaginary reflection of reality" to Marx's pronouncement that "man has found only the *reflection* of himself in fantastic reality of heaven where he sought a supernatural being" and that religion (in the fourth thesis on Feuerbach) could be explained "only by the self-cleavage and self-contradictoriness of the secular basis", i.e. that the origin of the religious-ideological consciousness lies in secular-human conditions and should not be understood on the basis of theological-imaginary criteria. But Marx also represents the contrary outlook, when this concerns the critical theory he himself founded or any progressive theory. This is not the place for a study of the problem of the extent to which the social consciousness of the bourgeoisie in the 16th, 17th and 18th centuries was theoretical or was permeated with ideological motifs.[82] There can be no doubt that without these there can be no revolution or the founding of a society in

---

[80] GI 49–50.

[81] MEGA I, 1, i, p. 614; Ph 257; for this issue see also Alfred G. Meyer: *Marxism. The Unity of Theory and Praxis*, Cambridge, Mass., Harvard University Press 1970, pp. 105–107.

[82] For this issue cf. Karl Korsch: *Karl Marx*, Frankfurt/M. 1967, pp. 34–36.

which it is possible to further human development. The postulate of
the need to examine the objective situation – and first and foremost,
production factors – in order to comprehend the character of philosophy,
is not vitally significant here, since it is clear that it is necessary to
start out from philosophy or theory in order to comprehend the com-
plexity of problems and to know the possibilities for social development.[83] Those who see Marx, in his historiosophical and sociological
thought, as advocating totality – in accordance with the recommenda-
tions of Marx himself – will not find it hard to understand his statement
that "the same spirit that builds philosophical systems in the brain of
the philosophers builds railroads by the hands of the workers."[84]

It is worth noting here that Marxological literature has recently
arrived at the same conclusions without seeing the Bauerian roots of
the issue.[85]

We may deduce from the above that Marx's conception – despite the
fact that it stresses different aspects from Bauerian ideas – and Marx's
criticism of Bauer the "theologian", who transforms secular matters
into theological questions, are close to the Bauerian theory on the two-
way connection between the consciousness and the reality which lies
outside it. As regards ideology it is possible to formulate this conclusion
as follows: the world is distorted because of its flawed social and
political order, and so is the ideological consciousness, which strives
to justify the gap, the oppression and discrimination. The ideology is
distorted not necessarily because it is the direct expression of a distorted reality, since we have already been made aware that Marx sometimes recognizes the independence of the consciousness. In other words:
as far as Marx is concerned, and in this he follows Bauer, it was clear
that any conception apart from his own was inflicted with the disease
of distortion, at least since the bourgeoisie had ceased to play the role
of the progressive class (this social outlook replaced Bauer's evaluations which were dictated by his antireligious considerations and his
attachment to Hegel). Hence the distortion existing in the world is
twofold and affects both reality and the consciousness. The sole
scholar who correctly evaluated this issue is Iring Fetscher, but because
of his belief that Marx advocates ideology as the reflection of reality,
he did not succeed in comprehending this problem to the full. Fetscher

[83] MEGA I, 1, i, p. 242; Ph 122.
[84] Idem. For this issue cf. George H. Sabine: *Marxism*. The Telluride Lectures 1957/58 at
Cornell University. Cornell University Press 1958, pp. 27–28.
[85] Paul Walton and Andrew Gamble: *From Alienation to Surplus Value*. London, Sheed
& Ward 1972, p. 17.

claims that "bourgeois ideology is a false reflection of a false reality. It is neither the true reflection of a false world nor the false reflection of a true world."[86] If he had studied his phrasing more closely he would have agreed that the term "reflection" has no significance in this context. But it should be noted that there is a certain connection between a world which aggravates alienation to intolerable dimensions and reduces man to animal existence, and the viewpoint that private property and the gap are external; between the reification of human relations, which is invisible to man, and transformation of the conscious factor "on the surface" into the decisive factor and the sole motive of historial development. This connection was established by Marx's philosophical principles according to which the ruling class is incapable – because of its objective situation – of a truly creative act, plumbing the depths of problems, that is to say uncovering the truth. The material power concentrated in the hands of this class enables it to impose on society ideological control and to impose on it its outlook and evaluation or, as Marx says: "The ideas of the ruling class are in every epoch the ruling ideas, i.e. the class which is the ruling *material* force of society is at the same time its ruling *intellectual* force."[87] In accordance with the above it is clear that this spiritual force constitutes a distorting and destructive element.

We have endeavoured to show the source of several of Marx's ideas which are anchored in Bauerian theories. But it is clear enough that Marx surpasses Bauer not only as regard his penetration to the heart of problems, his acuteness and his profound knowledge of the material. Through its connection with revolutionary praxis of the proletariat Marx's conception lost much of the subjectivity which characterized Bauer's ideas.

Marx's economic and sociological analyses lent the ideological question – and other issues in the sphere of society and forms of its consciousness – an objective sociological dimension. For these reasons Bauer, who sees religion as the dominant form of social consciousness and disregards many of its other aspects, falls far behind Marx. But this does not rule out the fact that Bauer exerted considerable influence on the consolidation of important Marxian conceptions on ideology.

[86] *Marx and Marxism*, p. 155.
[87] GI 60.

CHAPTER VI

MARX, FEUERBACH, BAUER

The problem of the relations between Marx on the one hand, and Feuerbach and Bauer on the other is more complex than is generally imagined. We have already seen on several occasions that it is useless to draw a straight line from Feuerbach to Marx and that Bauerian influences are evident in certain spheres in which it has been claimed that Marx bears affinity to Feuerbach.

At this point it is worth analysing several problems which have not yet been discussed, in order to arrive at our conclusions on this issue.

First and foremost let us discuss what is known in literature as the methodological principle of conversion or Feuerbach's transformative method. Ryazanov was the first to claim – in the introduction to the first volume of the historical-critical edition of the writings of Marx and Engels – that Marx wrote *Towards the Critique of Hegel's Philosophy of Right* on the basis of this method, which entails the converting of subject into predicate and of predicate into subject.[1] As regards religion, the significance of this theory is that God is not a subject, as theology claims, but that man should be set up in his place, while God becomes the predicate of man or, in other words: the qualities of God are but the qualities of man. The cogency of this premise is also valid for classic German philosophy, which transformed the absolute into the subject, while man was grasped as the predicate of the absolute; Feuerbach, of course, believed that this relationship should be reversed so that the absolute becomes the predicate of man. For Feuerbach, the Hegelian absolute is basically identical with thought which has been taken out of its human framework and made the subject of philosophy, while the being is grasped as the predicate of thought, but "the true relationship of thought to being is this only:

---

[1] MEGA I, 1, i, p. LXXIII.
[2] *Preliminary Theses on the Reform of Philosophy.* SWr 168.

being is the subject, thought the predicate."[2] Being is nothing but nature, including man.[3]

Ryazanov believed that Marx's critique of Hegel's political philosophy was an expression of the Feuerbachian method as expounded in *Preliminary Theses on the Reform of Philosophy* and *Principles of the Philosophy of the Future*. What is more, he believed it unthinkable that Marx could have written his essay on *Hegel's Philosophy of Right* without having first read the *Theses*, first published in *Anekdota* in February 1843. He therefore argued that Marx could only have commenced this work at the end of March-beginning of April 1843. Because of Ryazanov, almost all those engaged in critique of Hegel's political philosophy have linked Marx to Feuerbach and his method and reiterated the timetable determined by Ryazanov.[4]

But those who are unwilling to accept the theory regarding Feuerbach's influence over Marx's religious conception, also cannot content themselves with Ryazanov's arguments that Marx's political philosophy and Marx's critique of Hegel are dependent on Feuerbach's *Theses*. Suspicions are aroused by the seventh thesis, which is cited by Ryazanov: "The method of the reformative critique of *speculative philosophy* as such does not differ from that already used in the *Philosophy of Religion*."[5]

The question is: did Marx need to utilize Feuerbach's method of conversion, which has already been present in his studies of religion, in order to criticize Hegel and represent his views as mystification and as conversion of the true relations between civil society and the state, or, in the more general meaning: between the idea and the state, with its various manifestations?

It may be stated conclusively in this context that the transformatory method was typical of Bauer at least to the same degree as it characterized Feuerbach, at least where religion was concerned. Thus, for example, Bauer claimed that theology attributed human predicates to God, while philosophy aspired to abolish this situation which attested to the alienation of man from himself and his own essence, and wished

[3] Ibid. pp. 169–170. See also, ibid. pp. 153, 155, 162, 164–165; *Principles of the Philosophy of the Future*, ibid. §§ 1, 5, 8, 9, 10, 11.

[4] See for example, Louis Dupré: *The Philosophical Foundations of Marxism*, New York/Chicago, Harcourt, Brace & World 1966, pp. 87–108; Shlomo Avineri: *The Social and Political Thought of Karl Marx*, pp. 12–43; Karl Marx: *Critique of Hegel's Philosophy of Right*. Introduction by Joseph O'Malley, pp. IX–XIII, XXVII–XXXII, Cambridge University Press 1970; Robert Tucker: *Philosophy and Myth in Karl Marx*, pp. 102–105; David McLellan: *Marx before Marxism*, pp. 103–104.

[5] MEGA I, 1, i, p. LXXIII; SWr 154.

to regain man the subject, existing in his own right, man as a free sovereign individual, as the supreme creature who is not the predicate of another subject: "He", Bauer wrote, supposedly on Hegel, but in actual fact referring to himself, "does not wish to be like God, he wants to be the self – the self alone and to win infinity, freedom and self-sufficiency – which are desecration – and to enjoy them. This philosophy does not want any god or gods, as do pagans. It is interested only in human beings, in self-consciousness . . ."[6] Bauerian ideas of the same type are to be found in abundance in his various essays[7] from the period of Marx's dissertation. In addition Bauer and Marx had the opportunity of exchanging views on this question both in their personal encounters and in the letters they exchanged, while the lack of any contact between Marx and Feuerbach prevented such an exchange.

It is not surprising, therefore, that the principle of conversion appears at least twice in Marx's dissertation and one can only wonder at the fact that Ryazanov did not notice this. On one occasion the principle is formulated in a section on Plutarch and the second time in a discussion on the concept of the sage in Greek philosophy. In the first instance Marx says: "Ordinary thought always uses abstract predicates, which it separates from the subject. All the philosophers *converted the predicates themselves into subjects*."[8] On the second occasion he says: "Plato contemplates his attitude to reality in such a way that an independent kingdom of ideas reigns above reality (a world above reality is the self-subjectivity of the philosopher) and is obscurely reflected in it."[9] The first sentence is formulated in such a way that it needs almost no explanation: Plutarch is a kind of paradigm of the religious consciousness ("ordinary thought") which transforms the predicate into the subject, while philosophy – in contrast to theology – correctly grasps man as the subject and attributes to him those qualities attributed to God (such as freedom, sovereignty etc.). In the second case, i.e. that of Plato, the world above reality, the substantial world of the idea is a kind of subject, while the subjectivity of the philosopher is its predicate. The world of ideas infiltrates the empirical world, but this infiltration first goes through the stage of philosophical adaptation in the mind of the philosopher. Through the conversion method it is, of course, necessary to reverse the situation so that the subjective consciousness of

[6] Pos 151.
[7] ChS 35, 39; ThS 61–62; Syn I, p. VII.
[8] MEGA I, 1, i, p. 119.
[9] Ibid. p. 105.

the philosopher can be grasped as the authentic subject and creator of reality. The Bauerian motifs are strikingly evident, particularly since all of Marx's conceptions here revolve around the central axis of the free self-consciousness of the demiurge of reality.

At the same time, so it seems, one cannot exclude the possibility of Feuerbachian influence on Marx's *terminology*. Despite the harshness of his critique of religion, which is permeated with the principle of conversion, Bauer did not formulate this idea as clearly and unequivocally as did Feuerbach in an 1839 article, in which he wrote: "What are all the predicates – and what is the subject without the predicates? It is nothing but the totality of all its predicates. What are all the predicates, I say, which speculation and religion itself, attribute to the divinity, if not the notions of the human race – notions which man takes from his own king? Are not will, understanding, wisdom, essence, actuality, personality, love, power, presence in everything, if not the notions of mankind?"[10]

That Marx was acquainted with this article may be deduced from Bauer's letter to him of 11.12.1839;[11] it is possible that Marx utilized the phrasing of the conversion of predicate into subject and vice versa, but even this is to be doubted since, in his dissertation, Marx preferred Bauer's arguments regarding the hostility between philosophy and religion, the non-human character of religion, the self-consciousness as a supreme value etc., to Feuerbachian arguments.

The fact that Marx took a negative view of Feuerbach for quite some time is attested to by his refusal to approve the latter as a contributor to the journal of religious critique which he and Bruno Bauer planned to publish together.[12] This incident occurred in 1841 and there is not the faintest indication that Marx's attitude was more positive at the time he wrote his dissertation. Thanks to Bauer's success in persuading Marx to waive his opposition to Feuerbach, Jung was able to inform Ruge that Marx, Bauer and Feuerbach were preparing to publish an atheistic journal,[13] but Ruge did not need this information. He had already heard of the plan from Bauer and in one of his letters he writes: "*Bruno Bauer (and Marx)* [...] *and Feuerbach* have announced or are about to announce the rule of *the Montagne* and have taken up the standard of atheism ..."[14] The striking fact in this letter is that Marx's

---

[10] *Über Philosophie und Christentum*, SW I, 72.
[11] MEGA I, 1, ii, p. 235.
[12] Cf. Bauer's letter to Marx, 12 April 1841 (ibid. p. 253).
[13] Ibid. p. 261.
[14] *Briefwechsel und Tagebuchblätter*, p. 239.

name appears in parenthesis after that of Bauer: indisputable evidence that at that time Marx was regarded as Bauer's disciple. But anyone in need of further proof will find it in the letter Bauer sent to Ruge in which he notes jestingly that Marx is imprisoned together with him within the confines of the same theory – that of Jesus. Bauer reiterates the expression "imprisoned with me", when he writes of Marx as his collaborator in the writing of the *Posaune*.[15] The fact that Marx was Bauer's disciple as regards his views was well-known to German intellectuals at that time, and found expression in various publications.[16]

No change occurred in the relations between Bauer and Marx during 1842. What is more, the friendship and collaboration between them would appear to have reached their height in this year. This is attested to by the scheme for collaboration in the writing of the second half of the *Posaune;* the close relationship reflected in Marx's participation in the writing of articles for the *Rheinische Zeitung* and his entry into membership of its editorial board; Marx's frequent visits to Bauer in Bonn; Marx's defence of Bauer against Gruppe, published in the same year in the *Deutsche Jahrbücher* etc.[17] His cooperation with Bauer and the latter's clear influence on his anti-religious views, led Marx to write to Ruge on 20.3.1842 that in writing his section of the *Posaune*, he had "come into a certain conflict with Feuerbach, a conflict not on principle but on phrasing."[18]

But most important of all was the fact that Bauer increasingly dedicated his efforts to critique of the state and its institutions. We have already noted elsewhere his radical and revolutionary tendencies, the aim of which was drastic and violent change of the political situation in Germany. His political activity complemented his critique of religion and his atheistic views and created an additional basis for cooperation with Marx who, for his part, also attributed to politics the qualities of realization of theoretical-philosophical principles.[19] When Bauer asks "How did it happen that Feuerbach never dealt with politics?"[20] this question reflects the amazement of a man who re-

---

[15] Cf. Bauer's letter to Ruge, 6 December 1841.

[16] See, for example, *Bruno Bauer oder die Entwicklung des theologischen Humanismus unserer Tage*, p. 75.

[17] For this issue cf. Bauer's letter to Marx, 26 January 1842 (MEGA I, 1, ii, p. 266); *Noch ein Wort über "Bruno Bauer und die akademische Lehrfreiheit von Dr. O. F. Gruppe. Berlin 1842"* (MEGA, I, 1, i, pp. 397–400); A. Cornu: *Karl Marx und Friedrich Engels. Leben und Werk*, vol. I, pp. 268–269.

[18] MEGA I, 1, ii, p. 272.

[19] Ibid. p. 261.

[20] Cf. part one, ch. IX, n. 50.

garded political struggles and the onslaught on the establishment as an inseparable part of his life, while Feuerbach devoted almost no attention to politics. These differences were clear to the contemporaries of Feuerbach and Bauer. The absence of a systematic attitude towards politics may account, to a large extent, for the fact that Ruge preferred Bauer to the author of the *Essence of Christianity*.[21] In an article on Bauer published in the eighteen forties the view has been expressed that what Feuerbach does for man as an individual: liberation from external forces and alienation, – Bauer did for mankind as a whole and for the sake of history. It was claimed that Feuerbach saw the cause of alienation in religion alone while Bauer exposed alienation "as the principle common to every situation, all institutions and life in the Christian world." Whereas for Feuerbach theology is cancelled out in anthropology, Bauer sees its cancellation in cognition of the essence of man and its various manifestations, particularly in the sphere of history. For Bauer, in contrast to Feuerbach, the *Kritik der evangelischen Geschichte der Synoptiker* is the beginning of a turning point "not only in theology, but also in humanistic, political cognition in general."[22]

Marx too was convinced that Feuerbach did not pay enough attention to politics and was over-preoccupied with nature. Marx tended to accept the invalidation of idealist philosophy, particularly Hegelian, as carried out by Feuerbach, but believed that the path of politics was the sole one philosophy could follow in order to become truth;[23] this factor is missing in Feuerbach, and it is therefore impossible to realize the principles of philosophy, however beautiful they may be.[24]

It was not because of the influence of Feuerbach and his *Theses*, as many scholars claim in the wake of Ryazanov, that Marx began to occupy himself with Hegel's political theories.

Before we continue the discussion of this issue, let us turn to the anonymous work known as *Luther as Arbiter between Strauss and Feuerbach*, written in 1842, which appeared in Ruge's *Anekdota* at the beginning of the following year, and which serves as evidence that in

[21] Ruge: *Briefwechsel und Tagebuchblätter*, p. 247; Klutentreter: *Die Rheinische Zeitung von 1842/43...*, p. 31.
[22] *Bruno Bauer oder die Entwicklung des theologischen Humanismus unserer Tage*, pp. 55, 69.
[23] MEGA I, ii, ii, p. 308.
[24] Modern scholars take a similar stand in evaluating Feuerbach's attitude toward politics. Kamenka, for example, points out that Feuerbach contented himself with formulating a few phrases, such as that the God of religion and the spirit or the absolute of philosophy possess the same monarchistic pretensions; that the philosophical hierarchy creates a political hierarchy and vice versa, – and says that in actual fact Feuerbach never plumbed the depths of any political issue. Cf. E. Kamenka: *The Philosophy of Ludwig Feuerbach*, London, Routledge & Kegan Paul 1970, pp. 90–91.

1842 Marx was a sworn advocate of Feuerbach. In this essay, which Ryazanov attributed to Marx, there appears the famous statement that "there is no other road for you to *truth* and *freedom* except that leading through the stream of fire [i.e. the *Feuer-Bach*]. Feuerbach is the *purgatory* of the present times."[25] If Marx had written this essay, he would thus have been denying his own principles, which impelled him to object to Feuerbach's participation in the editing of the above-mentioned journal, and to state that his own theories differed from those represented by Feuerbach. But what is more important, by proclaiming that only through Feuerbach was it possible to arrive at the kingdom of truth, Marx would have simultaneously been doing two contradictory things: emphasizing the importance of politics for the liberation of man and society on the one hand and dedicating himself and his time to religious-theological problems detached from political questions, on the other.

Aparently out of a retrospective view, or because of his devotion to the principle that Feuerbach had greatly influenced Marx, as he claimed in his introduction, Ryazanov attributed this essay to Marx. The formal argument that Marx received payment for two articles he wrote for *Anekdota*, one of which had been identified while the other was unknown so that all the evidence pointed to this article, is unconvincing. Sass produced sufficient evidence to refute Ryazanov's claim.[26] Nowhere in Marx's writings and essays do we find a comment – however obscure – on this essay which he allegedly wrote. There is no evidence that Marx was seriously interested in Luther, as the numerous quotations from Luther in the essay would suggest. The number of pages for which Marx received payment from Ruge is not identical with the sum of the number of pages of the essay on the Prussian censorship[27] and the article on Luther, Strauss and Feuerbach. Sass's conclusion that Feuerbach himself was the author of the article is based on numerous arguments which we will not enumerate here: Feuerbach wrote to Ruge that he was sending him several lines on Strauss and on himself, the *Essence of Christianity* contains many quotations from Luther etc.

But there is an additional argument which Sass, for some reason, failed to perceive: in a letter to Fleischer written in February 1842

---

[25] MEGA I, 1, i, pp. 174–175; Ph 95.
[26] Hans-Martin Sass: *Feuerbach statt Marx. Zur Verfasserschaft des Aufsatzes "Luther als Schiedsrichter zwischen Strauss und Feuerbach"*. International Review of Social History. Vol. XII, 1967, pp. 108–119.
[27] *Über die neueste preussische Zensurinstruktion*, MEGA I, 1, i, pp. 151–173.

Ruge speaks of the differing views of Feuerbach and Strauss on the miracle which was the object of the above-mentioned article, and notes that "Feuerbach is a stream of fire and causes great trouble [referring to the rationalist theology which supports Strauss]."[28] The hint that it was Feuerbach who wrote the article on Luther, Strauss and himself is clear and it is also possible to deduce from the content of the letter that this article was then already in Ruge's hands. He found difficulty in publishing it in the *Deutsche Jahrbücher* and kept it for the *Anekdota*.

It is hard to understand how serious scholars, such as McLellan, could have dismissed the arguments raised in Sass's article claiming that they were unconvincing.[29]

The truth is that Marx began his article on the critique of Hegel's philosophy of right a whole year before Feuerbach's *Theses* appeared, as may be deduced from his letter to Ruge, dated 5.3.1842. In this letter Marx wrote that he had prepared for publication in the *Deutsche Jahrbücher* a critical article on the Hegelian law of nature, in which, first and foremost, he attacked the principle of constitutional monarchy as a completely unsuccessful combination of contradictory principles.[30] This motif was developed by Bruno Bauer in articles in the *Rheinische Zeitung* in the beginning of 1842, and it was only natural that Marx took an interest in the subject and arrived at approximately the same hostile attitude to the combination of parliamentary-constitutional rule and monarchy, as represented by Bauer. At the same time, it appears that there was reciprocal influence between Bruno Bauer and Marx as regards the formulation of political outlooks, and from Köppen's remarks to Marx[31] we learn that Bauer's article on the Christian state contained ideas voiced by Marx in personal encounters in the "Doktorklub".

Marx explicitly stated that his work on Hegel's philosophy of right was in its concluding stage and that it was in need of a few amendments and of being copied out in final draft. It is interesting to note that Ryazanov, who insisted on persevering in his theory that Marx's work was begun after he became acquainted with the *Theses*, is unwilling to accept Marx's word as reflecting the true situation and says: "We do not know at what stage Marx's work stood."

The fact that Marx continued to study Hegel's political philosophy

---

[28] *Briefwechsel und Tagebuchblätter*, pp. 260–261.
[29] *Marx before Marxism*, p. 108.
[30] MEGA I, 1, ii, p. 269.
[31] Ibid. p. 257.

is attested to by a letter dated 20.3.42, in which he writes of the reasons which prevented him from submitting the work for publication, and by his letter to Oppenheimer, of August 1842.[32]

We may deduce from all this that the theory of the decisive influence of Feuerbach's *Theses* and *Principles* – because of the conversion method they expounded – over Marx and his critique of Hegel's political theories, is but a legend which has misled many scholars.

The "transformative method" was to be found in the writings of Bauer, with which Marx was closely acquainted. It was also present, though not so strikingly, in the writings of Feuerbach in the eighteen thirties. Those who believe that Marx had need of Feuerbachian statements on conversion as regards philosophy i.e. that it was necessary to hand him on a platter that very same idea which was previously included in the critique of religion, do not properly appreciate Marx. The evidence of Marx himself – that he clearly understood the integral connection between the activity of the transformatory mechanism in politics and religion – should decide the question. He was referring to his idea that the same patterns lie at the basis of the phenomenon that the constitution does not create the people but vice versa, and at the basis of the principle – which applies to religion – that God does not create man but rather man creates God.[33]

It is clear that there is continuity on the question of the utilization of categories of conversion, and this may be ascertained from Marx's articles in the *Rheinische Zeitung*, again in contradiction to the views of Ryazanov, who wanted to emphasize what seemed to him the bequeathing of this category by Feuerbach to Marx.

In this context, Marx does not utilize terms such as subject and predicate. The reasons for this are clear. In his press articles Marx – for reasons related to the topical and empirical character of the discussion and for considerations connected with censorship – could not refer to political and legal problems in the same general-metaphysical, categorical way which characterizes the writing of *Towards the Critique of Hegel's Philosophy of Right*, which, furthermore, was not earmarked for publication, at least not in the immediate future.

Thus, for example, in his article on the law concerning the theft of wood, Marx expressed the view that the state does not act for the common good, but does everything possible to safeguard the rights of property owners – in this specific instance – of forest-owners. It does

---

[32] Ibid. pp. 272, 278.
[33] Cf. part two, ch. IV, n. 24.

not take into consideration the principles of reason and its universality and does not take into account the concept of honour, since it is guided by private interests. Since private property, according to Marx, does not attain to the point of view of the state "the state feels itself obliged to descend to the level of these measures of private property which conflict with reason and the law."[34] It is totally clear that, according to Marx's evaluation, the state and private property change places in the existing situation in complete contradiction to the conception which highlights the importance of the state and its universality. The state is transformed from subject to object, while the same logic operates with reference to property in opposite manner, converting it from object to subject. It transpires unequivocally, from Marx's statement that the social processes operating in the Rheingebiet are objectively-necessarily responsible for the behaviour of the state authorities, which "are forced to adapt to the limitations of private property". Elsewhere Marx notes that the members of the assembly of estates – an institution which the German bourgeois wanted to introduce but which did not as then exist – would be but representatives of private interests – who "will wish to and will inevitably succeed in transforming the state into the object of private interests."[35]

This idea – of a dominant private-propertied class and a society divided into classes with selfish interests, as against a state aspiring to be general but in actual fact serving as the instrument of capitalist elements – appears in other contexts as well [36]

There is another argument often cited in discussions of Feuerbach's influence over Marx, which cannot be accepted without reservations: it is claimed that Feuerbach influenced the formulation of Marx's critical view of Hegel. All the Young Hegelians were critical of Hegel, but they sometimes preferred to maintain their attachment to the author of the *Phenomenology*, to emphasize what they held in common with him and to represent their innovations in the sphere of historiosophy, atheism and politics as anchored in his teachings. At the same time they directed quite a few critical shafts at him.

Let us cite one of many examples of this approach: in an article published by Ruge in 1840, and dedicated to Hegel's *Philosophy of Right*[37] criticism was levelled against the rational model of the state as

---

[34] MEGA I, 1, i, p. 282.
[35] Ibid. p. 283.
[36] Ibid. pp. 278, 300, 303.
[37] *Zur Kritik des gegenwärtigen Staats- und Völkerrechts.* HJ 1840, No 151–156.

depicted in the latter work. Ruge claimed against Hegel that instead of basing philosophy of right on history, he had preferred to add the historical dimension by appending certain paragraphs on history to the end of the article. Thus – according to Ruge – the Hegelian state becomes an unchanging and closed being, binding in all situations, though it is well-known "that every form of state, and even the most streamlined, can only be the product of history."

Ruge deduced from this that Hegel had elevated certain facts of political life to be the level of the rational absolute which was located, as it were, outside history, whereas these facts themselves belong to it. Ruge also objected to the status which Hegel accorded to the monarch and to bureaucracy, and although he did not argue with the principle of constitutional monarchy, he argued that the importance of the king should be reduced and demanded that the authority of the legislative branch be imposed on the bureaucracy. Ruge believed that only joint rule of parliament and monarch reflected the idea of the sovereignty of the state. But Ruge's most vehement criticism of Hegel was voiced on the issue of the participation of the people in the life of the state. Ruge demanded the introduction of the principle of universal and free elections – in contrast to the postulates of the maintenance of an assembly of estates and absence of such elections.[38]

Ruge's article leaves no room for doubt that within the constitutional principle the monarchy forfeited its previous importance, was emptied of content and became mere symbolic rule, while the centre of gravity shifted to the participation of the people in power and to its determination of the composition of the authorities. In addition, Ruge demanded the introduction of freedom of expression and independence of the press as guarantees of the maintenance of free political life.

McGovern commented, with justification, that Ruge's views influenced the development of Marx's critical attitude both as regards Hegel and his political opinions and the institutions of his time.[39]

Does this mean that Feuerbach had no influence whatsoever over Marx? The answer is, of course, in the negative. Feuerbach's influence over Marx was emphasized by the latter himself and it would be unwise to disregard this evaluation. But the fact that Marx utilized the transformative method in his dissertation and in later writings, and that Bauer influenced him on this point, as on other issues, obliges us

---

[38] Ibid. No 152, pp. 1210–1211; No 153, p. 1221; No 154, pp. 1225–1228.
[39] Arthur McGovern: *K. Marx' First Political Writings. The Rheinische Zeitung 1842–1843.* In *Demythologizing Marxism.* Boston College Studies in Philosophy. Vol. II, 1969, p. 21.

to find a new basis for this problem, different from the accepted one.

In the *Economic and Philosophic Manuscripts* Marx pointed to three achievements of the author of *The Essence of Christianity*: proof that philosophy is nothing more than religion brought to and developed in reflection, and this is another form of the alienation of man's nature; the establishment of materialism and real science; that, as against the negation of Hegelian cancellation, which is but theologization of philosophy, he presented man as the creator of the reality within which he lives.[40] The two points, the first one and the third, are partially congruent and partially complement each other; the congruence applies to critique of Hegel as a covert theologian (or, as Feuerbach says in his first *Thesis*: "The secret of *theology* is *anthropology*, but *theology* itself is the secret of speculative philosophy"), while the complementary factor is reflected in the fact that sometimes stress is laid on Hegelian philosophy's representation of substance as God, and sometimes – on the fact that it represents the absolute spirit as something differing from the human consciousness and beyond it. The common denominator of all these factors is critique of Hegel, the view of his system as abstract, detached from man and from the human situation, transforming the consciousness of man into the self-consciousness of God. Marx explicitly states that he found these manifestations in *The Essence of Christianity*[41] but even without this explanation it is clear that if this book exerted any influence over Marx, it was not evident in the sphere of religion but rather in critique of the Hegelian system and the emphasizing of its negative aspects.

Marx was impressed by this critique, as may be ascertained from the section of his letter to Ruge of 20.3.1842, in which he noted his intention to introduce amendments into his article on Hegel, which had at first been earmarked for the *Posaune*, both as regards its parodistic tone and – what is more important in this context – out of a desire to free himself of the "oppressive imprisonment" to Hegel.

It transpires from the above that Marx commenced his work on the critique of Hegel's political philosophy in 1841, and completed the final draft in 1843 while in Kreuznach. Ryazanov's claim that the *Preliminary Theses* should be regarded as the starting point for Marx's article, is not valid because Feuerbachian influence does not play a decisive part here: the transformative method was employed by Marx from 1840 onwards. Marx's biographical data, as contained in his letters, confirms

---

[40] MEGA I, 1, iii, pp. 152–153; Ph 316–317.
[41] Ibid. p. 153; Ph 317.

this statement, since in March 1842 he had already finished the first draft of his work. On the other hand, we may deduce from his remarks in the preface to *A Contribution to the Critique of Political Economy* that when he secluded himself in his study after resigning from the *Rheinische Zeitung*, he continued his work on critique of Hegel's philosophy of right. That the final draft contained whole excerpts from previous works is attested to by erasure of the term "self-consciousness" which ceased to constitute a significant factor in Marx's conception after he and Bauer arrived at a parting of the ways.[42] This rule also applies to the conflict between the sovereign and the people, which appears in the previous version but which yielded place to a new conflict: between the sovereign and civil society.[43] And finally one more comment: Ryazanov claimed that Marx, during his stay in Kreuznach, not only read, in the course of four months, 62 volumes consisting of 20,000 pages and filled slightly less than 300 pages with his notes on these books,[44] but also wrote a manuscript which would take up 250 large pages in the edition of the works of Marx-Engels. It is clear that Ryazanov was in error, but it is hard to understand how those who followed him did not notice the error and failed to draw conclusions from the factual material and from comparison of texts.

The good relations between Marx and Bauer were disrupted towards the end of 1842; they were further disturbed at the beginning of 1843 and the two eventually arrived at a total breach. The ideological controversy between them, which commenced in the autumn of 1843 and continued for several years – and which will be discussed in the next chapter – was the culmination of this process.

Strangely enough, this affair began with a dispute between Marx, in his capacity as editor of the *Rheinische Zeitung*, and a group of teachers, journalists, writers and students who had organized themselves in Berlin into a group known as *die Freien*. Members of this group, which was organized while Bauer was in Bonn, included inter alia: Köppen, Stirner, Sass, Julius, Meyen, and Edgar Bauer, When Bruno Bauer returned to Berlin after his dismissal from Bonn University, he was treated as a hero by the group, and they appealed to him on all controversial questions.[45] *Die Freien* tended towards extremism, and admired the Jacobins and atheism and there were, among them,

---

[42] See for example MEGA I, 1, i, p. 418.
[43] Cf. ibid. p. 501.
[44] Cf. ibid. I, 1, ii, pp. 105–106.
[45] For all of this cf. John Henry Mackay: *Max Stirner. Sein Leben und Werk*, Berlin 1898, pp. 68–72, 76–90.

manifestations of sympathy for communist and socialist ideas, which
had reached Germany through France. Under Rutenberg's editorship
of the *Rheinische Zeitung*, many of their articles were accepted for
publication. The regime regarded them as deliberate provocation and
censorship became stricter. Marx learned a lesson from these events
and stopped *die Freien* from publishing extreme attacks on Christianity
and the establishment, particularly since, in his view, the level of the
articles was low and the argumentation lamentable.[46] Marx and Ruge
pinned hopes on Bauer as the man capable of restraining *die Freien*,
and thought that if he did not succeed, he would break off contact
with them.[47] But Bauer had no intention of responding to the appeals
of his friends who were living at a considerable distance from Berlin.
When Marx imposed a total ban on articles by members of the group,
and Ruge and the poet Herwegh quarrelled bitterly with them, Bauer,
after visiting Berlin and hearing what the group had to say, not only
failed to abandon the group but even defended them in discussions
with Ruge and Marx.[48] The last letter which Bauer wrote to Marx, on
13.12.1842 reflects no basic ideological differences, with the exception
of Bauer's forgiving attitude towards a group of people whom Marx
regarded as representatives of phraseology, who were therefore doomed
to failure.

The relations between the two did not immediately deteriorate from
understanding and ideological affinity to mutual criticism and tension.
In a letter he wrote to Ruge in March 1843, Marx lavished praise on
Bauer for his brilliant writing. He wrote of Bauer's book *Die gute
Sache der Freiheit und meine eigene Angelegenheit*: "In my opinion he
has never written so well" and described the latter's article on Ammon
as "splendid". Marx's reserved judgment on Feuerbach – as expressed
in this letter that he generally accepted the content of Feuerbach's
aphorisms but rejected his appeal to nature, preferring politics as the
means of realizing philosophical principles – has won great popularity,
while the fact that Marx's praise of Bauer originates in conscious
identification with his theories, has been totally ignored.

There is no way of ascertaining the entire course of events which led
to the total breach, since Marx's letters to Bauer, which could have
thrown light on the affair, were not preserved. But it is clear that the
breach was mutual. Marx's sharp criticism of Hegel was irreconcilable

---

[46] See Marx's letter to Ruge, 30 November 1842 (MEGA I, 1, ii, pp. 285–287).
[47] Ibid. p. 278; Ruge: *Briefwechsel und Tagebuchblätter*, p. 288.
[48] Ibid. p. 292; *Briefwechsel und Tagebuchblätter*, p. 290.

with Bauer's tendency to represent his theories as authentic Hegelianism.

In his article on Ammon, Bauer stressed the connection between truth and the people, but the height of his philosophical approach to the masses was simultaneously the point of transition to an outlook which placed exclusive emphasis on the pure intellectual critique of reality, a critique which is in contradiction to the desires of the passive masses who flock after material benefits and easily submit to the political and ideological-religious establishment. All this occurred at a time when Marx was beginning to see the masses, and first and foremost the proletariat, as the sole social force capable of detaching itself from deeply-rooted patterns of life and changing them from the foundations upwards.

Marx's move away from Bauer brought him closer to Feuerbach. It is no coincidence that wherever Feuerbach is accorded positive evaluation, or even more, we find, in the margins of the text, sharp criticism of Marx's former friend. *The Holy Family*, which consists wholly of an attack on Bauer, cannot serve here as an example, but for illustration of this situation let us turn to the *Economic and Philosophic Manuscripts*, where Marx lavished praise on Feuerbach after totally rejecting Bauerian criticism because of its connection with the Hegelian outlook and the absence of development of categories of logic. Not so important in this context is the fact that Marx claims that Bauer did not find an answer to Gruppe's question on the development of logic and left the issue to those who came after him,[49] whereas the truth is that Bauer, in *The Good Cause of Freedom*, never raised this issue at all. Marx was apparently referring to Marheineke, who demanded of Bauer that he prove the place of Hegelian ideas on religion in the entire system (including logic), but had no intention of inferring that Bauer had ignored logic.[50] It is more important to emphasize that Feuerbach was the man who disregarded the categories of logic and scarcely dealt with them at all, or, as Kamenka says: "Most of the traditional problems of philosophy were simply not discussed by Feuerbach; one of the central problems, the nature of logic, is hardly touched upon at all."[51]

This combination of criticism of Bauer, the former friend from whom Marx had begun to be estranged philosophically and emotionally, and the description of Feuerbach's views as close to Marx's emergent ideas

[49] Ibid. I, 1, iii, p. 151; Ph 315.
[50] Fr 194.
[51] *The Philosophy of Ludwig Feuerbach*, p. 90.

in the materialist-historical and communist spirit, is carried out in accordance with Marx's aim of presenting his theories as consistent with radical intellectual development and its latest manifestations. Despite his past as editor of the *Rheinische Zeitung*, Marx was not widely known and remained in the shadow of Bauer and Feuerbach, whose theories were regarded in Germany as the height of radical-oppositional thought. Marx was, at least for a time, in need of an authority on which he could rely in order to prove that his conclusions were correct.

But this is an ostensible connection based on appearance, or phrasing, while the most striking fact in this network of relationships is the lack of joint fundamental basis for the views of Marx and Feuerbach.

Thus, for example, Marx claims that "Feuerbach is the only one who has a *serious, critical* relation to Hegel's dialectic." This may be valid for Marx himself but is an incorrect statement where Feuerbach is concerned. It is necessary to erase the term "serious" in order to arrive at a sentence which is a faithful reflection of reality. Feuerbach, who started out as a Hegelian and in his paper directed against Lachmann, *Kritik des Antihegel*, defended the teachings of his mentor, later took up an oppositional stand as regards *all* the principles of the Hegelian system. He saw it as consistent and rational theology and nothing more,[52] based the Hegelian theory on man's consciousness of God as the self-consciousness of God, on the basis of Spinozian pantheism and claimed that pantheism was nothing but "the naked truth of theism[53] or "the negation of theology from the standpoint of theology".[54] Hegel's logic was also grasped by Feuerbach as "theology that has been turned into reason and presence"[55] and the system as a whole was represented as "lacking immediate unity, immediate certainty, immediate truth,"[56] since it tried to follow the path of synthesis of the finite and the infinite, the limited and the unlimited, the subjective and the objective, while Feuerbach sees the dialectical categories of Hegel as contradictions alone. For example: Feuerbach grasped the Hegelian absolute as "theological-metaphysical being or un-being, which is *not* finite, *not* human, *not* material, *not* determinate and *not* created, the world-antecedent nothingness posited as deed,"[57]

---

[52] *Principles of the Philosophy of Future*, SWr § 5, p. 178.
[53] Ibid. § 14, p. 192.
[54] Ibid. § 15, p. 194.
[55] *Preliminary Theses on the Reform of Philosophy*, ibid. p. 155.
[56] Ibid. p. 157.
[57] Ibid. p. 155.

and thus the whole development of the central category of Hegelian philosophy was lost. Feuerbach's statement that "everything is contained in Hegel's philosophy, but always together with its negation, its opposite"[58] also shows that he did not understand Hegel's dialectical way of thinking about development as negation together with preservation of the positive. Feuerbach's conclusion that Hegelian philosophy was an arbitrary combination of various methods, without the positive force of cohesion of diverse and opposing elements, is more than understandable in this context.[59] Nor should we wonder at Feuerbach's other conclusion that Hegel could not control the ideas which were absorbed into his philosophy and which originated in other thinkers, because he did not regard them with "absolute negation". "Only he who finds the courage to act with absolute negation", he wrote, "also finds the strength to create something *new*."[60] There can be no doubt that the latter statement applies to Feuerbach, who was almost incapable of seeing anything in Hegel's immense system except its allegedly theological character, utterly rejected its dialectical principles and believed that by returning to nature and emphasizing sensibility he could create a new philosophy.

In Marx's well-known letter to Feuerbach, dated 11.8.1844, in which he expresses admiration for the latter, expression is given to those two same tendencies which are evident in the *Manuscripts*:

a) Marx extensively criticizes Bauer whom he describes as "my friend of long standing (though now more estranged from me)".[61] Bauer was depicted as a pure spiritualist, fighting on behalf of criticism which had been transformed from a means into an end; the category of self-consciousness, which he advocated, was grasped as existing in its own right and totally detached from the living and active individual; Bauerian criticism was represented as directed against the masses etc. All this was done for one sole purpose: to demonstrate that Bauer played a negative role, both ideologically speaking and in the sphere of politics. In contrast Marx offers the work of Feuerbach, who formulated valuable theories on the unity of man with his fellow-men and thus laid the foundations for socialism.

b) In this fashion, all ties between Marx and Bauer were severed; on the other hand, Marx deliberately creates the impression that he and communism owe a great debt to Feuerbach, who may not have been a conscious communist, but through his views created the basis for the existence of a regime of social justice or, as Marx says: "[...] you have, whether intentionally I do not know – given a philosophical basis to socialism." Through such statements Marx linked his communist theory to Feuerbach, but they are no truer than the statement in which Marx attributed to Feuerbach a "serious attitude" to Hegelian dialectics.

On this issue there was an interesting sequence of events. Feuerbach took a serious view of Marx's evaluation that he was a communist on the basis of Feuerbach's use of the notion of man as the species being (*Gattungswesen*) or as communal man (*Gemeinmensch*) i.e. man as a creature with social links to his fellow-men. In an article he wrote shortly after receiving Marx's letter, and published in 1845,[62] he noted that, according to his understanding, man was simultaneously an individual or "egoist" and a creature with links to others, and as such he – man – whether he wished it or not, was a communist.

In response to Feuerbach's self-evaluation, Marx pointed out his error. Feuerbach, he claimed, has used the term "communist" incorrectly. A communist was a member of a revolutionary party, working for the collapse of the existing social order, while Feuerbach, who engaged only in theory, could not be classified among such people.[63] As Marx saw it, Feuerbach had formulated thoughts on the links between men, which were positive in themselves, but belonged within the framework of the trivial belief that "men need and always have needed one another." In other words: Marx objects to the image of Feuerbach as a communist, an image he himself had created; Feuerbach's error lay in the fact that he had had faith in Marx's statement.

Furthermore, since Bauer accepted Feuerbach's self-definition and claimed that Feuerbachian communism had grown out of the cancellation of man as an individual, his transformation into part of a collective and the imposition of the authority of the human race on him,[64] Marx launched an attack on him, accusing him of making his critical work easier by attacking abstract images, like those of Feuerbach, unrelated to the subject of communism, instead of tackling the true communism.[65]

We can learn from this incident that Marx understood the difference

---

[62] *Das Wesen des Christentums in Beziehung auf den "Einzigen und sein Eigentum".* Wigands Vierteljahrsschrift, Leipzig 1845. No. 2.
[63] GI 53–54.
[64] LF 105, 128–131.
[65] GI 54.

between his own beliefs, which were not restricted to description of the social condition but aspired to revolutionary praxis for the sake of the basic transformation of reality, and the ideas of Feuerbach, which were merely theoretical or, to be more exact, ideological since the lack of the trend to radical change made them a checking force. It transpires, therefore, that Marx ostensibly based his communist theories, which drew inspirations from various different sources (von Stein, Hess, Engels, Saint-Simon etc.) – for the reasons mentioned above – on the anthropological Feuerbachian theory, but was conscious of the fact that Feuerbach's belletristic and pathetic formulations, his theory of man as living in "I – you" relations alone as a happy sensuous entity – were so abstract that they were inapplicable as individual social and political praxis.[66]

This is also valid for the statement in the *Manuscripts* regarding Feuerbach's scientific and materialistic approach. Feuerbach's influence over Marx could not have been significant on this point, if we take into consideration the fact that the Feuerbachian nature, which constituted the foundation of human life, was represented as primeval, and as something on which man's social praxis had left no stamp.[67] This statement was also valid for the theory of consciousness which, for Marx, is not merely a theoretical process, but serves the needs of human life. Marx saw in contemplative philosophy the expression of man's self-alienation[68] while for Feuerbach "in the place where the sense begins, religion and philosophy end and the simple and named truth is obtained in their place."[69] And elsewhere: "The task of philosophy and science consists [...] *not* in transforming *objects* into *thoughts* and ideas, but in making *visible* i.e. *objective* – what is *invisible* to *common eyes.*"[70]

Against the background of conceptions of this type, indubitably close to positivism, it is possible to understand the statement of Engels, who also advocated materialism of this kind,[71] that after the appearance of the *Essence of Christianity* "the enthusiasm was universal: we

---

[66] For this issue see Hans-Martin Sass: *Feuerbachs Prospekt einer neuen Philosophie.* Revue Internationale de Philosophie. Bruxelles 1972. No 101, p. 269.

[67] E; *Das Wesen der Religion*, SW I, 418–422, 426–439.

[68] Pol 243, 245.

[69] *Das Wesen des Christentums in Beziehung auf den "Einzigen und sein Eigentum"*, SW I, 349.

[70] SWr 232.

[71] For this issue cf. Iring Fetscher: *Marx and Marxism*, pp. 267–270.

all immediately became Feuerbachians,"[72] but this characterization most definitely does not apply to Marx.

In the *Manuscripts* Marx already took issue with Feuerbach and expounded the theory that work is the essence of man; because of the importance of this issue in Hegel's system, he also claims that Hegel adopts the standpoint of modern political economy. The reality surrounding man is not grasped in this context as an objective factor, external to man but as shaped by his labour and Marx goes as far as to grasp man as the immediate object of natural science.[73] This critique reaches a higher level in the *Holy Family*, which Marx openly declared to be directed against Bruno Bauer and his supporters and in which Marx widely employs Feuerbachian terminology. There, Marx attacks the simplistic view of nature, which characterizes the authors of the articles printed in the paper Bauer edited, who see in nature a factor which has been shaped once and for all, which is unchanging, and the sole purpose of which is to supply man's needs. As against this he claimed that nature is part of society and its history, that it is constantly changing because of man's creative work and the development of industry and that the social praxis leaves its stamp on the reality within which man lives.[74] It is not surprising, therefore, that Marx speaks in that article at length about English and French eighteenth century materialism, which made a considerable contribution to the evolvement of socialism, and says not one word about Feuerbach in this context.[75] We may therefore concur with Korsch who said that "in his views as expressed in the *Holy Family* Marx was formally coming out against Bruno Bauer but to the same extent against Feuerbach, as demonstrated by his comments against the *unsatisfying character of a merely naturalistic, and not a historical and economic materialism.*"[76]

In the *German Ideology*, written several months after the *Holy Family*, Feuerbach was demoted to the level of Bruno Bauer. It transpires that in contrast to what was attributed to him in the *Manuscripts*, he does not advocate a critical approach to the categories of dialectics but rather the contrary: his views suffer from an antidialectical, contemplative, antihistorical approach; they are contemp-

[72] *Ludwig Feuerbach und der Ausgang der klassischen deutschen Philosophie*, p. 272.
[73] MEGA I, i, iii, p. 123; Ph 312.
[74] Ibid. p. 327; HF 201.
[75] Ibid. pp. 306–308; HF 175–177.
[76] *Karl Marx*, p. 153.

tuous of praxis, perpetuate the alienation of man, take up the stand-point of the bourgeoisie etc.[77]

It transpires from all this that Feuerbach did not exert decisive influence over the consolidation of Marx's views, a fact which has already been noted by serious Marxologists.[78] Only on one issue is Feuerbachian influence evident: as regards the changing of Marx's attitude towards Hegel from positive to critical and sometimes to emphatically negative – but here too the Feuerbachian influence was restricted since Marx was also influenced by other elements, and despite his anti-Hegelian proclamations, was dependent on the ideas of the author of the *Phenomenology*. He sometimes makes use of them and employs a dialectical approach which draws inspiration from Hegel's system.[79] In other areas Marx uses Feuerbachian terminology, referring to naturalism, humanism, species being, but the content behind these terms differs significantly from the Feuerbachian version.

In contrast to the accepted view on the Feuerbachian sources of Marx's thought, this interpretation of Marx's intellectual development leaves room to other influences, among which Bauerian ideas play a prominent part. Furthermore: a balanced picture obtained from per-ception of these facts, also leaves room for other viewpoints, which apparently also exerted influence over the formulation of Marx's thought (those of Edgar Bauer, Moses Hess, Wilhelm Schulz and others).

---

[77] GI 53–60; see also *Theses on Feuerbach*, Pol 243–245.

[78] Cf. for exmaple, J.-Y. Calvez: *La pensée de Karl Marx*, p. 121; see also Nicolas Lobko-wicz: *Theory and Praxis. History of a Concept from Aristotle to Marx*, p. 251.

[79] Löwith has recently pointed this out in his analysis of the Hegelian dialectical issue of mediation and immediacy which Marx follows to a large extent, while Feuerbach almost totally ignored it. Cf Karl Löwith: *Vermittlung und Unmittelbarkeit bei Hegel, Marx und Feuerbach*. Revue Internationale de Philosophie, 1972, No 101, pp. 308–335.

CHAPTER VII

THE POLEMIC BETWEEN MARX AND BAUER

The controversy between the viewpoints of Marx and Bauer, which was sparked off by the publication of *On the Jewish Question*, written in the autumn of 1843, reached its height a year later, when Bauer wrote a series of articles in the *Allgemeine Literaturzeitung*, and Marx wrote the *Holy Family*. Bauer was the first to criticize Marx's communist theories and this should be emphasized in the light of the prevailing theory that Stirner was the first critic of Marxian philosophy.[1] The truth is that Bauer preceded Stirner, though only by a few months. The anti-communist motif was to appear for years in Bauer's historical essays as well, and particularly in those writings dealing with radical movements in Germany in the eighteen forties.

The sharp change of direction in his views in 1843 is explained by Bauer as the result of the indifference of the masses, whom the radicals including Bauer himself – had tried to activate without properly ascertaining the nature of these masses.[2] The closing down of the radical papers did not shock the wider public, nor did it arouse angry reaction. Rather the contrary: the radical movement disappeared, as if it has never existed, and its place was taken by the liberal-bourgeois movement, which advocated tried and moderate methods and loyalty to principles on which the regime was founded.[3]

Bauer was disappointed at the passivity of the masses, their failure to carry out great deeds on behalf of progress, and their choice of a stand in favour of religion and conservatism. "It is in the masses [...] that we should seek the true enemy of the spirit. All the great projects of history so far have failed in advance and have not achieved real success because the masses displayed interest in them and enthusiasm,

---

[1] Rudolf Hirsch: *Der erster Kritiker Marxens*. Zeitschrift für Religions- und Geistesgeschichte, IX (1937), pp. 246–256.
[2] *Vollständige Geschichte der Parteikämpfe in Deutschland während der Jahre 1842–1846*, vol. II, Charlottenburg 1847, p. 80.
[3] Ibid. pp. 234–236.

or else came to a disappointing end because the idea discussed within their framework contented itself with a superficial conception, thus ensuring itself of mass support."[4]

The masses are not seen by Bauer solely in social terms; he sees the term as encompassing those circles known as "intellectual" to the extent that they live in a state of illusion as to the nature of the world and the ideology which governs it,[5] i.e. have not arrived at a state of criticism, as envisaged by Bauer, which comprehends the anti-human essence of the Christian-civil world. At the same time it is clear that for Bauer the proletariat is the main representative of the masses[6] since it constitutes the element which has been impoverished both materially and spiritually speaking;[7] for these reasons it cannot be trusted. On this point Bauer strongly attacks communism for pinning its political and social hopes on the masses and the proletariat in particular.

Bauer takes issue with the theory disseminated by Hess and Marx that the proletariat is a progressive class, whose objective situation inevitably brings in its wake the liberation of society as a whole as the result of its own emancipation. According to Bauer, the proletariat, like most other classes, with the exception of criticism which is fighting for the liberation of the selfconsciousness, is guided by its own interest and has no common denominator with other estates of the existing society. Because it is absorbed by monotonous physical labour it lacks universal horizons, (in contrast to the claim of communism), and is in fact split into atoms and, as such, is in need of education, however minimal rather than the slogans of communist revolution and the solution of the problem of society as a whole through radical changes in the social structure.[8]

Unlike Marx, who emphasized the oppositional and revolutionary character of the working class, Bauer does not doubt that the masses always consider their own advantage and that their conception is determined, in the last analysis, by income. Bauer anteceded Herbert Marcuse and his theory of one-dimensional man who is given to the manipulation of the establishment, having adapted to the conditions of capitalist society, when he, Bauer, wrote: "Competition leads to one-sided concentration of capital [. . .] and the masses who recognize no

---

4 *Neueste Schriften über die Judenfrage*, ALZ No 1 (1843), p. 3.
5 Ibid. p. 2.
6 GM, ALZ, No 10 (1844), p. 42.
7 *Vollständige Geschichte der Parteikämpfe...*, vol. II, pp. 13–29.
8 GK, ALZ, No 8 (1844), p. 26; GM 42–43.

supreme value except for their own sensual existence, will they hesitate to submit to capital and to its rule, if it promises them employment and life?"[9]

The masses are not capable of understanding their own situation in the world and they cling to prejudices. For this reason it is not the thinkers with a pure philosophical approach and abstract ideas who have the chance of winning their favour – the precondition for absorption of their ideas in this cultural milieu – but those who disseminate simplistic ideas. In other words: only easily-digestible assumptions and statements can reach the consciousness of the masses and win popularity. Bauer was referring here to dogma and he used this term frequently. It was his opinion that for radicals and communists dogmatic concepts are idols and the masses willingly submit to them and allow them to rule their lives.[10] Thus only dogmatic ideology (every ideology is of dogmatic tendencies, but communism elevates dogma to a supreme principle) can serve as the programmatic basis for a wide mass movement, since the masses will understand a limited number of trivial statements, suited to their capabilities and emphasizing their interests, while no other viewpoint has any chance of finding acceptance. On the contrary: if any viewpoint is popular with the masses, its very popularity attests to its dogmatic quality. Dogmas disseminated by the regime supply ready formulae to the masses who are incapable of thinking and do not wish to think, finding it more convenient that the leadership do so in their place. "The unity of society is no longer disturbed since there is only *one* dogma which serves as the expression of the whole truth and as such it dominates all the brethren to the same extent."[11]

Bauer's criticism of communism and the communist society which might emerge some day – he thought such a development would bring catastrophe to human society – is characterized by the same intellectual acuteness which is evident in all his theories. He starts out from the view that the slogan that "the workers create everything and therefore have the right to everything" is a supreme example of dogma, since this idea implies that other sections of the population do not suffer but enjoy profit and the exploitation of the workers. Bauer defines this approach as "a unique pathological viewpoint." He likens the communist revolution to healing of the body through amputation of limbs;

[9] GM 46.
[10] *Hinrichs politische Vorlesungen*, zweiter Band, ALZ, No 5 (1844), pp. 23–24.
[11] GM 48.

the body symbolizes the proletariat while the diseased limbs are other social strata. A communist society would impose a regime of political chaos, since it is based on an ideology which denies the very need for the existence of a state and, in order to unite the masses, disseminates slogans of fraternity and universal equality. But Bauer cast doubt on the existence of an authentic egalitarian society and claimed that it was only an illusion, since spiritual and physical deeds differ from individual to individual so that the comparison, which entails abolition of individual specificity, is not implementible in the long run. "The contradiction within the human race – the cessation of unity through the specific change – is preserved even within the kingdom of the non-differentiable masses, in which this species is immersed, and it constitutes a threatening force . . ."[12]

Despite his serious approach to the theory that the state would be cancelled within communist society, Bauer was aware of the fact that a communist regime would develop tendencies to expansion of power and imposition of authority, and hence his vacillation between two stands on this issue. This conclusion is reflected in his belief that for sake of the existence of unity and cohesion, the authorities will employ all the measures at their disposal, particularly in order to suppress the natural tendency of human beings to satisfy their specific needs. For this purpose laws of despotism, an extensive bureaucracy and intensified police force will be employed, and their intervention in all affairs becomes one of the rules of existence within the new social framework. "The members of the new society", Bauer writes, "obtain police rule in return for sacrificing all means of existence. The police at last attains universal power and knowledge of events, which the police force of the former state could not achieve despite its efforts in struggles against the liberty and ingenuity of the individual."[13]

Bauer reiterates the statement of the communist Weitling: "The government of the people is nothing but a pleasant illusion", and emphasizes that the belief that every individual, including the milk-maid, is capable of conducting the affairs of the state is more than utopian; in actual fact nothing will change in this respect: power will be concentrated in the hands of a tiny minority, which will exploit the alleged principles of equality for the sake of its own objectives.

Bauer also held that though communism might object to fiscal oppression and the impoverishment of the masses, the bureaucracy, which

---

[12] Idem.
[13] *Vollständige Geschichte der Parteikämpfe...*, vol. I, p. 42.

would control the administration and the economy, would foil any attempt to combat these phenomena. The outcome would be the opposite: "Taxes, which according to Weitling's theory, would be abolished in his society will reach a height such as society has never known, because this army of officials will have to be much larger than any previous horde of bureaucrats."[14]

On this occasion Bauer gives expression to his belief that socialism, which places emphasis on the masses, disregards those people who are endowed with self-consciousness and as such advance the affairs of society, culture and the state. The socialist programme does not recognize the great significance of the human spirit and stresses production and material matters or, as Bauer puts it: "As to the spirit and the self-consciousness, this proposal knows nothing of them, at least as long as the issue is not recognition of the wisdom and perspicacity of the regime for elimination of any force competing with its exclusive authority."[15]

Bauer attacks communism for individualist reasons, clearly deriving from his subjectivist outlook: fulfilment of the hopes of the masses through communist theory is a kiss of death to human specificity, which differs from person to person and to the human spirit and the human species. Communism provides the regime with authorization for the ordering of all social relations and particularly production relations, and thus places at its disposal the means of destroying the unique character of various kinds of human beings. Scepticism as to the creative possibilities of the spirit, according to Bauer, is the main source of the proposal that society be constructed on a socialist basis. "Is there only competition between capital and labour?", Bauer asks, "or does the spirit also possess the necessary force to take part in this competition?"[16]

Bauer's criticism of communism exposes, to a certain degree, his own intellectual weaknesses. To his mind, the creative intelligentsia, guided by its knowledge of the complex problems of the world thanks to the critical self-consciousness, was the sole force shaping human history, and he detached it completely from the other social estates. Thus he arrived at a total confrontation between a very narrow sector of intellectuals and the masses, who were remote from representation of a rational outlook on cultural and political affairs. His stand on the

[14] Ibid. p. 41.
[15] GM 47.
[16] Idem.

question of self-consciousness is strange, to say the least, since this consciousness appears as a factor separate from the actual man and his social life.

Yet, despite all this, Bauer's critique contains a considerable degree of prophesy. One hundred and thirty years ago he envisaged a communist regime in which man was deprived of his liberty and lived under the strict supervision of the institutions which supposedly acted on his behalf to safeguard his interests. Analysis of Bauer's critique of the essence of dogmatic communism leaves no room for doubt as to the nature of this regime, which rules through anti-democratic measures and employs coercion as its support. The evaluation of communist ideology as based on specifically dogmatic principles, with the aim of reaching the consciousness of as many people as possible, also appears now to be based on a retrospective view, summing up historical events. Bauer's acumen is also evident in those chapters of his critique in which he expresses his belief that an outlook centred on the proletariat as a universal eschatological force will be transformed into an outlook aimed at that same proletariat (this was, as we know, what happened to dogmatic Marxism, particular in its Soviet version. This issue has been discussed by Iring Fetscher, who dwelt on the role of Engels, Kautsky, Lenin and Plekhanov in shaping the image of this type of Marxism).[17]

Bauer's approach should be regarded as a consistent protest against the intervention of state-communist factors in social life – intervention of the state is possible only in an atheistic-critical state, based on the principles of Bauer's own thought. Bauer leaves no room for doubt as to his opposition to the subjugation of the private-actual man to universality and he accuses Feuerbach of linking the individual to the human species and imposing the general authority on him in all matters.[18] Bauer's outlook demands, above all, preservation of the interests of the individual, but to the same extent it is the standpoint of an intellectual, concerned to highlight the role of intellectuals in the life of society and the nation. Another reason which led Bauer to level criticism against communism is the theory of class consciousness, as reflected in *Towards the Critique of Hegel's Philosophy of Right. Introduction*. Bauer, who regarded the self-consciousness as a universal phenomenon, could not reconcile himself to its fragmentation according to the class structure of society, and accused communism of ruining

[17] *Marx and Marxism*, pp. 148–181.
[18] GM 44–46.

the work of criticism, the aim of which was to overcome fragmentation and to restore to man his alienated consciousness.[19]

It is interesting to note that Bauer, in contrast to Marx, does not openly attack his former friend in his articles in the *Allgemeine Literaturzeitung* and does not mention him by name. What Marx wrote about covert criticism against Feuerbach in this paper[20] is even more valid as regards Marx himself. This in abundantly clear from Bauer's arguments on the Jewish problem. In response to Marx, who characterized Bauer's outlook on Judaism as theological, Bauer argued that he saw the Jewish question in a many-faceted way – both as a religious-theological problem and as an issue of political significance.[21] Hence the Marxian criticism which claims that "Bauer thus demands, on the one hand, that the Jew give up Judaism and man give up religion in order to be emancipated as a *citizen*. On the other hand he holds that from the *political* abolition of religion there logically follows the abolition of religion altogether,"[22] and suspects him of far-reaching concessions to the existing state, since he finds identity betwen the two types of emancipation. But in Bauer's opinion this is not valid. Bauer returns more emphatically than before to the theory formulated in the *Jewish Question*, that the existing state, which he calls Christian, is based on excessive rights; he does not want to abolish religion as one of these rights but rather the category as a whole.[23] The constitutional state is in no way identical with the proposed atheistic state. Bauer repeats this theory, which appeared in the *Jewish Question*, in order to acquaint Marx with his error as to identification of political and human emancipation. In the *Jewish Question* he noted that the abolition of the state religion in France after the July revolution had transformed the Jews into free citizens, but that this did not spell the end of the conflict between Jews and Christians. Political life is dominated by the principles of privilege, lack of true freedom and the classification of citizens into oppressors and oppressed, or, as Bauer says: "Universal liberty is not the law in France. The Jewish question has not, therefore, found its solution since legal freedom (all citizens being equal) is restricted by the religious privileges which rule life and fragment it,

---

[19] For the Young Hegelian's concept toward consciousness, cf. Dieter Hertz-Eichenrode: *Massenpsychologie bei den Junghegelianern*. International Review of Social History, vol. VII, 1962.

[20] ET 185.

[21] GK 23.

[22] MEGA I, 1, i, p. 579; Ph 220.

[23] GK 23–24.

and this lack of liberty in its turn affects the law and forces it to lend authorization to the division of citizens into oppressors and oppressed."[24] As was his wont, Bauer saw the excessive rights of religious, political and social groups as religious in essence, but, as the above context demonstrates, he was referring explicitly to the political and social privileges introduced under the rule of Louis Philippe. This is also attested to by the following Bauerian statement: "Constitutional liberalism is the method of granting privileges, of restricted freedom based on interest. Its basis is prejudice and its essence is religion."[25] Thus the abolition of alienation should be carried out not only in the sphere of religion but also on the political and ideological plane – an approach which is consistent with Bauer's general principles. Thus also in the *Allgemeine Literaturzeitung*, Bauer explains to Marx that he is doing him an injustice by placing the liberation of man in the Bauerian conception on the same basis as the western bourgeois-parliamentarian state. Bauer argues that the French Revolution was a "symbol" and "imaginary expression" of the work of criticism and yet differed from it in many ways: the revolution advocated atheism in theory, but in practice at its height, in Robespierre's day, reconciled itself to the principles of religion; it abolished feudalism, but was enslaved by national egoism; it became involved in contradictions, when, despite its humanistic outlook, it employed blind terror which needlessly claimed victims. Even the Enlightenment movement which, intellectually speaking, prepared the Revolution, was flawed since it based itself on substance and ignored the self-consciousness and its liberation.[26] Bauerian critique on the other hand remains as consistent atheism and is not ready to renounce its principles; it unrestrainedly advocates humanism and for this specific reason objects to the principles of constitutionalism and to any regime which grants excessive rights to any group and in which there is classification into oppressors and oppressed; it advocates the liberation of man, from the intellectual and political aspect etc.

It is clear that Bauer does indeed, in principle, support the ideas of the French Revolution, but he wishes to emphasize those elements which distinguish his outlook from the bourgeois-democratic revolution, such as the abolition of religion and any ideological system etc. The reference to the constitutional regime is out of place, since the revolu-

---

[24] Jud 45.
[25] Ibid. p. 101.
[26] GK 22–25.

tion went so far as to abolish this form of regime. Bauer's objection to
the principle of constitutional monarchy as a regime of privileges cannot therefore apply to the democratic republic and hence Marx's
counter-arguments, when he cites the example of the United States
which carried out political emancipation in accordance with Bauer's
political ideal but where religion nevertheless flourished. Private property and egoism existed there and as a result the country was far away
from human emancipation.[27]

But precisely because of the emphasizing of the uniqueness of
criticism, which seeks to liberate man completely and to create a new
world which is in contrast to the old one, Bauer adds a new dimension
to the problem of emancipation. He adds nothing to the political
principles of the democratic revolution, but the stressing of critique of
the illusory existence of man in a society in which the conventional
falsehood of ideology and "religiosity" reigns as the preferred status
of various groups, and the demand to break away from the old Judeo-
Christian world, cause his outlook to be represented within a more
radical framework than the theories of human liberation of the French
Revolution. It transpires from this that Marx's criticism of Bauer may
be basically correct but misses several Bauerian ideas, which cannot be
classified through the division into supporters of political emancipation
and the view of it as human emancipation on the one hand, and supporters of human, i.e. socialist, emancipation on the other.

It was undoubtedly Marx who caused Bauer to launch his critique of
communism. Bauer was aware of the fact that the radical movement,
which disintegrated in 1843, when its larger part gave up the idea of
bringing about change from below – through violent revolutionism –
and became a liberal-civil movement, nevertheless served as the basis
for evolvement of a trend which was socially and politically speaking
just as radical, and in which communist ideas developed. Bauer takes
issue with the ideas of Saint Simon, Fourier and Weitling, but when he
says that "recently the masses have been singled out to do a great
deed"[28] it is clear that he is referring to Marx and not to those who
disseminated socialist-utopian ideas in the past. This conclusion is
further substantiated by Bauer's statement that (Marxian) communism
had accepted Feuerbach's theory that it was necessary to champion
the cause of the human species against the specificity of the individual.[29]

[27] MEGA I, 1, i, pp. 581–585; Ph 222–227.
[28] GM 42.
[29] Ibid. pp. 44–46.

Bauer's disappointment with the masses for abiding in a state of religiosity and under the domination of ideological patterns, and because of their acceptance of the prevailing situation; his disillusionment with radicalism which had changed from a wolf into a placid and self-satisfied lamb in the image of conciliatory and compromising bourgeois liberalism; his opposition to communism for cooperating with the masses in order to impose dogmatic ruling and ideological principles, worse than the old conservative principles – all these factors impelled Bauer to give up the idea of active participation in political life in order to translate his views into actuality, and to retreat to the principle of pure criticism which does not contaminate itself by contact with reality. The first signs of this approach were already evident in 1842: "When existing relations are totally opposed to the idea, where can it survive if not in the pure self-consciousness, which has saved itself from corruption and bears within itself the true forms of its being?"[30] But the tendency which was latent in a period of ideological onslaught on the establishment, at a time when the trend to revolutionary change was predominant, became the central motif of his thought from 1844, when Bauer arrived at the conclusion that it was necessary to act with caution in the face of the masses and of all the political and ideological movements which were striving to realize their plans by means of the masses. Bauer attributes to himself what at various times was attributed to the struggles of the Germans: that these struggles were of a purely ideological-literary nature without immediate political implications.[31] He thought that it was a mistake that this fact was forgotten at decisive moments and that theory was seen as practical action. But when Bauer claimed that criticism "never pandered to the masses"[32] he himself was forgetting that there were times when he identified truth with the people. His evasive statements that there was a time "when it [Bauerian theory] was not yet capable of depriving the masses of their belief that it shared a common interest with them"[33] cannot change this fact.

Bauer's retreat from the revolutionary praxis would seem to have been caused by his hostility towards the masses for allowing themselves to be manipulated by the regime, and by the failure of the radical movement which, according to Bauer, achieved nothing or, as he

[30] B 81.
[31] GK 16–17.
[32] Ibid. p. 18.
[33] Idem.

says, became aware that "the game was a game" and nothing more.[34]

Another reason for the transformation of Bauerian critique into pure criticism, operating in the sphere of the self-consciousness alone and deliberately remaining as remote as possible from reality, was its awareness that there was no point to revolutionary change, since the miserable social and cultural situation could not be altered in this way. The political revolution necessarily recruits the masses to implement its schemes and the consequence is that only external changes occur. The rule of one group is replaced by a regime which bestows excessive rights on another group, but the essence remains unchanged: the regime of privilege, vested interests and manipulations remains.

According to Bauer, theory should place itself in opposition to any other outlook and to reality as a whole; it should level criticism at the corrupt world from afar, in order to break away from it. Furthermore: criticism should reexamine itself from time to time lest it become involved in ties with the world around it. "Theory criticized itself all the time and tried not to proclaim slogans or to be caught up by its enemies' assumptions."[35] This viewpoint derives from the theory that the Judeo-Christian-bourgeois world is based on a living fabric of mutual interests which, through coercion and the dissemination of distorted ideas, defend the existence of this world. But unlike any other outlook, including the most radical one, namely communism, Bauerian theory cannot make an alliance with the masses so as to depose the institutions of this world.[36] Bauer deduced from this fact that he should represent a critical standpoint *outside* the world and not within it. The programmatic-strategic significance of this theory is that Bauerian criticism cannot collaborate with any social class or political group so as to implement the postulates related to its hostility towards reality. As a result "the good cause of freedom" becomes "the cause of Bauer himself", and it is no coincidence that Bauer gave his book this title (*Die gute Sache der Freiheit und meine eigene Angelegenheit*). Alone and isolated by choice, Bauer stands on the Olympus of pure criticism, remote from the happenings of the world. It is not, therefore, surprising, that Marx directed his shafts against him.

In the *Holy Family* Marx revealed all the real and imaginary sins of Bauer, and demonstrated on this occasion his excellent memory when enumerating his misdemeanours. Thus, for example, Marx recalls that

---

[34] *Hinrichs politische Vorlesungen*, p. 23.
[35] GK 20.
[36] GM 42.

Bauer, when a theologian tried to cite evidence of the immaculate conception of Mary; that he regarded the angel seen in Jacob's dream as the
embodiment of God; that he justified the existence of the Prussian
state as an absolute state; that in *Kritik der evangelischen Geschichte der
Synoptiker* he presented the self-consciousness in place of actual man
etc.[37] Instead of concentrating on a relevant discussion, Marx prefers
to conduct sorties into Bauer's ideological past and confuses all the
views which Bauer ever held, as if to demonstrate that Bauer was
actually repeating himself. This impression is strengthened by perusal
of the following Marxian statements: "For the theologian Bauer it is
self-evident that criticism should, in the long term, be *speculative
theology*, since *he*, the *critic* is a theologian by profession;"[38] "Herr
Bauer, the docent in theology"; "Herr Bauer, a *genuine* [...] *theologian*
or *theological* critic".[39] In order to leave no doubt as to the tendencies of
Bauer's outlook, Marx notes: "Herr Bauer's last stage is not an anomaly
in his development; it is the *return* of his development *into itself* from
its *estrangement.* [...] Returning to its starting-point, absolute *criticism*
ended the *speculative circular motion* and thereby its own *life's career.*"[40]

Marx, who was closely acquainted with Bauer's thought, knew, of
course, that Bauer not only had not returned to the theological stage
of his development, but that he had arrived at a characteristically
atheistic standpoint. But all means were acceptable in order to condemn Bauer, and hence the citing of his views from the days when all
the Young Hegelians pinned their hopes on the Prussian monarchy, as
if they characterized Bauer alone, with the intention of persuading
Marx's audience that Bauer was a political traitor. If Marx had devoted
more thought to the method to be employed in his polemic with
Bauer, he would undoubtedly have arrived at the conclusion that all of
his historical arguments were irrelevant and totally superfluous, particularly since Bauer's intellectual weaknesses, as revealed in the *Allgemeine Literaturzeitung*, supplied sufficient evidence that his views
could not be accepted.

As could have been expected, Marx set himself the aim of emphasizing
the role of the masses in historical advancement and the creation of a
better political and social regime, in comparison with the prevailing
situation. In order to achieve this aim, he had to criticize the Bauerian

---

[37] MEGA I, 1, iii, pp. 281, 286; HF 144–145, 148, 151.
[38] Ibid. p. 276; HF 138.
[39] Ibid. pp. 278, 284; HF 140, 148.
[40] Ibid. p. 320; HF 192.

theory that it was the critic, with his free and developed self-consciousness, who created ideological changes which could, in the long term, open up a new historical era. The positive aspect – the masses as a factor shaping history, and particularly along progressive and revolutionary lines – and the negative aspect: the cancellation of the ideological significance of the intellectuals like Bauer, who were detached from the masses, for the achievement of progress – are of one piece as far as Marx is concerned. Those who are unwilling to accept the idea of the decisive role of the masses in history, turn to the outstanding personality and vice versa.

For Marx, the Bauerian conception is a paradigm of arrogant intellectualism, which sees its main strength in independence of the masses and of material interests, when in actual fact this standpoint reflects an inability to bring about any real change and is an expression of the impotence of the German petit bourgeoisie where the abolition of absolutism and feudalism is concerned. This motif was later developed in *The German Ideology*, mainly directed against Stirner. "It [the critique] has drawn its relative fame from critical debasement, rejection and transformation of *definite* massy objects and persons. It now draws its absolute fame from the critical debasement, rejection and transformation of the mass in general."[41]

Marx attacks the Bauerian standpoint from several directions. First he refers to the Bauerian concept of the masses and establishes that this is a static and unchanging category, whereas the true situation is completely different: there are not many traits common to the masses during the French Revolution on the one hand and the masses of several centuries ago on the other. Bauer's approach, he says, suffers from disregard for history and from lack of understanding of its development. Secondly: Bauer attributes to the masses interestedness while theory is characterized by lack of interest towards events in social life. Marx argues against Bauer's theory that the projects of theory – because of lack of interestedness and remoteness from socio-economic factors – do not win the recognition of the masses and that history, in which the masses take part, does not create worthy projects – that it is precisely the lack of interestedness and close contact with the masses which should be regarded as the main cause of the failure of pure theory. "The 'idea' always disgraced itself insofar as it differed from the 'interest'."[42] On the other hand, the material interest, which

41 Ibid. p. 249; HF 105.
42 Ibid. p. 253; HF 109.

found expression in the idea formulated in accordance with its objectives led to the mobilization of the masses in order to pave the way for a political-social regime realizing its principles. History shows, according to Marx, that in the past, for example during the French Revolution, there was illusory unity between the idea, which was bourgeois in essence and universal in form, and the interest in authentic and universal emancipation of the masses. A true unity is possible only when there is total congruence of the idea and interest of the masses.[43] Thirdly: Bauer's idealistic conception, which draws inspiration from Hegel, does not regard history as the arena of real events, but rather as the battleground of ideas, detached from any material basis. Such a viewpoint, which does not apply where Bauer and even more so Hegel are concerned, is extended by Marx to all of reality and he thus arrives at the conclusion that "the *absolute criticism* has learnt from Hegel's *Phenomenology* at least the art of changing *real objective* chains that exist *outside me* into mere *ideal*, mere *subjective* chains existing *in me*, and thus to change all *exterior* palpable struggles into pure struggles of thought."[44] Therefore the Bauerian school is tilting against windmills while reality is not affected by the struggle being conducted on the spiritual, almost celestial plane. Fourthly: the masses are defined thus on the basis of his quantitative assumption that they far outnumber small groups, of intellectuals for example. But what is important is their empirical appearance in contrast to Bauer's metaphysical approach, or, as Marx says: "The 'mass' is therefore distinct from the *real* masses and exists as the 'mass' only for 'criticism'." The word "Masse" in German has several meanings, both physical mass and the masses. The real masses were grasped during the French Revolution as the "people", the bourgeois estate and the workers being classified together in this category, but with the development of capitalism there was increasing differentiation, until it became clear that the wage-earners and property-owners were in conflict. In this context Marx develops his communist theory, the preliminary foundations of which were laid down in *Towards the Critique of Hegel's Philosophy of Right. Introduction*, on the revolutionary significance of the proletariat. But there he presented an abstract idea without real historical and sociological content, whereas here, in *The Holy Family*, he was giving expression to his historical-dialectical approach. Marx analyses the conditions for a proletarian revolution and compares them with the

[43] Idem.; HF 109–110. See also ibid. pp. 298–299; HF 164–166.
[44] Ibid. p. 254; HF 111.

French Revolution which was essentially bourgeois in character; he emphasizes the objectivity of the process of accumulation of revolutionary factors and the factor of the practical and theoretical consciousness of the plight of the proletariat and again expounds the theory, that Bauer ridiculed, on the inability of the proletariat to arrive at self-liberation without the liberation of society as a whole from inhuman conditions.[45]

It is interesting to note at this point that Marx makes use of the Bauerian theory on the universal nature of alienation, when he attributes alienation to both proletariat and bourgeoisie.[46] The sole difference between the two is that capitalists, feeling at ease and their own masters, recognize alienation as their own force and enjoy in it the outward appearance of human existence, while the proletariat is destroyed by alienation and recognizes in it its own helplessness; thus the distinction is only on the spiritual level. This theory is a classic example of the combination of a metaphysical motif – the universality of alienation – with statements of sociological nature: the rule of private property as the cause of the plight of the wage-earning class, whose behaviour is determined by its situation, and this is dependent on the entire organization of bourgeois society.[47]

In his discussion of the bourgoisie, the proletariat and the conflicts of bourgeois society, Marx reveals his superiority to Bauer, particularly in those sections in which he analyses historical events such as the revolutions in France at the end of the eighteenth century and in 1830 and in the chapters relating to economic and social issues, for example the structure of the capitalist economy and the changes in it since the eighteenth century. Instead of Bauer's abstract conflicts: spirit and "mass", mankind and the individual, self-consciousness and substance, he offers a historical and sociological formulation of the development of bourgeois society, private property and classes.

At the same time, Marx gave a distorted picture of Bauer's views: by depicting his approach as theological – the self-consciousness issue was seen as a manifestation of idealism and idealism as theology in philosophical guise – by bringing in ideas which Bauer had long since abandoned, and by tackling his views as expressed in the four articles – of the *Allgemeine Literaturzeitung* – which were but a drop in the bucket in comparison with the dozens of books and articles he had

[45] Ibid. pp. 206–207; HF 52–53.
[46] Ibid. p. 206; HF 51.
[47] Idem.; HF – idem.

written previously and which are representative for all his theories. It is obvious that it was convenient for Marx to take issue with those of Bauer's views which highlighted the pure character of theory and the conflict between the spirit and the masses, instead of arguing with those of his theories which belonged to his radical stage. But, in addition to this motive, i.e. to reduce Bauer's theories ad absurdum and thus to make his polemical task easier by alternatively presenting factual motifs and caricatured versions of theories, – Marx was also influenced by his desire to break away from Bauer, who had influenced him so strongly during that precise radical stage.

Bauer's response to Marx's attack was lukewarm. In his article *Charakteristik Ludwig Feuerbachs* he devoted some 50 pages to Feuerbach, whom he continued to regard as his main enemy, and only 5 pages to Marx. This was the first time that Bauer explicitly referred to Marx and to his own critique of his views in *The Holy Family*. Bauer claims that Marx (and Engels as well) did not comprehend that his criticism was directed against all the transcendent forces which had till then held mankind in a regime of oppression and humiliation, precluding it from living a human life, and that he had fiercely attacked religion in general and the state in its various manifestations, since he had expounded the principles of the self-consciousness and attacked the substance. Before his time the substance had been grasped as a sacred force, the foundation of religion and the state, whereas he had proved that it was but a human creation with the self-consciousness as its starting point. Bauer argues against Marx that the latter had ignored his achievements and successes in his struggle against political and church institutions and was focusing only on his literary and journalistic activity in the *Allgemeine Literaturzeitung*, thus detaching his critique from its radical background and development.[48]

According to Bauer, Marx, through utilizing such methods, had created the impression that criticism was dogmatic, but the truth was that it was Marx himself who was the dogmatist, who for purposes of polemic created the image of his opponent which was convenient for himself.[49]

Bauer vehemently rejects the Marxian criticism that the self-consciousness is detached from actual man, that it is speculation, arriving at caricature of itself, and claims that Marx employs derogatory terms instead of responding factually to arguments. But the truth is that

[48] LF 138–139.
[49] Ibid. p. 140.

Bauer himself was also guilty of failing to respond in relevent fashion to Marx's arguments, since he apparently decided to pay him back in his own coin. "Marx", he wrote, "supplied us with a play, in which he himself appears in the end as an entertaining comedian."[50]

Marx's reaction to Bauer's answer appears in a section of *The German Ideology* which is entitled *Saint Bruno*. The main idea of this chapter had already been formulated in *The Holy Family* as follows: "*Ideas* can never lead beyond an old world system but only beyond the ideas of the old world system. Ideas cannot *carry anything out* at all. In order to carry out ideas men are needed who dispose of a certain practical force."[51] To Bauer's conception of self-consciousness, which sets up, in place of real human beings and their real consciousness, the "absolute spirit" in its subjectivist version, the "abstract phrase" and "thought" – he attributes various characteristics of ideology: it is a distorted viewpoint which sees in the idea the sovereign force in the world; it is convinced that a change of consciousness will lead to change and even a change of direction in the structure of the social world; it ignores the true relations prevailing in society and the real factors shaping the quality of these relations etc.[52]

Marx is saying nothing that was not said in his previous criticism: again he stresses Bauer's dependence on Hegel and Feuerbach's superiority to Bauer. Apart from this Marx reiterates several times that criticism is detached from the critic since the self-consciousness is detached from man and, in this specific instance, from Bauer himself.

The controversy between Bauer and Marx won the attention of the press. The writer Julius, for example, believed that Marx was trying to save practical humanism from Bauer by offering Feuerbachian argumentation.[53] But the details attest to the fact that Julius was not an expert on this issue. Thus, for example, when he attributes to Feuerbach Marx's stand on material factors in the life of society, Julius' anger against Marx was directed mainly at Marx's view of Bauer as a theologian since, according to Julius, Bauer was unwilling to accept the theory on the historical role of the proletariat and rejected Marxian historical materialism. As far as Julius is concerned, it is far more important to defend the human individual, who

---

[50] Ibid. p. 143.
[51] MEGA I, 1, iii, p. 294; HF 160.
[52] GI 101–103, 106–109, 114.
[53] *Der Streit der sichtbaren mit der unsichtbaren Menschenkirche, oder Kritik der Kritik der kritischen Kritik.* Wigands Vierteljahrsschrift, 1845, Vol. II, pp. 326–333.

is the sole substance in the world, than to rely on the masses, or the abstract human species lacking any specificity.

The anonymous author of the lengthy article on Bauer mentioned several times above[54] points out that Bauer's views on pure theory and on the masses in opposition to it, did not necessarily grow out of his previous convictions, and gave expression to the belief that Bauer's latest views had deservedly been criticized by Marx.[55] At the same time, the writer of the article was not unaware of the fact that Bauer had influenced Marx. It transpires from his remarks that it is incorrect to stress constantly the contradictions between Marx and Bauer, since Marx's theories, particularly on the state, contain numerous Bauerian elements. In his view, Marx drew inspiration from the view of the existing state as a body based on privilege, as expressed in *The Good Cause of Freedom* and in Bauer's other articles. "In the *Deutsch-Französische Jahrbücher*", he wrote, "Marx realized the Bauerian principle in relation to the state more consistently and liberated him from the theological approach more fundamentally than did Bauer himself.[56] With the exception of this general statement, he cited no concrete examples, but the very fact that he expounded the theory of Marx's dependence on Bauer is interesting and noteworthy. It is to be regretted that with the passing of time this theory disappeared almost entirely from the field of vision of Marxian scholars.

[54] See part one, ch. V, p. 41, and n. 25, 26; also part two, ch. VI, n. 16 and 22.
[55] *Bruno Bauer oder die Entwicklung des theologischen Humanismus unserer Tage, pp.* 81–82.
[56] Ibid. p. 75.

BIBLIOGRAPHY

A. BRUNO BAUER'S WORKS CITED IN THE TEXT

D. F. Strauss: Das Leben Jesu (Review), JWK 1835, Vol. 2, pp. 879ff.
Der mosaische Ursprung der Gesetzgebung des Pentateuch. ZspT, Vol. 1, 1836, Part I, pp. 140ff.
Der Pantheismus innerhalb des Rationalismus und Supranaturalismus. Ibid., pp. 267ff.
Der alttestamentliche Hintergrund im Evangelium des Johannes. Ibid., Part II, pp. 158ff.
Das "Antitheologische" am Hegelschen Begriff der hebräischen Religion. Ibid., pp. 247ff.
Die Prinzipien der mosaischen Rechts- und Religionsverfassung. Ibid., pp. 297ff.
E. W. Hengstenberg: Die Authentie des Pentateuch (Review), ibid., Vol. 2, 1837, pp. 439ff.
Die Urgeschichte der Menschheit nach dem biblischen Bericht der Genesis. Ibid. Vol. 3, 1838, pp. 125ff.
Bähr: Symbolik des mosaischen Kultus (Review), ibid., pp. 485ff.
D. F. Strauss: Das Leben Jesu Vol. II (Review), JWK 1836, Vol. I, pp. 681ff.
C. S. Matthies: Erklärung des Briefes Pauli (Review), ibid., pp. 108ff.
D. F. Strauss: Streitschriften etc. (Review), ibid., 1838, Vol. 1, pp. 817ff.
Kritik der Geschichte der Offenbarung. Vol. 1, Part I-II: *Die Religion des Alten Testaments in der geschichtlichen Entwicklung ihrer Prinzipien dargestellt*. Berlin 1838.
A. F. Gfrörer: Die heilige Sage (Review), JWK 1840, Vol. 1, pp. 223ff.
Die evangelische Landeskirche Preussens und die Wissenschaft, Leipzig 1840.
Kritik der evangelischen Geschichte des Johannes, Bremen 1840.
Der christliche Staat und unsere Zeit, HJ Leipzig 1841, No 135–140, pp. 537ff. Reprinted in *Feldzüge der reinen Kritik*, Frankfurt/M. 1968, pp. 7ff.
Kritik der evangelischen Geschichte der Synoptiker. Vol. I-II, Leipzig 1841, Vol. III, Leipzig 1842.
Die Posaune des jüngsten Gerichts über Hegel, den Atheisten und Antichristen. Ein Ultimatum, Leipzig 1841. Reprinted in *Hegelsche Linke*, Stuttgart-Bad Cannstatt, 1962, pp. 123ff.
Theologische Schamlosigkeiten, DJ, Dresden 1841, No 117–120, pp. 465ff. Reprinted in *Feldzüge der reinen Kritik*, pp. 44ff.
Die Parteien im jetzigen Frankreich, RhZ Köln, 23.1.1842, No 23, Beiblatt.
Die deutschen Sympathien für Frankreich. Ibid., 6.2.1842, No 37, Beiblatt.
Was ist Lehrfreiheit? Ibid., 12.4.1842, Beiblatt.
Th. Romer: Deutschlands Beruf in der Gegenwart und Zukunft (Review). Ibid., 7.6.1842, No 158, Beiblatt.

Bekenntnisse einer schwachen Seele, DJ, Dresden 1842, No 148–149, pp. 589ff. Reprinted in *Feldzüge der reinen Kritik*, pp. 70ff.

D. F. Strauss: Das Leben Jesu. Vol. I-II (Review), DJ, Leipzig 1842, No 165–168, pp. 66off.

Die gute Sache der Freiheit und meine eigene Angelegenheit, Zürich-Winterthur 1842.

Hegels Lehre von der Religion und Kunst von dem Standpunkte des Glaubens aus beurteilt. Leipzig 1843.

Die Judenfrage, Braunschweig 1843.

D. F. Strauss: Die christliche Glaubenslehre etc. (Review), DJ, Leipzig 1843, No 21–24, pp. 81ff.

Leiden und Freuden des theologischen Bewußtseins, An, Zürich-Winterthur 1843. Vol. II, pp. 89ff. Reprinted in *Feldzüge der reinen Kritik*, pp. 153ff.

Bremisches Magazin für evangelische Wahrheit gegenüber dem modernen Pietismus. (Review), Ibid., pp. 113ff.

Th. Kliefoth: Einleitung in die Dogmengeschichte (Review), ibid., pp. 135ff.

V. Ammon: Die Geschichte des Lebens Jesu mit steter Rücksicht auf die vorhandenen Quellen (Review), ibid., pp. 160ff.

Das alte neue Testament, ibid. pp. 186ff.

Die Fähigkeit der heutigen Juden und Christen frei zu werden, 21 Bogen aus der Schweiz, Zürich-Winterthur 1843. Reprinted in *Feldzüge der reinen Kritik*, pp. 175ff.

Das entdeckte Christentum. Zürich-Winterthur 1843. Published by Ernst Barnikol, 1927, under the title *Das entdeckte Christentum im Vormärz*.

Geschichte der Politik, Kultur und Aufklärung des 18. Jahrhunderts. Vol. I: Deutschland während der ersten vierzig Jahre des 18. Jahrhunderts. Charlottenburg 1843.

Hinrichs politische Vorlesungen (Review), ALZ, Charlottenburg 1844, No 5, pp. 23ff. Reprinted in *Feldzüge der Kritik*, pp. 196ff.

Die neuesten Schriften über die Judenfrage. Ibid., 1844, No 4, pp. 10ff.

Hinrichs politische Vorlesungen, Vol. II (Review), Ibid. No 5, pp. 23–25. Reprinted in *Feldzüge der reinen Kritik*, pp. 196ff.

Was ist jetzt Gegenstand der Kritik? Ibid., No 8, pp. 18ff. Reprinted in *Feldzüge der reinen Kritik*, pp. 200ff.

Die Gattung und die Masse, Ibid. No 10, pp. 42ff. Reprinted in *Feldzüge der reinen Kritik*, pp. 213ff.

Briefwechsel zwischen Bruno Bauer und Edgar Bauer während der Jahre 1839–1842 aus Bonn und Berlin, Charlottenburg 1844.

Charakteristik Ludwig Feuerbachs, Wigands Vierteljahrsschrift, Leipzig 1845, Vol. III, pp. 86ff.

Vollständige Geschichte der Parteikämpfe in Deutschland während der Jahre 1842–1846. Vol. I-II, Charlottenburh 1847.

Die humanistische Bildung der Deutschen in der zweiten Hälfte des 18. Jahrhunderts. Vierteljahresschrift für Volkswirtschaft, Politik und Kulturgeschichte, Berlin 1876. Vol. 13/4.

Jesus und die Cäsaren, Berlin 1880.

B. MARX'S WORKS CITED IN THE TEXT

Differenz der demokritischen und epikureischen Naturphilosophie nebst einem Anhange, MEGA I, 1, i, Frankfurt/M. 1927, Edited by D. Ryazanov, pp. 5ff.

Aus den Vorarbeiten zur Geschichte der epikureischen, stoischen und skeptischen Philosophie, Ibid. pp. 84ff.

(Ludwig Feuerbach) *Luther als Schiedsrichter zwischen Strauss und Feuerbach*, Ibid. pp. 174f.

Bemerkungen über die neueste preußische Zensurinstruktion, Ibid. pp. 153ff.

Die Verhandlungen des 6. rheinischen Landtags. Erster Artikel. Debatten über Preßfreiheit und Publikation der Landständischen Verhandlungen, Ibid. pp. 179ff.

Der leitende Artikel in der Nr. 179 der Kölnischen Zeitung, Ibid. pp. 232ff.

Der Kommunismus und die Augsburger Allgemeine Zeitung, Ibid. pp. 260ff.

Verhandlungen des 6. rheinischen Landtags. Dritter Artikel. Debatten über das Holzdiebstahlsgesetz, Ibid. pp. 266ff.

Über die ständische Ausschüsse in Preußen, Ibid. pp. 321ff.

Noch ein Wort über: "Bruno Bauer und die akademische Lehrfreiheit von Dr. O. F. Gruppe. Berlin 1842", Ibid. pp. 397ff.

Kritik des Hegelschen Staatsrecht (§§ 261–313), Ibid. pp. 403ff.

Ein Briefwechsel von 1843, Ibid. pp. 557ff.

Zur Judenfrage, Ibid. pp. 576ff.

Zur Kritik der Hegelschen Rechtsphilosophie. Einleitung, Ibid. pp. 607ff.

Exzerpte 1840–1843, MEGA I, i, ii, Frankfurt/M. 1929. Edited by D. Ryazanov, pp. 98ff.

Briefe und Dokumente, Ibid. pp. 184ff.

Ökonomisch-philosophische Manuskripte aus dem Jahre 1844, MEGA I, 1, iii, Berlin 1932. Edited by V. Adoratskij, pp. 33ff.

Die heilige Familie, Ibid. pp. 175ff.

Grundrisse der Kritik der Politischen Ökonomie, Berlin 1953.

Das Kapital, Vol. I-III, Berlin 1951.

Writings of the Young Marx on Philosophy and Society. Edited and Translated by Loyd D. Easton and Kurt H. Guddat, Garden City, N.Y., Doubleday & Co. 1976.

Basic Writings on Politics and Philosophy, Edited by Lewis S. Feuer, Garden City, N.Y., Doubleday & Co. 1959.

The Difference Between the Democritean and Epicurean Philosophy of Nature. In Norman D. Livergood's *Activity in Marx's Philosophy*. The Hague, Martinus Nijhoff 1967.

Critic of Hegel's "Philosophy of Right". Translated by A. J. and J. O'Malley. Edited with an Introduction by Joseph O'Malley. Cambridge University Press 1970.

The German Ideology, Moscow, Progress Publishers 1964.

The Holy Family. Edited by R. Dixon, Moscow 1956.

Early Texts. Translated and edited by David McLellan. Oxford, Basil Blackwell 1971.

On Religion, New York, Schoken Books 1957.

A Contribution to the Critique of Political Economy, London, Lawrence & Wishart 1971.

C. HEGEL'S WORKS CITED IN THE TEXT

Hegels theologische Jugendschriften. Edited by Hermann Nohl, Tübingen 1907.

Jenenser Realphilosophie I, edited by Johannes Hoffmeister, Leipzig 1932.

Jenenser Realphilosophie II, edited by Johannes Hoffmeister, Leipzig 1931.

Jenaer Schriften 1801–1807, Theorie Werkausgabe, Frankfurt/M., Suhrkamp Verlag 1970.

Vorlesungen über die Philosophie der Religion. Zweite verbesserte Auflage, 1840.

Begriff der Religion. In *Vorlesungen über die Philosophie der Religion*, Vol. I edited by Georg Lasson, Leipzig 1925.

Vorlesung über die Philosophie der Weltgeschichte, edited by Georg Lasson, Leipzig 1919.

Vorlesungen über die Ästhetik, edited by Fr. Bassenge, Berlin 1955.
Vorlesungen über die Philosophie der Geschichte, Theorie Werkausgabe, Frankfurt/M., Suhrkamp Verlag 1970.
Berliner Schriften, Theorie Werkausgabe, Frankfurt/M., Suhrkamp Verlag 1970.
Lectures on the Philosophy of Religion, vol. I-III, translated by E. B. Speirs and J. Burdon Sanderson, London, Routledge & Kegan Paul 1968.
The Phenomenology of Mind, translated, with an introduction by J. B. Baillie. Introduction to the Torchbook Edition by George Lichtheim, New York and Evanston, Harper & Row 1967.
Science of Logic, 2 vols., translated by W. H. Johnston and L. G. Struthers, London, George Allen & Unwin; New York, The Macmillan Company 1951².
Lectures on the History of Philosophy, 3 vols., translated by E.S. Haldane, London, Routledge & Kegan Paul 1955.
The Logic of Hegel. The Encyclopaedia of the Philosophical Sciences, Part One, translated by William Wallace, sec. edition, Oxford University Press. Reprinted 1965.
Philosophy of Mind. The Encyclopaedia of the Philosophical Sciences, Part Three, translated by William Wallace, with foreword by J. N. Findlay, Oxford, at the Clarendon Press 1971.
The Philosophy of History, translated by J. Sibree, with a new introduction by C. J. Friedrich, New York, Dover Publications 1956.
Hegel's Philosophy of Right, translated with notes by T. M. Knox, Oxford University Press, 1969.

D. OTHER SOURCES

(Anon.): *Hengstenberg und das Judentum*, HJ Leipzig 1840, pp. 971ff.
(Anon.): *Bruno Bauer oder die Entwicklung des theologischen Humanismus unserer Tage. Eine Kritik und Charakteristik*. Wigands Vierteljahrsschrift, Vol. II, III, Leipzig 1845, pp. 52ff.
Auch ein Berliner: *Zwei Vota über das Zerwürfniß zwischen Kirche und Wissenschaft*, DJ 1842, No 7, 8, pp. 25ff.
Bauer, Edgar: *Bruno Bauer und seine Gegner*, Berlin 1842.
—: *Der Streit der Kritik mit der Kirche und Staat*, Bern 1844.
—: *1842*, ALZ, vol. 8, 1844.
Cieszkowski, August: *Gott und Palingenese*, Berlin 1842.
Ein Berliner: *Vorläufiges über "Bruno Bauer, Kritik der evangelischen Geschichte der Synoptiker"*, DJ, No. 105, 1841, pp. 417f.
Feuerbach, Ludwig: *Gedanken über Tod und Unsterblichkeit*, edited by W. Bolin and Fr. Jodl, Stuttgart 1903.
—: *Ueber Philosophie und Christentum in Beziehung auf den der Hegelschen Philosophie gemachten Vorwurf der Unchristlichkeit*, SW, vol. I, Leipzig 1846, pp. 42ff.
—: *Zur Beurtheilung der Schrift: "Das Wesen des Christentums"*, Ibid. pp. 248ff.
—: *Ueber das "Wesen des Christentums" in Beziehung auf den "Einzigen und sein Eigenthum"*, ibid. pp. 342ff.
—: *Ueber Philosophie und Christentum*, SW, vol. II, Leipzig 1846, pp. 179ff.
—: *Kritik der Hegelschen Philosophie*, ibid. pp. 185ff.
—: *Vorläufige Thesen zur Reform der Philosophie*, ibid. pp. 244ff.
—: *Grundsätze der Philosophie der Zukunft*, ibid. pp. 269ff.
—: *Das Wesen des Christentums*, SW, vol. VII, Leipzig 1849³.
—: *Vorlesungen über das Wesen der Religion*, SW, vol. VIII, Leipzig 1851.
—: *The Essence of Christianity*, translated by George Eliot, Introduction by

Karl Barth, Foreword by H. Richard Niebuhr, New York, Harper Torch-
  books, Harper & Brothers 1957.
—: *Ludwig Feuerbach in seinem Briefwechsel und Nachlass*, herausgegeben von
  Karl Grün, vol. I., Leipzig & Heidelberg 1884.
—: *Selected Writings of Ludwig Feuerbach*. Translated with an Introduction by
  Zawar Hanfi. Garden City, N.Y., Anchor Books, Doubleday & Co. 1972.
Göschel, Karl Friedrich: *Aphorismen über Nichtwissen und absolutes Wissen im
  Verhältnis zum christlichen Glaubenserkenntnis*, Berlin 1829.
Glossy, Karl: *Literarische Geheimberichte aus dem Vormärz*, Wien 1912.
Hansen, Joseph (editor): *Rheinische Briefen und Akten zur Geschichte der politi-
  schen Bewegung 1830–1850*, Osnabrück 1967.
Julius, G.: *Der Streit der sichtbaren mit der unsichtbaren Menschenkirche oder
  Kritik der Kritik der kritischen Kritik*, Wigands Vierteljahresschrift, vol. II,
  Leipzig 1845, pp. 326ff.
Löser, W.: *Die reine Kritik und ihre Bewegung. Zur Charakteristik der von Bruno
  Bauer und seinen Anhängern in jüngster Zeit eingeschlagenen Richtung*, Leipzig
  1845.
Dr. Modus: *Der Posaunist und das Centrum der Hegelschen Philosophie*, DJ 1842,
  No 136-7-8, pp. 542ff.
Opitz, Theodor: *Bruno Bauer und seine Gegner. 4 kritische Artikel*, Breslau 1846.
—: *Die Helden der Masse, Charakteristiken*, Grünberg 1847.
Prutz, Robert: *Zehn Jahre. Geschichte der neuesten Zeit. 1840–1850*, vol. I,
  Leipzig 1850.
Rhenius, D.: *Kritik der evangelischen Geschichte der Synoptiker von B. Bauer*. DJ
  1842, No 219, 220, 221, pp. 875ff.
Richter, Friedrich: *Die Lehre von den letzten Dingen*, Breslau 1833.
Rosenkranz, Karl: *Enzyklopädie der theologischen Wissenschaft*, Halle 1831.
—: *Kritik der Schleiermacherschen Glaubenslehre*, Königsberg 1837.
Ruge, Arnold: *Preussen und die Reaktion. Zur Geschichte unserer Zeit*, Leipzig
  1838.
—: *Der Pietismus und die Jesuiten*, HJ 1839, pp. 284ff.
—: *Zur Kritik des gegenwärtigen Staats- und Völkerrechts*. H.J. 1840, No 151–156.
—: *Nachschrift zu: Vorläufiges über "Bruno Bauer, Kritik der evangelischen Ge-
  schichte der Synoptiker"* DJ 1841, pp. 418ff.
—: *Die evangelische Landeskirche Preussens und die Wissenschaft*, HJ 1841, pp.
  537ff.
—: *Hegel's Lehre von der Religion und Kunst, vom Standpuncte des Glaubens aus
  beurtheilt*, DJ 1842, pp. 579 ff.
—: *Bruno Bauer und die Lehrfreiheit*, Anekdota, Zürich-Winterthur 1843, pp.
  119ff.
—: *Briefwechsel und Tagebuchblätter*, edited by P. Nerrlich, vol. I, Berlin 1886.
Sass, Friedrich: *Berlin in seiner neuesten Zeit und Entwicklung*, Leipzig 1846.
Stahl, Friedrich Julius: *Philosophie des Rechts nach geschichtlicher Ansicht*. Vol. I,
  Die Genesis der gegenwärtigen Rechtsphilosophie, Heidelberg 1830.
—: *Der christliche Staat und sein Verhältnis zu Deismus und Judentum*, Berlin
  1847.
Strauss, David Friedrich: *Streitschriften zur Verteidigung meiner Schrift über das
  Leben Jesu und zur Charakteristik der gegenwärtigen Theologie*, Tübingen 1837.
—: *Das Leben Jesu kritisch bearbeitet*, 2 vols., Tübingen 1835–1836.
—: *Die christliche Glaubenslehre in ihrer Entwicklung und im Kampf mit der
  modernen Wissenschaft*, Tübingen 1840.
Stuhr, P. F., H. Leo: *Lehrbuch der Universalgeschichte*, HJ, 1839, pp. 184ff.

E. OTHER WORKS

Adams, H. P.: *Karl Marx in His Earlier Writings*, New York, Russel & Russel 1965.
Avineri, Shlomo: *The Social and Political Thought of Karl Marx*, Cambridge University Press 1970.
—: *Hook's Hegel*. In *Hegel's Political Philosophy*, edited by Walter Kaufmann, New York, Atherton Press 1970.
—: *Hegel's Theory of the Modern State*, Cambridge University Press, 1972.
Barion, Jacob: *Ideologie, Wissenschaft, Philosophie*, Bonn 1966.
Barnikol, Ernst: *Das entdeckte Christentum im Vormärz. Bruno Bauers Kampf gegen Religion und Christentum und Erstausgabe seiner Kampfschrift*, Jena 1927.
—: *Bruno Bauers Kampf gegen Religion und Christentum und die Spaltung der vormärzlichen preussischen Opposition*, Zeitschrift für Kirchengeschichte 46, Gotha 1927, pp. 1ff.
—: *Bruno Bauer. Studien und Materialien*, Assen, Van Gorcum & Co. 1972.
Barth, Hans: *Wahrheit und Ideologie*, Zürich 1945.
Benz, E.: *Hegels Religionsphilosophie und die Jungshegelianer. Zur Kritik des Religionsbegriffe von Karl Marx*, Zeitschrift für Religions- und Geistesgeschichte, vol. 7/1955, pp. 247ff.
Bergh van Eysinga, G. A. van den: *Aus einer unveröffentlichen Biographie von Bruno Bauer*, Annali, Anno Sesto, Milano, Feltrinelli 1963, pp. 329ff.
Berlin, Isaiah: *Karl Marx, His Life and Environment*. Oxford University Press, 1963.
Beyer, Wilhelm R.: *Hegel-Bilder. Kritik der Hegeldeutungen*, (Ost) Berlin 1967.
Bloch, Ernst: *Subjekt-Objekt. Erläuterungen zu Hegel*, Frankfurt/M. 1962.
—: *Das Prinzip Hoffnung*, 3 vols, Frankfurt/M. 1968.
Bockmühl, Klaus: *Leiblichkeit und Gesellschaft. Studien zur Religionskritik und Anthropologie im Frühwerk von Ludwig Feuerbach und Karl Marx*, Göttingen 1961.
Brazill, William J.: *The Young Hegelians*, New Haven and London, Yale University Press 1970.
Camus, Albert: *L'Homme révolté*. Paris 1951.
Calvez, Jean-Yves: *La pensée de Karl Marx*, Paris 1956.
Cornu, Auguste: *Karl Marx und Friedrich Engels. Leben und Werk*. 3 vols. (Ost) Berlin 1954, 1962, 1968.
Daumer, Georg Friedrich: *Geheimnisse des christlichen Altertums. Mit einer einleitenden Rede von Karl Marx*. Wissenschaftliche Bibliothek des proletarischen Freidenkertums. Vol. IX, Dresden 1924.
Drews, Arthur: *Die Leugnung der Geschichtlichkeit Jesus in Vergangenheit und Gegenwart*, Karlsruhe in Baden 1926.
Dupré Louis: *The Philosophical Foundations of Marxism, New York/Chicago*, Harcourt, Brace & World 1966.
Engels, Friedrich: *Luwdig Feuerbach und Ausgang der klassischen deutschen Philosophie*, Karl Marx-Friedrich Engels. *Werke*, vol. 21 (Ost)Berlin 1962.
Erdmann, J. E.: *Philosophie der Neuzeit*, vol. II, Berlin 1896.
Fetscher, Iring: *Marx and Marxism*, New York, Herder & Herder 1971.
Friedrich, Manfred: *Philosophie und Ökonomie beim jungen Marx*, Berlin 1960.
Fleischmann, Eugène: *La philosophie politique de Hegel sous forme d'un commentaire des fondements de la philosophie du droit*, Paris 1964.
—: *La science universelle ou la logique de Hegel*, Paris 1968.
Garaudy, Roger: *Dieu est mort*, Paris 1962.

Gebhardt, Jürgen: *Politische Ordnung und menschliche Existenz*. In *Festgabe für Eric Voegelin*, München 1962.
—: *Politik und Eschatologie. Studien zur Geschichte der Hegelschen Schule in den Jahren 1830–1840*. Münchener Studien zur Politik, I/1963.
Gollwitzer, Helmut: *Die marxistische Religionskritik und der christliche Glaube*, Marxismusstudien 4/1962.
McGovern, Arthur: *K. Marx' First Political Writings. The Rheinische Zeitung 1842–1843*. In *Demythologizing Marxism*. Boston College Studies in Philosophy, vol. II, 1969, pp. 19ff.
Harris, H. S. *Hegel's Development Toward the Sunlight 1770–1801*, Oxford, Clarendon Press 1972.
Hartmann, Nicolai: *Die Philosophie des deutschen Idealismus*. Vol. II, *Hegel*, Berlin-Leipzig 1929.
Haym, Rudolf: *Hegel und seine Zeit*. Hildesheim 1962.
Heine, Heinrich: Sämtliche Werke, Berlin 1911, vol. VIII, *Zur Geschichte der Religion und der Philosophie in Deutschland*.
Hertz-Eichenrode, Dieter: *Der Junghegelianer Bruno Bauer im Vormärz*, Berlin 1957 (Dissertation).
—: *Massenpsychologie bei den Junghegelianern*, International Review of Social History, vol. VII, Amsterdam 1962.
Hillmann, Günther: *Marx und Hegel. Von der Spekulation zur Dialektik*, Frankfurt/M. 1966.
Hirsch, Rudolf: *Der erster Kritiker Marxens*, Zeitschrift für Religions- und Geistesgeschichte, IX/1937, pp. 246ff.
Holbach, P. H. D.: *Le Christianisme devoilé*, Paris 1761.
Hook, Sidney: *From Hegel to Marx. Studies in the Intellectual Development of Marx*, The University of Michigan Press 1968[3].
Hyppolite, Jean: *Studies on Marx and Hegel*, London, Heinemann Educational Books 1969.
Iljin, Iwan: *Die Philosophie Hegels als kontemplative Gotteslehre*, Bern 1946.
Kamenka, Eugene: *The Philosophy of Ludwig Feuerbach*, London, Routledge & Kegan Paul 1970.
Kaufmann, Walter: *Hegel. A Reinterpretation*. New York, Doubleday & Co. 1965.
Kägi, Paul: *Genesis des historischen Materialismus*, Wien 1965.
Kegel, Martin: *Bruno Bauer und seine Theorien zur Entstehung des Christentums*, Leipzig 1908.
Kempski, Jürgen von: *Bruno Bauer. Eine Studie zum Ausgang des Hegelianismus*. Archiv für Philosophie, I/1962.
Klutentreter, Wilhelm: *Die Rheinische Zeitung von 1842/43 in der politischen und geistigen Bewegung des Vormärz*. Dortmunder Beiträge zur Zeitungsforschung, vol. 10, part one, 1966.
Knox, T. M.: *Hegel and Prussianism*. In *Hegels Political Philosophy*, edited by Walter Kaufmann, New York, Atherton Press 1970.
Koch, Lothar: *Bruno Bauers "kritische Kritik". Beitrag zum Problem eines humanistischen Atheismus* (Dissertation), Köln 1969.
Koigen, David: *Zur Vorgeschichte des modernen philosophischen Sozialismus*, Bern 1901.
Koren, J. Henry: *Marx and the Authentic Man*, Pittsburg, Duquesne University Press 1967.
Korsch, Karl: *Karl Marx*, Frankfurt/M. 1967.
Koselleck, Reinhart: *Staat und Gesellschaft in Preussen 1815–1848*. In *Staat und Gesellschaft im deutschen Vormärz 1815–1848*, Stuttgart 1952, pp. 79ff.

Kratkiy nauchno-ateisticheskiy slovar', Moscow 1964.
McLellan, David: *The Young Hegelians and Karl Marx*, London, Macmillan 1969.
—: *Marx before Marxism*, London, Macmillan 1970.
Lenk, Kurt: *Ideologie. Ideologiekritik und Wissenssoziologie*, Neuwied 1971[5].
Lenin, V. I.: *O znachenii woinstwoyushchego materializma*, Sochineniya, Izd. IV, tom 33, Moscow 1953.
Lichtheim, George: *The Concept of Ideology and other Essays*, London, Random House 1954.
Litt, Theodor: *Hegel. Versuch einer kritischen Erneuerung*[2], Heidelberg 1961.
Lobkowicz, Nicolas: *Marx Attitude Toward Religion*, The Review of Politics, vol. 26/1964.
—: *Theory and Praxis. History of a Concept from Aristotle to Marx*. Notre Dame-London, University of Notre Dame Press 1967.
Löwenstein, Julius: *Vision und Wirklichkeit, Marx contra Marxismus*, Basel und Tübingen 1970.
Löwith, Karl: *From Hegel to Nietzsche*, Garden City, N. Y., Doubleday & Co. 1967.
—: *Man's Self-alienation in Early Writings of Marx*, Social Research 21/1954.
—: *Vermittlung und Unmittelbarkeit bei Hegel, Marx und Feuerbach*, Revue Internationale de Philosophie, vol. 101, 1972.
—: *Die Hegelsche Linke*, Stuttgart-Bad Cannstatt 1962.
Lukács, Georg: *Beiträge zur Geschichte der Ästhetik*, Berlin 1954.
—: *Die Zerstörung der Vernunft*, Berlin 1955.
—: *Schriften zur Ideologie und Politik*, Neuwied 1967.
Lübbe, Hermann: *Die politische Theorie der Hegelschen Rechte*, Archiv für Philosophie, Stuttgart 1960.
—: *Die Hegelsche Rechte. Texte*. Stuttgart-Bad Cannstatt 1962.
Mackay, John Henry: *Max Stirner, Sein Leben und Werk*, Berlin 1898.
O'Malley, Joseph: *Critique of Hegel's Philosophy of Right by Karl Marx, Introduction*, Cambridge University Press 1970.
Mannheim, Karl: *Ideology and Utopia*, London, Routledge and Kegan Paul 1954.
Marcuse, Herbert: *Reason and Revolution. Hegel and the Rise of Social Theory*, Boston, Beacon Press 1968[5].
—: *Über die philosophischen Grundlagen des wirtschaftswissenschaftlichen Arbeitsbegriff*. In *Archiv für Sozialwissenschaft und Sozialpolitik, vol. 69, part 3, 1933*.
Maréchal, Sylvain: *Dictionnaire des athées anciens et modernes*, Paris An. VIII(1800).
Mayer, Gustav: *Friedrich Engels. Eine Biographie*, Haag 1934.
—: *Die Junghegelianer und der preussische Staat*, Historische Zeitschrift, vol. 121'1920.
—: *Die Anfänge des politischen Radikalismus im vormärzlichen Preussen*. In *Radikalismus und bürgerliche Demokratie*, Frankfurt/M. 1968.
—: *Marx und der zweite Teil der Posaune*, Archiv für die Geschichte des Sozialismus und der Arbeiterbewegung, vol. 7/1916.
Meyer, Alfred: *Marxism. The Unity of Theory and Praxis*, Cambridge, Mass., Harvard University Press 1970.
Miller, Sepp, Sawadzki, Bruno: *Karl Marx in Berlin*, Berlin 1956.
Milić Vojin: *Das Verhältnis von Gesellschaft und Erkenntnis in Marx' Werk*. In *Ideologie*, edited by Kurt Lenk, Neuwied 1971.
Nigg, Walter: *Geschichte des religiösen Liberalismus*, Zürich 1937.
Ollman, Bertell: *Alienation. Marx's Concept of Man in Capitalist Society*, Cambridge University Press 1971.
Pelczynski, Z. A.: *Hegel Again*. In *Hegels Political Philosophy*, New York, Atherton Press 1970, pp. 8off.

Petrović, Gajo: *Marx in the Midtwentieth Century*, New York, Anchor Books, Doubleday & Co. 1967.
Plant, Raymond: *Hegel*, London Allen & Unwin, 1973.
Popitz, Heinrich: *Der entfremdete Mensch*, Frankfurt/M. 1967.
Post, Werner: *Kritik der Religion bei Marx*, München 1969.
Rawidowicz, S.: *Ludwig Feuerbachs Philosophie-Ursprung und Schicksal*, Berlin 1931.
Reding, Marcel: *Der politische Atheismus*, Wien-Graz-Köln 1971[2].
—: *Marxismus und Atheismus*, in *Marxismus-Leninismus, Geschichte und Gestalt*, Vortragsreihe der Freien Universität Berlin 1961, pp. 16off.
Ritter, Joachim: *Hegel und die französische Revolution*. In *Metaphysik und Politik, Studien zu Aristoteles und Hegel*, Frankfurt/M. 1969.
Rosenberg, Hans: *Arnold Ruge und die "Hallischen Jahrbücher"*, Archiv für Kulturgeschichte, vol. 20, pp. 292ff.
Rosenzweig, Franz: *Hegel und der Staat*, 2 vols., München-Berlin 1920.
Sabine, George H., *Marxism*, The Telluride Lectures 1957/58 at Cornell University Cornell University Press 1958.
Sass, Hans-Martin: *Bruno Bauers Idee der Rheinischen Zeitung*, Zeitschrift für Religions- und Geistesgeschichte, 1967.
—: *Feuerbach statt Marx. Zur Verfasserschaft des Aufsatzes "Luther als Schiedsrichter zwischen Strauss und Feuerbach"*, International Review of Social History, vol. XII, 1967, pp. 118ff.
—: *Feuerbachs Prospekt einer neuen Philosophie*, Revue Internationale de Philosophie, Bruxelles 1972, vol. 101.
Schacht, Richard: *Alienation*, New York, Doubleday 1970.
Schaper, Ewald: *Religion ist Opium fürs Volk*, Zeitschrift für Kirchengeschichte, 1940, pp. 425ff.
Schlawe, Fritz: *Die junghegelsche Publizistik*, Die Welt als Geschichte 11/1960, pp. 30ff.
Schläger E.: *Bruno Bauer und seine Werke*, Internationale Monatsschrift. Zeitschrift für allgemeine und nationale Kultur, vol. I, Chemnitz 1882.
Schnabel, Franz: *Deutsche Geschichte im 19. Jahrhundert*, vol. 3, Freiburg 1954.
Schweitzer, Albert: *Geschichte der Leben-Jesu-Forschung*, vol. I, München-Hamburg 1966.
Seeger, Reinhart: *Friedrich Engels. Die religiöse Entwicklung eines Spätpietisten und Frühsozialisten*, Halle 1935.
—: *Herkunft und Bedeutung des Schlagwortes: Die Religion ist Opium für das Volk*, Theologische Arbeiten zur Bibel-, Kirchen- und Geistesgeschichte, Halle 1935.
Sens, Walter: *Die irreligiöse Entwicklung von Karl Marx*. Christentum und Sozialismus. Quellen und Darstellungen, Halle 1935.
Stuke, Horst: *Philosophie der Tat. Studien zur Verwirklichung der Philosophie bei den Junghegelianern*, Stuttgart 1963.
Tucker, Robert: *Philosophy and Myth in Karl Marx*, Cambridge University Press 1971.
Walton, Paul and Gamble, Andrew: *From Alienation to Surplus Value*, London, Sheed & Ward 1972.
Weber, Max: *Methodologische Schriften*, Frankfurt/M. 1968.
Weil, Eric: *Hegel et l'État*, Paris 1950.
—: *Säkularisierung des politischen Denkens*, Marxismusstudien, Vierte Folge, Tübingen 1962.
Wildermuth, Armin: *Marx und die Verwirklichung der Philosophie*, 2 vols., Haag 1970.

INDEX

Adams, H. P., 151n
Alexander the Great, 21
Allgemeine Literaturzeitung, 4, 223, 224n, 225n, 229, 230, 234, 237, 238
Altenstein, Karl, Frh. von Stein zum, 21, 44, 59, 111
Ammon, Christian Friedrich, 215, 216
Anekdota zur neuesten deutschen Philosophie und Publizistik, 54n, 64n, 78n, 105n, 117n, 140n, 203, 207–209
Annali, 44n
Archiv für die Geschichte des Sozialismus und der Arbeiterbewegung, 130n
Archiv für Kulturgeschichte, 35n
Archiv für Philosophie, 44n
Archiv für Sozialwissenschaft und Sozialpolitik, 11n
Aristotle, 26, 149, 151, 152, 155, 156
Avineri, Shlomo, 9n, 111n, 166n, 189n, 203n

Bakunin, Michail, 189
Barion, Jacob, 180n, 191n
Barnikol, Ernst, VII, 7, 8n, 9 ,14, 15, 60n, 119n, 127n, 130n, 134n
Barth, Hans, 180, 191n
Bassenge, Fr., 26n
Bauer, Edgar, 12, 13, 46, 53n, 58, 59n, 60n, 61n, 127, 214, 222
Bauer, Egbert, 127
Benz, E., 140
Bergh van Eysinga, G. A. van den, VII, 44n, 61n, 63n
Berlin, Isaiah, 188n
Berliner, Ein (Ps.), 54
Beyer, Wilhelm R., 34n
Blanc, Louis, 188
Bloch, Ernst, 10, 163
Bloch, Joseph, 197n
Bockmühl, Klaus, 146n, 148

Böhme, Jacob, 26
Bolin, W., 28n
Brazil, William J., 13, 41n
Bruno, Giordano, 29
Buhl, Ludwig, 131

Calvez, Jean-Yves, 138n, 169n, 222n
Camus, Albert, 33, 46n
Carritt, E. F., 111
Cieszkowski, August, 9, 12, 32, 157
Cornu, Auguste, 5n, 35n, 44n, 119n, 130n, 131, 148n, 156n, 206n

Daub, Karl, 28
Daumer, Georg Friedrich, 144, 145
Democritus, 133, 149, 153
Deutsche Jahrbücher für Wissenschaft und Kunst, 6, 36, 52n, 54n, 59, 63n, 79n, 119, 206, 209
Deutsch-Französische Jahrbücher, 240
Dortmunder Beiträge zur Zeitungsforschung, 120
Drews, Arthur, 96
Dupré, Louis, 203n

Eichhorn, Johann Albrecht Friedrich, 60
Engels, Friedrich, 4, 6n, 13, 15, 16, 45, 99, 109, 132, 148, 188, 197, 202, 220, 228, 238
Epicurus, 133, 134, 149, 150, 153
Erdmann, Johann Eduard, 19, 21n, 27b, 28n, 36
Evangelische Kirchenzeitung, 19n

Fetscher, Iring, 146n, 200, 220n, 228
Feuerbach, Ludwig, 8, 12, 14, 28, 33, 34, 59, 96–102, 119, 120n, 128, 134, 138, 140, 145, 146, 148, 162, 163, 166, 167, 174, 175, 177, 180, 181, 189, 199, 202–213, 215–222, 228, 229, 231, 238, 239

Fichte, Johann Gottlieb, 66, 74, 82–84
Fichte, Immanuel Hermann, 160
Filon, 48
Fischer, Kuno, 160
Fleischer, Karl Moritz, 208
Fleischmann, Eugène, VII, 112n, 113n, 193n
Fourier, Charles, 231
Friedrich, Manfred, 148n, 166n
Friedrich II, 114
Friedrich Wilhelm III, 109
Friedrich Wilhelm IV, 59, 115

Gabel, Joseph, 192n
Gabler, Georg Andreas, 28, 30, 34, 36
Galai, Haia, VII
Galilei, Galileo, 29
Gamble, Andrew, 200n
Gans, Eduard, 35
Garaudy, Roger, 165
Gebhardt, Jürgen, 8n, 18n, 33
Gesellschaft, Die, 163n
Glossy, Karl, 5n
Gollwitzer, Helmut, 138n
Göschel, Karl-Friedrich, 27, 28, 34, 36
Grün, Karl, 99n, 188
Grünberg, Carl, 130n
Gruppe, Otto Friedrich, 206, 216

Haller, Albrecht von, 115
Hallische Jahrbücher für deutsche Wissenschaft und Kunst, 43n, 62n, 113n, 115n,
119, 211n
Hansen, Joseph, 120n
Hardenberg, Karl August, Fürst von, 111,
115
Harris, H. S., 165n
Harstick, Hans-Peter, VII
Hartmann, Nikolai, 25n
Haym, Rudolf, 18, 111
Hegel, Georg Wilhelm Friedrich, VII, 11n,
18, 19n, 22–29, 32–34, 37, 39, 40, 43, 60,
62–69, 71–73, 75–80, 82–84, 86, 91, 99–
101, 103, 106, 109–113, 118, 129–132,
134, 146, 149, 151–153, 155, 156, 159,
160, 162, 163, 165, 167, 170, 171, 177,
180, 190, 193, 203, 204, 207, 209, 211–
214, 217, 218, 221, 222, 236, 239
Heine, Heinrich, 1, 65, 141
Hengstenberg, Ernst Wilhelm, 18, 19, 42,
44, 59, 63, 174
Hertz-Eichenrode, Dieter, 6n, 14, 18n,
19n, 229n

Herwegh, Georg, 215
Hess, Moses, 12, 13, 32, 34, 121, 129, 138,
141, 188, 220, 222, 224
Hillmann, Günther, 148n, 156n, 157
Hirsch, Rudolf, 223n
Historische Zeitschrift, 11n
Holbach, P. H. D., 84, 90, 140
Homer, 57
Hook, Sidney, 11, 12
Hotho, H. G., 18, 19, 62
Hyppolite, Jean, 163n, 165n

Iljin, Iwan, 26
Internationale Monatsschrift, 17n
International Review of Social History,
208n, 229n

Jacobi, Friedrich Heinrich, 40, 63
Jahrbücher für wissenschaftliche Kritik, 19,
36, 37n, 38n, 39n
Jodl, Fr., 28n
John (Evangelist), 50, 52
John the Baptist, 48
Jong Edz., Frits de, VII
Julius, Gustav, 214, 239
Jung, Georg Gottlieb, 128, 129, 205

Kägi, Paul, 180n, 193n
Kamenka, Eugene, 207n, 216
Kant, Immanuel, 66
Kapp, Friedrich, 98
Kaufmann, Walter, 18n, 165n
Kautsky, Karl, 228
Kegel, Martin, 47n
Kempski, Jürgen von, 44n
Kierkegaard, Sörgen, 35n
Klutentreter, Wilhelm, 120n, 207n
Knox, T. M., 111n
Koch, Lothar, 14
Koigen, David, 11, 57n
Kołakowski, Leszek, VII
Konradi, 28
Köppen, Friedrich, 44, 131, 209, 214
Koren, Henry J., 163
Korsch, Karl, 199n, 221
Koselleck, Reinhart, 35n
Kreuzzeitung, 8
Kuhlmann, Georg, 188

Lachmann, Karl, 217
Lasson, Georg, 24n, 63
Lenin, V. I., 9, 35, 146, 228
Lenk, Kurt, 198n

Leo, Heinrich, 192
Lieber, Hans-Joachim, VII
Lichtheim, George, 180n
Litt, Theodor, 68n
Livergood, Norman D., 150n
Lobkowicz, Nicolas, 145, 222n
Louis Philippe, 120, 230
Löwenstein, Julius L., 198n
Löwith, Karl, 8, 14, 35n, 98, 163, 222n
Lübbe, Hermann, 35
Lukàcs, Georg, 10, 11, 12
Luke (Evangelist), 53
Luther, Martin, 17, 207, 208, 209

Mackay, John Henry, 214n
Mannheim, Karl, 181, 182
Marcusse, Herbert, 11, 163, 165n, 166n, 224
Maréchal, Sylvain, 140
Marheineke, Philipp Konrad, 18, 19, 28, 36, 62, 66, 129, 216
Mark (Evangelist), 53
Marxismusstudien, 113n, 138n
Matthew (Evangelist), 53
Mayer, Gustav, 4, 5, 6n, 11, 99n, 118n, 119n, 130
McGovern, Arthur, 212
McLellan, David, 13, 138n, 148, 203n, 209
Meyen, Eduard, 127, 131, 214
Meyer, Alfred G., 199n
Michelet, Karl Ludwig, 19
Milić, Vojin, 198n
Miller, Sepp, 127n, 131n
Modus, Dr, 63
Münchener Studien zur Politik, 18n

Napoleon, I Bonaparte, 105, 110
Neander, Daniel Amadeus, 17
Nerrlich, P., 36n
New Moral World, 6n
Nietzsche, Friedrich, 9
Nigg, Walter, 9, 10n, 18n
Noack, Ludwig, 21n
Nohl, Hermann, 26n, 33n

Ollman, Bertell, 179n
O'Malley, Joseph, 203n
Oppenheimer, Joseph, 210

Paul (Evangelist), 120
Pelczynski, Z. A., 111n
Petrović, Gajo, 163n
Plant, Raymond, 166n

Plato, 151
Plekhanov, G. V., 228
Plutarch, 133, 134, 204
Popitz, Heinrich, 156n, 178
Popper, Karl Raimund, 111
Post, Werner, 138n
Proudhon, Pierre-Joseph, 188
Prutz, Robert, 59, 61, 99, 115n

Rawidowicz, S., 97n, 102n
Reding, Marcel, 143, 146n
Review of Politics, The, 145n
Revue Internationale de Philosophie, 220n, 222n
Rheinische Zeitung, 3, 6, 119, 121n, 122, 123n, 131, 159, 168, 198, 206, 209, 210, 214, 215, 217
Rhenius, D., 59n
Richter, Friedrich, 28, 29, 32
Ritter, Joachim, 111n
Robespierre, Maximilien de, 99, 105, 230
Rosenberg, Hans, 35n
Rosenkranz, Karl, 19, 30, 31n, 34
Rosenzweig, Franz, 110n
Rousseau, Jean-Jacques, 164, 193
Ruge, Arnold, 6, 12, 13, 32, 34, 36, 49, 50, 54, 60, 63, 97, 99, 107, 113, 115, 119n, 120, 128, 129n, 131n, 135, 138, 193, 196, 205, 206-209, 211-213, 215
Rutenberg, Adolf, 44, 120, 131, 215
Ryazanov, D., 12, 127, 202-204, 207-210, 213, 214

Sabine, George H., 200n
Saint Simon, Claude Henri, Comte de, 220, 231
Sass, Hans-Martin, 119n, 120, 208, 209, 214, 220n
Sawadzki, Bruno, 127n, 131n
Schacht, Richard, 179n
Schaper, Ewald, 140
Schelling, Friedrich Wilhelm von, 26, 30
Schläger, E., 17n
Schlawe, Fritz, 35n
Schleiermacher, Friedrich Daniel Ernst, 17, 18, 40, 63, 64
Schmidt, Conrad, 197n
Schnabel, Franz, 17n, 46n
Schulz, Wilhelm, 222
Schweitzer, Albert, 9, 32n, 45
Seeger, Reinhart, 94n, 141, 176n
Sens, Walter, 130n
Social Research, 163n

Spinoza, Baruch, 68, 69, 72–74, 104, 190
Staats- und Gesellschaftslexikon, 8
Stahl, F. I., 115
Starkenburg, Heinz, 197n
Stein, Karl, Reichsfrh. von und zum, 111, 115
Stein, Heinrich von, 220
Stirner, Max, 6n, 12, 131, 214, 223, 235
Strauss, David Friedrich, 20, 21, 27, 29–34, 36–38, 40, 41, 46–48, 50, 52–54, 131, 138, 208, 209
Stuhr, P. F., 117
Stuke, Horst, 9, 12, 13, 35n, 73n, 103, 119, 123, 198n

Themistocles, 157
Timmer, Charles, B. VII
Tucker, Robert, 169n, 177, 203n

Vanini, Lucilio, 29
Vatke, Johann Karl Wilhelm, 19
Vierteljahresschrift für Volkswirtschaft, Politik und Kulturgeschichte, 18n
Voltaire, François Marie, 84

Wagener, Hermann, 8
Walton, Paul, 200n
Weber, Max, 15n
Weil, Eric, 111n, 113n
Weisse, Christian Hermann, 53, 62, 160
Weitling, Wilhelm, 188, 226, 227, 231
Welcker, Karl Theodor, 60
Welt als Geschichte, Die, 35n
Wigands Vierteljahresschrift, 41n, 219,n 239n
Wildermuth, Armin, 148n
Wilke, Christian Gottlob, 53

Zeitschrift für Kirchengeschichte, 140n
Zeitschrift für Politik, 11n
Zeitschrift für Religions- und Geistesgeschichte, 119n, 140n, 223n
Zeitschrift für spekulative Theologie, 19, 37n, 42n, 48n, 51n, 62n
Zeller, Eduard, 62